the celtic church in britain

by Leslie Hardinge

Published for the
Church Historical Society

LONDON S·P·C·K
1972

No. 91 in the
Church Historical Society series

First published in 1972
by S.P.C.K.
Holy Trinity Church
Marylebone Road
London NW1 4DU

Printed in Great Britain by
Willmer Brothers Limited, Birkenhead

SBN 281 02483 9

TO F. O. RITTENHOUSE
*educator, administrator and friend
this book is affectionately dedicated*

Contents

Preface   xi

Abbreviations   xvii

INTRODUCTION
The Rise of the Celtic Church in Britain   1
The Missionary Outreach of Celtic
     Christianity   7
The Celtic Church and the See of Rome   17

1   THE ROLE OF THE SCRIPTURES   29

2   MAJOR DOCTRINES   53

3   THE CHRISTIAN YEAR   75

4   DIVINE SERVICES   101

5   MINISTRY   123

6   DISCIPLINE   135

Contents

7 MONASTICISM 153

8 MONASTERIES 173

9 CONCLUSIONS 201

Appendix 209

Notes 217

Bibliography 235

Index 259

illustrations

The West Cross of Monasterboice   iii

Illustration of the Parable of the
    Multiplication of the Loaves and
    Fishes
From the High Cross of Moone   xi

St Mark Seated
From Gospel Book no. 51, St Gall   xvii

The Twelve Apostles
From the High Cross of Moone   1

Daniel in the Lions' Den
From the High Cross of Moone   7

Map: Missionary Movements of
    Celtic Christians, A.D. 500–1000   13

The Arrest of Christ
From the South Cross of Monaster-
    boice   17

A Scribe
From Ms. 1395, St Gall   29

The first page of the *Liber ex Lege Moisi*   *facing* p.44

St Mark the Teacher
From Gospel Book St Gall   53

Flight into Egypt
From the High Cross of Moone   75

A page from the Latin Commentary
of A.D. 815   *facing* p.77

The Chrismating of Christ
From a broken cross at Kells   101

Adam and Eve, Cain and Abel
From the South Cross of Monaster-
    boice   123

The Sacrifice of Isaac
From the Scripture Cross of Durrow   135

The Founding of the Monastery
From the Scripture Cross of Clonmac-
    noise   153

Soldiers Guarding Christ's Tomb
From the Scripture Cross of Clonmac-
    noise   173

The "axehead" tonsure   195

Noah's Ark
From the West Scripture Cross,
    Killarney   201

The Fall of Adam and Eve
From St Declan's Church, Ardmore   209

The Eagle
From folio no. 27, the Evangelical
    Symbols from the Book of Kells,
    Trinity College, Dublin   235

pReface

Studies in the Celtic Church are attaining increasing importance, not only among scholars, archaeologists, theologians, historians, and linguists, but also among general readers. The books on Celtic topics, both popular and technical, multiply year by year. The anniversary of the landing of Columba fourteen centuries ago, celebrated in so many ways in 1963, has aroused great interest.

The purpose of this work is twofold: to investigate the sources so as to discover what Celtic Christians actually believed and practised; and to arrange the available facts so as to present a systematic picture of this aspect of Christianity. Due emphasis will be placed on those points which are unique.

The expression "Celtic Church", as used in this work, connotes that group of Christians which lived in the British Isles before the coming of the Italian mission of Augustine (A.D. 597), and continued for about a century, or a little more, in an independent state. The term "church" is a handy title for this body of believers, and has no suggestion that they constituted anything of an organization with a centralized government or an acknowledged head. "Britain" is employed as a simple designation of the entire British Isles, as, during the period under review, Ireland was known as "lesser Britain".[1]

Certain appellations are used with special meanings. The names of countries, such as England, Wales, Scotland, Ireland, Germany, and France, and of counties, such as Cornwall, Somerset, and Devon, indicate the localities suggested by their twentieth-century meanings. This is done for clarity. In original quotations, in which, for example, the Irish are called Scots, the context will reveal the correct significance. "Old-Irish", always hyphenated, points to works written before about eight hundred. "Glossator", "commentator" and "theologian", connected with the glosses preserved in the *Thesaurus Palaeohibernicus*, are general titles for the clerics who wrote them. They are used interchangeably for variety. Although these glosses were written by two or three hands, they all come within the Old-Irish period. They are regarded as containing what might for convenience be called the consensus of Celtic opinion on topics theological. In the context of Christian studies, "Celtic" invariably means "Celtic Christian". The word "beliefs" is a simple heading for the doctrinal and moral concepts which were the dynamics of the conduct of Celtic Christians, while "practices" indicates their outward religious acts, both in worship and behaviour, which grew out of such beliefs.

The Celtic Church began at a date unknown. In this investigation the starting-point is the mission of Patrick some time towards the end of the fourth and the beginning of the fifth century. The investigation of the beliefs and practices of the Christianity which he professed, and which he probably gained from his father and grandfather who were both clergymen, will have as its starting-point the usages and doctrines of the mid-fourth century. During the larger portions of the fifth and practically the entire sixth century the Celtic Church was apparently cut off from Western Christianity, and developed points of view which were different from those of the broad stream of believers in Mediterranean lands. Subsequent to their contact with continental Christianity at the very end of the sixth century the Celts continued their independence until they were, section by section, gradually absorbed by the Church of the Romans.

The end of the independence of the segments of the Celtic Church took place at different times. Southern Ireland was the first to throw in its lot with the representatives of the Italian mission. If a date is to be set, perhaps 632 would be suitable. Northumbria, through its king and leaders, gave up Celtic usages following the

Council of Whitby, 664. Northern Ireland surrendered to the eloquent appeals of Adamnan and accepted Roman customs at the very end of the seventh century, 695. The Christians in Scotland, with their headquarters at Iona, felt the heavy hand of King Nectan, who in 717 banished the Columbate brethren from their island retreat and established at Iona those who followed Roman traditions. But there were still remnants of these independent Christians in Scotland when Margaret became queen in the second quarter of the twelfth century, at which time they threw in their lot with Canterbury. Some time about 768 the Celts of South Wales, that is, Somerset, Devon, and Cornwall, appear to have joined forces with the Anglo-Roman Church, while North Wales (modern Wales), accepted Catholic views about 777.

When the Celts assumed Roman usages, they surrendered their independence. The Celtic Church was no longer purely "Celtic", but became Anglo-Roman-Celtic. Its uniqueness receded with the passing years. It is the purpose of this study to seek for those beliefs and practices which these Celtic believers professed before they were modified by seventh and eighth-century traditions from continental Europe.

That they held special doctrines and usages, differing in several respects from those of Italian Christianity, is vouched for by the sources.

The weight of this evidence tends to underline the fact that there existed fundamental and far-reaching differences between the Celtic and Roman Churches. Rome was ignorant of these discrepancies until the opening decade of the seventh century. It seems reasonable to conclude that the Celts were, for their part, also unaware of the beliefs and usages of the Roman Christians. The purpose of the historian is to discover what those differences were.

A vast literature has sprung up during the past century on various aspects of the Celtic Church. Monumental bibliographies have been compiled, among which J. F. Kenney, *The Sources of the Early History of Ireland; Ecclesiastical* I, and Wilfrid Bonser, *An Anglo-Saxon and Celtic Bibliography, 450–1087* deserve special mention. They greatly aid the historian who is kept up to date with the help of the bibliographies published annually in the *Journal of the Irish Historical Society*, under the inspiration of Ludwig Bieler.

But among the almost twenty-five thousand books and articles listed the present investigator has not been able to find a single volume devoted solely to a consideration of the beliefs and practices of the Celtic Christians. Passing allusions to, and studies of, concepts and acts of worship and conduct there are, but the only work even nearly touching the plan of this book is F. E. Warren, *The Liturgy and Ritual of the Celtic Church,* and it was written over eighty-five years ago. But, as its title suggests, it deals with only one important phase, which is actually outside the scope of this book. It is hoped that the following pages will be a first step in filling the need for a brief, comprehensive handbook on the topic of the beliefs and practices of the Celtic Church. It should be emphasized that this study excludes the liturgy and the institutions of the Celts which constitute a phase too vast to be touched in this work, and must be left to another investigation.

The sources for this study may be listed under seven heads. Histories and geographies, by Patrick, Gildas, Nennius, Bede and Adamnan, Dicuil and Giraldus Cambrensis, while not specifically such in the modern sense, reveal insights into the thinking and acting of the Christians during the times of these authors.

Narratives, which were but oral traditions written down later, are replete with clues. Comminatory stories, containing anachronisms, nevertheless reveal what the writers believed were the actual facts of the case. Reflecting traditional memories of the clerical scribes, they are often very useful contributions to an understanding of early conditions and backgrounds. The critical historian must try cautiously to demythologize these accounts.

The *Lives* of saints, a large number of which have been preserved, also often full of anachronisms and propaganda, reveal conditions, not always of the saint's age, but of the times of the writers. These biographies are occasionally in the form of homilies. They were probably read long ago, by the light of sputtering candles, to monks relaxed over their suppers, and present points which the historian is able to weave into the tapestry he is preparing.

Scattered over the pages of Celtic Christian literature many poems and verses may be found, containing religious ideas which are illuminating. The ancient *Annals* are indispensable mines of information. Although they are more accurate for the compiler's own age, they also show, here and there, what the Celtic Christians believed and practised. Legislation, both civil and ecclesiastical, the *Liber ex Lege Moisi*, laws, penitentials, and rules, also are vital sources.

Glosses, crowding between the lines of Old-Irish biblical texts and commentaries on the Scriptures, being suggestions for sermonic development, are the finest indexes for the theological views of these ancient Christians. Written in Old-Irish, preserved inviolate in continental libraries, they crystallize the concepts of the Celtic Church.

These sources are listed in the Bibliography. While the present investigator is not competent to assess their age or merits on the grounds of comparative linguistics or progressive palaeography, he is constantly thankful to the experts in these fields whose altruistic labours have made his task so much simpler, and whose works are gratefully acknowledged in the footnotes on almost every page. He would also like to take this opportunity to thank the Reverend Professor C. W. Dugmore, D.D., and Charles Duggan, PH.D., both of King's College, London, and most especially Kathleen Hughes, PH.D., of Newnham College, Cambridge, for their invaluable help and unfailing encouragement during the pleasant years devoted to the preparation of this book. He owes a debt of gratitude to a number of kindly librarians who have eased his labours. Special mention is due to Mr Dennis Porter of the Bodleian Library in Oxford whose genial helpfulness is noted with gratitude.

A word of thanks is also due to my artist friends, Clyde Provonsha and C. M. Hubert Cowen, for the line drawings and initial letters and chapter headings which add so much interest to the opening pages of each chapter. And finally, thanks are especially due to my wife Miriam for her countless hours in checking references and proof-reading endless drafts of the manuscript! The errors of judgement and fact which this book must contain are mine, and for them I crave the indulgence of my readers.

LESLIE HARDINGE

aBBReViations

AA SS BOL   *Acta Sanctorum Bollandiana*
AB   *Analecta Bollandiana*
ACC   *Amhra Choluimb Chille* (see WS)
Acta Sanct.   *Acta Sanctorum Hiberniae*
Adomnan*   *Life of Columba* (ed. Anderson)
AFM   *Annals of the Four Masters* (ed. O'Donovan)
AI3F   *Annals of Ireland, 3 Fragments* (ed. O'Dovonan)
ALI   *Ancient Laws of Ireland* (ed. Hancock)
ASC   *Anglo-Saxon Chronicle* (ed. Whitelock)
ATig   *Annals of Tigernath* (ed. Stokes)
AU   *Annals of Ulster* (ed. Hennessy)
Bede, HE   *A History of the English Church and People* (see Sherley
              Price)
Bede, Cuthbert   *Life of St Cuthbert*
BNE   *Bethada Naem nErenn* (ed. Plummer)
BOH   *Baedae Opera Historica* (ed. Plummer)
Bury, Patrick   *The Life of St Patrick*, by J. B. Bury
Butler, Lausiac   *Lausiac History of Palladius*, by E. C. Butler

---

* Adomnan is the spelling adopted by O. A. Anderson, and refers exclusively to Anderson's *Adomnan's Life of St Columba*. In every other use in this book the traditional spelling, Adamnan, will be used. In the footnotes *Adomnan* will be found.

CMH   *Cambridge Medieval History*
Confession   of St Patrick (see White)
CQR   *Church Quarterly Review*
DCA   *Dictionary of Christian Antiquities* (ed. Smith)
DACL   *Dictionnaire d'Archéologie Chrétienne et Liturgie* (ed. Cabrol)
DIAS   Dublin Institute of Advanced Studies
DTC   *Dictionnaire de Théologie Catholique* (ed. Vacant)
EHR   English Historical Review
ERE   *Encyclopedia of Religion and Ethics* (ed. Hastings)
Eriu   *Journal of the School of Irish Learning*, Dublin
Gildas, De Excidio   *De Excidio et Conquestu Britaniae* (Gildas)
HBS   Henry Bradshaw Society
HS Councils   *Councils and Ecclesiastical Documents Relating to Great Britain and Ireland* (ed. Haddan and Stubbs)
HS   Historians of Scotland
HE   *Historia Ecclesiastica*
IER   *Irish Ecclesiastical Record*
IHS   *Irish Historical Studies*
ITQ   *Irish Theological Quarterly*
JBL   *Journal of Biblical Literature*
JEH   *Journal of Ecclesiastical History*
JES   *Journal of Ecclesiastical Studies*
Jonas, Columban   *Vita S. Columbani*
Joyce, Social History   *A Social History of Ancient Ireland*
JRHAAI   *Journal of the Royal Historical and Archaeological Society of Ireland*
JRSAI   *Journal of the Royal Society of Antiquaries of Ireland*
JTS   *Journal of Theological Studies*
Kenney, Sources   *The Sources for the Early History of Ireland*
KM   Kuno Meyer
KM, Saip   *Selections from Ancient Irish Poetry*
LCBS   *Lives of the Cambro-British Saints* (Rees)
Letter   of St Patrick to Coroticus
LHP   *Lausiac History of Palladius* (tr. Lowther Clarke)
LSBL   *Lives of the Saints from the Book of Lismore* (see WS)
MD   *Martyrology of Donegal* (ed. Todd and Reeves)
MG   *Martyrology of Gorman* (see WS)
MGH   *Monumenta Germaniae Historica*

MHBP	*Medieval Handbooks of Penance* (ed. McNeill and Gamer)
MO	*Martyrology of Oengus* (see WS)
MT	*Martyrology of Tallaght* (ed. Best and Lawlor)
NPNF	*Nicene and Post-Nicene Christian Fathers*
O'Curry, *Lectures*	*Lectures on the Manuscript Materials of Ancient Irish History* (ed. O'Brien)
O'Curry, *Manners*	*On the Manners and Customs of the Ancient Irish*
PG	*Patrologia Graeca* (ed. Migne)
PL	*Patrologia Latina* (ed. Migne)
PRIA	Proceedings of the Royal Irish Academy
RB	*Revue Bénédictine*
Reeves, *Antiquities*	*Ecclesiastical Antiquities of Down, Connor, and Dromore*
Reeves, *Columba*	*The Life of St Columba, founder of Hy, written by Adamnan, ninth abbot of that monastery*
R. Tall.	*Rule of Tallaght* (ed. Gwynn)
TLP	*The Tripartite life of Patrick* (ed. WS)
TP	*Thesaurus Palaeohibernicus: A Collection of Old-Irish Glosses* (ed. WS)
Tallaght	See Gwynn and Purton
PSAS	*Proceedings of the Society of Antiquaries of Scotland*
RC	*Revue Celtique*
THSCymm	*Transactions of the Historical Society of Cymmrodorion*
Todd, *Patrick*	*St Patrick, Apostle of Ireland*
TRHS	*Transactions of the Royal Historical Society*
TRIA	*Transactions of the Royal Irish Academy*
UJA	*Ulster Journal of Archaeology*
VSH	*Vitae Sanctorum Hiberniae* (Plummer)
VSB et G	*Vitae Sanctorum Britanniae et Geneologiae* (Wade-Evans)
Walker, *Columban*	*S. Columbani Opera*
Warren, *Liturgy*	*The Liturgy and Ritual of the Celtic Church*
WS	Whitley Stokes
WS. ACC	*Amhra Choluimb Chille*
ZCP	*Zeitschrift für celtische Philologie*
+	death of

Footnotes in general are printed at the end of the book, numbered throughout each chapter (pp.217–34). But notes which are closely related to the text are printed at the foot of the page.

introduction
the RISE OF the celtic
church in BRItain

Christianity tiptoed into Britain. It left no written records of its entry, but here and there its footprints may be traced in the soil of these islands.*

Archaeological evidence of Christianity in Roman Britain is meagre. A fragment, containing a Christian cryptogram, attests the witness of Christians before the peace of Constantine.[1] The foundations of what were probably two small churches of this period have so far been discovered at Silchester[2] and Caerwent.[3] The chi-rho monogram has been found in several places: worked into mosaics; carved on building stones, rings, and lamps; and painted on the walls of houses. It is found most frequently in southern England.[4] Excavations since 1947 in London,[5] and from 1949 at the Roman villa of Lullingstone,[6] on the Darent, have revealed other possible Celtic Christian remains. Christian symbols found at Lullingstone house chapel are the earliest in any building in Britain. Similar house chapels have been unearthed in Gaul.[7]

* The purpose of this chapter is to consider briefly the evidences bearing on the origin of Celtic Christianity so as to form a framework for the study of its beliefs and practices.

Among the precious remains in Scotland are the three Kirkman-
drine gravestones.[8] Excavations at the east end of the church at
Whithorn have revealed what might well be a fifth-century place of
worship.[9] Three possible Celtic Christian artifacts were unearthed at
Traprain Law in East Lothian.[10] But these fragments of archaeological
evidence tell only of the presence of Christians before the fifth century, they do not establish that an organized Church existed, nor do
they show any particular place of origin for Celtic Christianity.

Written records of the presence of early Christians are extremely
meagre. The earliest statements are merely passing illusions by a few
church fathers.[11] The first hint of a group of organized believers
in Britain is in the story of the Council of Arles (314), convened
by the Emperor Constantine. Three bishops, a presbyter, and a deacon
are recorded as having come from Britain, but even this statement is
open to question.[12] It should be stressed that this council met independently of the bishop of Rome, who was not present. A copy of its
decisions was sent *fratri Sylvestro*.[13] British clerics were also present
at the Council of Rimini (359). Three of them were so poor that they
accepted financial aid from the Emperor.[14]

Gildas lamented that British Christians were plagued by Arianism,[15] while Germanus and Lupus are believed to have come to their
aid against Pelagianism. Germanus is believed to have returned with
Severus (444–5) at the request of British Christians, possibly to help
in their combat with Pelagianism, or perhaps to encourage them to
bear up under the blows of the Picts and Scots.[16] Who authorized
these visits has yet to be established.[17] But from the middle of the
fifth century nothing further was heard of British Christians until
the arrival of Augustine one hundred and fifty years later. That
Christians were in Britain during the fourth and fifth centuries is
known, but when or whence they came cannot yet be established.

Scarcely had the tramp of the feet of the departing Romans died
away than the Picts and Scots surged into northern England. The
people fled, their farms ravaged, their homes in ashes.[18] Decades
of fluctuating war and peace followed. About the middle of the
fifth century the desperate British leaders solicited help from the
pagan Saxons. Soon the guests from the Continent had become the
masters of England. When Augustine landed in Britain in 597 the
country was virtually heathen. What Christians there were had fled
to the far west.

But even traces of these Christian settlements in Wales before the coming of Augustine are slight and scattered.[19] On the lonely moors of Cornwall Christian settlers have left traces of their existence in several caves. The Picts of southern Scotland probably received the faith through the preaching of Ninian.[20] Ninian's name is embedded in several place-names scattered over Scotland and the Western Isles.[21]

The presence of Christians in Scotland during the fifth century is also vouched for by Patrick's complaint to Coroticus that his soldiers were "apostate".[22] About a century after Ninian's death Kentigern laboured in the region now known as Glasgow. He is even more of a shadowy figure than Ninian. Jocelyn, his biographer, confessed that he had found some things "contrary to sound doctrine and the Catholic faith" in the old biography of Kentigern. Being "grieved and indignant that the life of so priceless a prelate ... should be tainted with heretical passages", he rewrote his story, seasoning "the barbarous composition with Roman salt".[23] Ailred recorded that he had used similar methods in his *Life* of Ninian.[24] This tendency of later hagiographers must be kept in mind when seeking for the beliefs and practices followed by early saints. The faith and works of a sixth-century Celtic saint evidently appeared "contrary to sound doctrine and the Catholic faith" to a pious writer of the twelfth century. What these "heretical passages" might indicate will be considered later. When Columba arrived there were few, if any, Christians still surviving in Scotland. It would appear that it was from Ireland that the faith was successfully reintroduced into Scotland.

But how Christianity came to Ireland in the first place is not known. By the end of the fourth century a few representatives of the faith had apparently reached its shores. The old Irish writers had little doubt that there had been Christians in Ireland before Patrick began his missionary work. Tirechan, in a homily on the life of Patrick, mentioned archaeological remains of liturgical objects, glass chalices under a stone altar.[25] There are also notices, in the *Book of Armagh*, of Christian clerics in Ireland before the saint's arrival who later pledged the support of their churches to Patrick.[26] Patrick himself recorded that he had laboured "to confirm the people". This might well mean those previously baptized by others. He also noted that he had travelled into pagan regions in which no Christian had previously preached.[27]

At the end of the fourth and the beginning of the fifth centuries conditions on the Continent seem to have forced numbers to flee westward. Kuno Meyer rightly pointed out that among these refugees there were probably Christians. Virgilius Maro recorded that Huns invaded the Goths with the result that the depopulation of the entire Empire commenced. This was completed by the Huns and Vandals and Goths and Alans, "owing to whose devastation all the learned men on this side of the sea fled away, and in transmarine parts, i.e. in Hiberial[28] and wherever they betook themselves, brought about a very great advance of learning to the inhabitants of those regions".[29] Ecclesiastical loan words modified in Irish would attest such intercourse.[30]

During the fifth and sixth centuries, while the Continent and even Britain were ravaged by sporadic wars, Ireland in its seclusion appears to have been the bastion of learning and Christianity. During these troubled years many British students received a kindly welcome and hospitable entertainment from the Irish schools.[31] The lot of Christians in Ireland was improved by the coming of Patrick, a Briton, born of three generations of clergy about 388.* Patrick's grandfather was ordained a priest about 325. The Christianity practised by Patrick's ancestors and by the saint himself would reflect no further modifications in faith and works than would be held by Christians generally, during the early fourth century.

When Palladius, ordained and authorized by Celestine, came to Ireland (c. 431), he "baptized a few in that place[32] and founded three churches".[33] But the "Irish already believing in Christ"[34] did not rally about Palladius, who withdrew from the island and died during the following year. It seems that the attitude of the Celtic Christians in Ireland towards the emissary of Pope Celestine,[35] was similar to that shown by the Celtic Christians of England a century and a half later towards Augustine.

The churches which Patrick established in Ireland continued after his death, but were apparently not many in number. Wilfrid taunted Colman and his friends, saying: "Do you imagine that they, a few men in a corner of a remote island, are to be preferred before the universal Church?"[36] And the letter of Pope Honorius addressed

* The problems connected with Patrick are outside the scope of this chapter. For a discussion see the writings of L. Bieler, J. B. Bury, J. Carney, M. Esposito, and others listed in the Bibliography.

to the Irish "earnestly warned them not to imagine that their little community, isolated at the uttermost ends of the earth, had a monopoly of wisdom over all the ancient and new churches throughout the world".[37] When the clerics at the court of Alfrid were trying to convert Adamnan to the Roman practices, Adamnan "was earnestly advised by many who were more learned than himself not to presume to act contrary to the universal customs of the church, whether in the keeping of Easter or in many other observances, seeing that his following was very small and situated in a remote corner of the world".[38] In his letter to his superior at Iona, Cummian gave his reasons for deserting the usage of the Celts in favour of that of Rome. He discussed the unity of Catholic countries and contrasted them with "the little party formed by the Britons and Scots, who are almost at the very end of the world, and but a mere eruption, so to speak, on its surface".[39]

These charges could easily have been countered had the Celtic Church had a large following. The picture that seems to emerge from the sources is of a comparatively small band of enthusiastic missionaries wielding an influence greatly disproportionate to their numbers, doing a work quite out of keeping with their size, and maintaining their zeal for an impressively long period.

The time during which British Christianity is lost sight of (450–597), was an important one for the development of Western Christian thinking. Many changes took place. It does not seem likely that the recommendations of Nicea or the definitions of Augustine and other great councils and teachers were known to Patrick and the Christian communities he established. L. Gougaud might well be right in thinking that there was no such thing as a Celtic Church with a unified system of beliefs and practices.[40] Christianity in the far west of Europe during the unsettled decades of the fifth and sixth centuries would concern itself only with providing principles for a simple and helpful way of life. With little centralized control conmmunities would develop their own emphases and views, and ecclecticism and pragmatism would mark the early beliefs and practices of Celtic Christians. As teachers developed, they interpreted the Scriptures as they felt best.*

---

* See the discussion of this point in chs. 4 and 6.

the missionary outreach of celtic christianity

Bede's story of the Church in Britain brings his readers face to face with the Celtic attitude toward evangelism. He records that Augustine began his approach to the indigenous British Christians "by urging them to establish brotherly relations with him in Catholic unity, and to join with him in God's work of preaching the Gospel to the heathen".[41] But the Celts refused. This has been interpreted as indicating their lack of zeal for the conversion of the pagan Saxons. But conquerors have seldom been eager to accept the religion of the conquered. The records suggest that Celtic Christians at large were eager to propagate their faith. This may be established from Bede's own records. And one of the canons attributed to Patrick stressed that "one's country is first to be taught, after the example of Christ; and afterwards if it does not make progress, it is to be abandoned".

After his second attempt to persuade the Celtic Christian leaders to co-operate with him proved futile. Augustine laid down his ultimatum. Here is his final statement as Bede has preserved it, and Bede's own comment on its result. Augustine invited the British Christians "to join with us in preaching the word of God to the English. But the bishops refused these things, nor would they recognize Augustine as their archbishop".[42] The last sentence is the crux of the matter. The British Christian leaders would not submit to

Augustine. It was a matter of authority and not merely of a lack of zeal for evangelism. To have complied with the request for the former they evidently felt would have amounted to submission to the latter.

Notwithstanding all this, one of the main characteristics of Celtic Christians during the seventh century was the stress they laid upon missionary activity. Far and wide the "pilgrims for God" ranged the islands of the western seas, lashed by storms. Their frail coracles bore them from Ireland to the land of the pagans of North Britain, untamed in heathenism. Across into the Continent ravaged by war, the representatives of the Celtic Church carried the gospel. For the British evangelist "to voyage over the seas, and to pace over broad tracts of land was not so much a weariness as a delight", Gildas recorded.[43] They often embarked in the smallest of currachs, allowing the winds and currents to bear them where they would. Some must have found unmarked graves in the rough waters of the north Atlantic. With no assistance from a missionary base at home, into lands unknown, the pilgrim evangelists journeyed. They lived where they were able to find shelter; they ate what they received from hospitable strangers. Here is a story, although of a later date, which is typical of any point during the period of Celtic missionary activity:

> Three Scots came to king Alfred in a boat without any oars, from Ireland, whence they had stolen away, because they desired, for the love of God, to be in a state of pilgrimage, they recked not where. The boat in which they came was wrought of two hides and a half, and they took with them food sufficient for seven nights; and on the seventh night they came to land in Cornwall, and then went straightways to king Alfred.[44]

And so Celtic Christians, in gratitude for the faith they had received, travelled from their homes, *propter nomen Domini*, making always *peregrinatio pro Dei amore*.

Interest in this type of evangelism probably started in Ireland through the influence of Patrick's example. His words must have stirred the hearts of his people: "Who was it that called me, fool though I be? ... that ... I should faithfully be of service to the nation to whom the love of Christ conveyed me ..."[45] This labour, he affirmed, he had "learnt from Christ my Lord".[46] He looked back after his eventful life and testified that his only reason for returning to Ireland was the gospel and God's promises.[47]

Those who revered Patrick's memory followed his lead. Later Celtic preachers used arguments taken from biblical precedents when advocating missionary enterprise. The *Old-Irish Life of Columba* sketched the saint's career in the form of a sermon probably read on the occasion of his festival. The speaker introduced his theme by discussing the call of Abraham to go from Ur to the Promised Land. He presented three reasons why similar pilgrimages should be made in his time.[48] God's grace might call men to service in foreign lands; other missionaries might make appeals; a "soul-friend" might suggest such a trip. To these, three further reasons might be added: the ascetic urge to find the "desert"; the Celt's love of adventure; or the expulsion of those who maintained the old usages in face of the gradual Romanization of the Celtic Church. These motives, singly or in combination, scattered hundreds of pilgrim-missionaries into distant lands. The movement probably started with Columba in 563. Place names, and dedications of churches across Europe and its islands demonstrate the extent to which these evangelists travelled.

Columba's contribution towards the conversion of Scotland and the accomplishment of his followers in Christianizing their Anglo-Saxon neighbours is, from the viewpoint of world history, the most momentous achievement of the Irish section of the Celtic Church.[49] In 563,[50] at the age of forty-one, Columba left Ireland for Iona with a dozen[51] helpers.

King Bruide is credited with having given Iona to Columba as a missionary base.[52] From it Columba's followers and successors spread their settlements into remote parts of Scotland,[53] and out to the western islands.[54] And so the long task of bringing the northern heathen tribes into the Christian fold began. But not only did the Columban church reach out to evangelize Scotland, it also spread its influence into England. By 632 Augustine's disciple Paulinus, after founding an outpost of Christianity in Northumbria, was forced by a rise of paganism and war to flee south, leaving Hames the deacon to try to maintain the faith. After the departure of Paulinus the Christianity in the north of England passed into another phase.[55] While Oswald had been in exile at Iona, the brethren had instructed him carefully in "the teachings of the Scottish church".[56] When he became king, he apparently disregarded whatever remnants of

Kentish Roman Christianity might still have remained, and sent to his old friends at Iona for a missioner to instruct the Northumbrians in the Celtic Christian faith.[57] The first Celtic preacher to respond was too exacting and met with little success before he returned home disgruntled. The brethren at Iona held a council to discuss their next move. One of their number made the point that the spread of the gospel among pagans would be hastened by tact and patience.[58] The others noted his insight into the situation and decided that he would be a suitable missionary. So Aidan was immediately ordained and sent to Northumbria.

It was probably about 635[59] that Aidan arrived. As had Columba before him, Aidan picked an island off the coast as his base. It was from Lindisfarne that light penetrated pagan Northumbria. On occasion King Oswald himself acted as Aidan's interpreter in the work of evangelizing his subjects. From the north, Celtic Christian beliefs spread into the kingdom of the Middle Angles, and thence into Essex. Here Fursey from Ireland had pioneered Christianity.[60] The brethren of Lindisfarne spread the knowledge of the cross from the Forth to the Thames. There were, however, large areas of Britain which remained rough and pagan.

On the day Aidan died in 651, the young lad Cuthbert requested entrance into the Christian community at Melrose. He was destined to become the most illustrious missionary of that celebrated settlement. Sometimes on horseback, more often on foot, Cuthbert sought out distant villages and everywhere preached the gospel,[61] leaving behind him "a fame which no Churchman north of the Humber has surpassed or even rivalled".[62] When the initial success of Augustine and his followers failed to fulfil its promise, it was the group of missionaries from Iona, establishing their base on "the Holy Island of Lindisfarne, the true cradle of English Christianity",[63] that gave the faith a precarious foothold up into Scotland and down into England.[64]

Celtic missionaries also laboured on the Continent. About the time Columba established Iona, Columbanus was born in what is today Leinster.[65] His first schooling was under Sinell on the island of Clauin, in Lough Erne.[66] He moved on to the Christian school of Bangor on Belfast Lough, about 580, for further study with Comgall.[67] "After he had been many years in the cloister he longed to go into strange lands",[68] and with twelve companions crossed

England and reached Gaul. Preaching and teaching as he and his friends were able, living and toiling with any who shared hospitality with them, the Celtic clerics entered Burgundy the next year. King Sigibert, grandson of Clovis, welcomed Columbanus and gave the ruins of the ancient Roman castle of Anegray (Anagrates) in the Vosges, as a site for the first Celtic monastery on the Continent.[69] Austere to severe, the regulations which Columbanus drew up bound his fellows to rigid lives of stern discipline. Their food was simple, their labours exhausting, their devotions long sustained. Either refraction or forgetfulness was immediately punished.[70]

From this Christian household the salutary principles of religion and education, the blessings of mercy and tolerance, the disciplines of justice and righteousness flowed gently into the turgid stream of Gallic life. Multitudes journeyed to listen to the Irish teacher and stayed to believe. But opposition from angry pagans and jealous Roman clerics drove them eventually through the region which is today called Switzerland[71] and on into Italy. King Agilulf donated Bobbio[72] to Columbanus. Here the Irishmen built up a Christian settlement and laid the foundations of what was to become the most famous Celtic house in Italy.

But not only did the missionaries from Ireland travel across Scotland and down into England and on into the Continent, they also turned their eyes northward. To the isles of the western seas as far away as Iceland and beyond they sailed their tiny craft. Maol Rubha, born into the same clan as Columba, crossed into Scotland in 671[73] and established a settlement at Applecross in the region known today as Ross-shire, between Loch Garron and Loch Torridon.[74] He preached both in Scotland and also in Skye and other islands of the Hebrides. Dying in his eightieth year,[75] Maol Rubha left a reputation almost as glowing as that of the great Columba himself.[76]

Celtic pilgrims soon occupied islands lying to the extreme north of Scotland. The ancient Norwegian chronicler noted that "these islands were at first inhabited by the Picts and *papae*", and "the *papae* have been named from their white robes, which they wore like priests; whence priests are all called *papae* in the Teutonic tongue. An island is still called after them Papey. But, as is observed from their habit and the writings of their books abandoned there, they were Africans, adhering to Judaism."[77] Here is a very early record of Celtic Christian settlers who were accused of "adhering to Judaism". This expression is used to indicate observers of the Jewish Sabbath. This evidence suggests that early Celtic Christians followed this custom.* These pioneers were Christians who tenaciously held to their ancient beliefs and had been banished by tyrants such as King Nectan.†

From the outer Hebrides or from the northern Orkneys, or it might even have been from Ireland itself, the Irish missionary-settler-hermit-adventurers sailed up into the Atlantic looking for a "desert" in which to fulfil their pilgrimage. The Irish geographer Dicuil wrote (c. 825) that a priest had told him that "for nearly a hundred years hermits dwelt, [in the Faroes] from our Scottia (Ireland) ... But the Norsemen had slain every one of them."[78] So it was believed that as early as 725 Celtic settlers had lived on the Faroes.

But not satisfied with these outposts in the ocean, more daring pilgrims travelled on to Iceland:

> But before Iceland was inhabited (by settlers) from Norway, there were there the men whom the Norwegians call *Parpar*; these were Christian men, and it is believed that they had come from the west beyond the sea, because Irish books, and bells, and croziers, were found (left) behind them, and many other things besides, so that one might know they were Westmen.[79]

Olaf's *Saga* added "that they were Christian men, and had come from the west beyond the sea".[80] Theodoric observed in his *Historia* that they were "very few"[81] in number. The Norwegian chronicler noted as of the date 872:

> And then the land (which is now called Iceland) began to be inhabited for the first time, except that a very few men from the island of Ireland, that is lesser Britain, are believed to have been there in ancient times, from certain indications found; namely their books, and certain utensils.[82]

While these Celtic pilgrims[83] were not missionaries in the strictest sense, even in death their books testified to succeeding pagan peoples of the Christian faith which they had professed.

The Celtic predilection for change occasionally was a source of

---

* See ch. 6 below.
† See ch. 3 below.

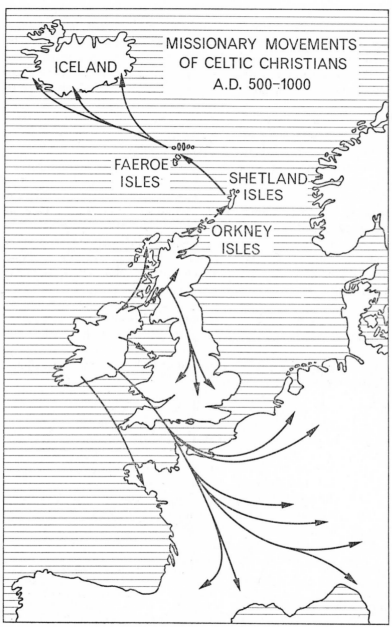

MISSIONARY MOVEMENTS
OF CELTIC CHRISTIANS
A.D. 500-1000

ICELAND

FAEROE
ISLES

SHETLAND
ISLES

ORKNEY
ISLES

B

difficulty. The penitential of Cummean ruled against "any wandering and unstable man", and decreed that he "shall be healed by permanent residence in one place".[84] There are records of trips even to the Holy Land and Rome in later centuries. But these were not always viewed with favour, as this quatrain in Old-Irish suggests:

> Going to Rome? Going to Rome?
> 'Twill bring no profit, only trouble.
> The King thou there wouldst quest
> Not found shall be, if he go not in thy breast.[85] *

A similar sentiment was expressed on the virtue of long journeys in order to find God: "Since God is near to all who call upon Him, no necessity is laid on us to cross the sea. For one can approach the kingdom of heaven from every land."[86] These sentiments seem to reflect a swing away from a regard of pilgrimages, especially to Rome, as ways for deepening devotion. There were those who contentedly sighed:

> All alone in my little cell without a single soul in my company.
> Beloved pilgrimage before going to the tryst with Death.[87]

And it was for this that Cormac, son of Culennan, made his choice, singing for many of his friends:

> Shall I choose, O King of the mysteries,
> After the delight of downy pillows and music,
> To go upon the rampart of the sea,
>
> Turning my back upon my native land?
> Shall I be in poverty in the battle
> Through the grace of the King, a King without decay,
> Without great honour, without my chariot,
> Without gold, or silver, or horse?

---

* Finian of Clonard was told by God's angel when desiring to go to Rome: "What would be given thee at Rome", saith he, "will be given to thee here. Go and renew faith and belief in Ireland after Patrick" (LSBL, 224). Does this mean that there had taken place some sort of apostasy in Ireland after the passing of Patrick? (See Todd, *Patrick*, 503.) Gildas, David, and Cadoc are supposed to have helped establish the second order of Irish saints.

Shall I launch my dusky little coracle
On the broad-bosomed glorious ocean?
Shall I go, O King of bright Heaven,
Of my own will upon the brine?

Whether it be roomy or narrow,
Whether it be severed by crowds or hosts—
O God, wilt Thou stand by me
When it comes upon the angry sea?[88]

Individual response to a divinely placed inner drive to spread the faith, singly or in groups, impelled Celtic missionaries to go forth. Without credentials or material support, self-reliant and trusting in God they accomplished more than their numbers would warrant. Spontaneity, lack of traditionalism, and individuality were the features of this movement.

With the gradual Christianizing of the peoples of the Continent the motives for making journeys outside Celtic lands changed. As Roman Christianity spread during the seventh and succeeding centuries, Celtic missionary pilgrims encountered more and more representatives of the Church of Rome, and after initial suspicion, and sometimes hostility, many eventually joined with them.

But not only did this missionary and pilgrim travel in itself indicate an important phase of the practice of Celtic Christians, it also provided opportunity for a comparison to be made between their beliefs and those of Roman Christian communities.

the celtic church
and the see of rome

Frequently the remark is encountered that Celtic Christianity had no fundamental differences with Roman Christianity. This view should be set against the ancient records of the contacts between Celtic Christians and the representatives of the bishop of Rome.* Wherever and whenever these initially took place there was conflict. By creed and temperament the Celts were seemingly unable to adapt themselves easily to the suggestions of others. Used to interpreting the Scriptures in their own way and following their traditional manners, they were not immediately ready to change.

Without consultation with them Augustine was granted jurisdiction over the Celtic Christians by Pope Gregory. The Roman pontiff ruled: "All the bishops of Britain, however, we commit to your charge. Use your authority to instruct the unlearned, to encourage

---

* Writing of Wilfrid and his training under the influence of Lindisfarne, Margaret Deanesly said of the attitude of the Celtic Church towards Rome: "There was no hostility, no suspicion, of the see of Peter; . . . Rome was a place of pilgrimage, very holy, very distant" (*The Pre-Conquest Church in England*, 83).

In contrast with this view Nora Chadwick stated the basic issues thus: "The fundamental and far-reaching nature of this great spiritual and intellectual contest between the Celtic Church and the adherents of Roman usage can hardly be overestimated" (*Studies in the Early British Church*, 14).

the weak, and correct the obstinate."[89] In 601 Gregory sent Augustine the pallium and a letter in which he declared: "You, my brother, are to exercise authority in the name of our Lord and God Jesus Christ both over those bishops whom you shall consecrate, and any who shall be consecrated by the Bishop of York, and also over all the British bishops."[90] Two categories of bishops are here noted, those to be consecrated under Roman jurisdiction, and "the British bishops" of Celtic tradition. Augustine was arbitrarily placed over the latter, but his authority was not accepted by them. Gregory went as far as to deny that episcopal authority existed among Celtic Christians. "You", he assured Augustine, "are the only bishop"[91] of the Church in England.

In opening his discussion with the leaders of the Celtic Christians, the emissary of the bishop of Rome learnt to his surprise that, besides a difference in the date for celebrating Easter and the mode of tonsure, there were "certain other of their customs ... at variance with the universal practice of the church".[92] A century later Bede noted that the Celtic Christians differed from the Roman "*in many other observances*".[93] These consisted not merely of ritual, they included also "doctrines"[94] ("*disciplinis ac moribus*, rendered so by L. Sherley-Price).

At their second meeting the rift between the two parties widened. The Celtic leaders consulted "a wise and prudent hermit", who told them that Augustine must meet his Celtic brethren as equals by rising to greet them. Should he fail to do this, the hermit warned, "do not comply with his demands".[95] It turned out that the Italian remained seated and submitted four demands. The Celtic "bishops refused these things, nor would they recognize Augustine as their archbishop".[96] The last sentence is vital. The Celtic Christians were unwilling to submit to the authority of Augustine, as the representative of the Roman Church, and by their subsequent actions showed their determination to maintain their independence.

Laurentius, who succeeded Augustine as archbishop of Canterbury, also worked for unity with the Celtic Church. He "sought also to extend his pastoral care to the original inhabitants of Britain, and to the Scots of Ireland adjacent to this island of Britain. For having learned that in their own country the life and customs of the Scots and of the Britons were unorthodox ... he wrote a letter jointly with his fellow bishops ..."[97] This statement is very important as it indicates two items: first, that early in the seventh century the Celtic Christians in Ireland did not differ in "life and customs" from their brethren in England and Wales with whom Laurentius had closer contacts, and also that Roman Christians regarded Celtic Christianity as "unorthodox". A copy of the pastoral epistle has been preserved in which Laurentius confessed:

> Until we realized the true situation, we had a high regard for the devotion of the Britons and Scots, believing that they followed the customs of the universal Church; but on further acquaintance with the Britons, we imagined that the Scots must be better. We have now, however, learned through Bishop Dagan on his visit to this island, and through Abbot Columbanus in Gaul, that the Scots are no different to the Britons in their behaviour. For when Bishop Dagan visited us, he not only refused to eat with us, but even to take his meal in the same house as ourselves.[98]

Rome and its representatives were apparently unaware of the actual beliefs and practices of Celtic Christians. It would seem natural, therefore, that the Celts were also ignorant of the peculiar beliefs and practices of the Roman Church. This fact is fundamental to all study of life and works of the Celtic Christians. They had lived for so long cut off from the Western Church that they were unaware of the changes which had taken place in theology and ritual. Commenting on the outcome of the appeal made by Laurentius, a century and a quarter later, Bede sighed that "the present state of affairs shows how little he succeeded".[99] Neither party would give way.

Even as late as the seventeenth century Cardinal Caesare Baronius, Librarian of the Vatican (+ 1607) echoed the Roman viewpoint. Laurentius, he said, laboured "with might and main for the purpose of extricating the Britons and Scots from their schism, and reconciling them to the Catholic Church".[100] That this difference was recognized as an actual schism at the time was noted by Bede. He lamented that "even in our own days the Britons pay no respect to the faith and religion of the English, and have no more dealings with them than with the heathen".[101]

With the enthronement of Theodore of Tarsus in 668 as the seventh archbishop of Canterbury the cause of Roman Christianity received its most successful champion. He was commissioned by the Pope "to draw together a new people in Christ, and establish them in

the Catholic and Apostolical faith".[102] Theodore's attitude towards
the Celtic Christians was shown both by his legislation and by his
actions. In the first canon of his famous penitential he recommended
that, "If one has been ordained by heretics, if it was without blame
(in the matter) he ought to be re-ordained".[103] That Theodore
lived up to his own rules is witnessed by his dealings with Bishop
Chad who had been ordained with the help of Celtic bishops and
became an adherent of Roman usages:

> During his visitation, Theodore consecrated bishops in suitable
> places, and with their assistance he corrected abuses wherever he
> found them. When he informed[104] Bishop Chad that his consecra-
> tion was irregular, the latter replied with the greatest humility:
> "If you consider my consecration as bishop to have been irregular,
> I willingly resign the office, for I have never thought myself
> worthy of it. Although unworthy, I accepted it solely under
> obedience." At this humble reply, Theodore assured him that he
> had no wish to deprive him of his office, and completed his conse-
> cration according to Catholic rites.[105]

At the time of Chad's consecration, "Wini was the only bishop in all
Britain who had been canonically consecrated".[106] His consecration
had been carried out in Gaul, evidently because in 665 the Roman
party in Britain was still very small. Wini had actually been assisted
by two bishops in the consecration of Chad. But Theodore regarded
this consecration of Chad as "heretical". Eddius, who denounced the
Celtic Christians as *schismatici Britanniae et Hiberniae*, sneered at
Chad as having been consecrated by Quartodecimans. He added a
most revealing detail, that Theodore "fully ordained Chad through
every ecclesiastical grade"[107] to demonstrate the Roman feelings.

Theodore also ruled that baptism performed by Celtic clerics should
be regarded as invalid: "A person from among these nations, or anyone who doubts his own baptism, shall be baptized."[108] Communion was restricted. "If any one gives the communion to a
heretic, or receives it from his hand ... he shall do penance for an
entire year",[109] Theodore further legislated. The "heretics" with
whom he had to deal were, in the main, Celtic Christians.

About the middle of the seventh century, Ronan, a champion of
the Roman Easter, sought to bring Finan, a successor of Aidan of
Lindisfarne, into line with Rome. But Finan became a "more deter-

mined and open adversary of the truth", Bede regretted.[110] When Wilfrid, a student of Lindisfarne, returned from a visit to the Imperial City, he was an ardent convert to Roman usage, convinced that what he had learned in Italy "ought to be preferred above all the traditions of the Scots".[111] His biographer noted that Wilfrid had discovered the correct computation of Easter "which the schismatics of Britain and Hibernia did not know, and many other rules of ecclesiastical discipline".[112] About this time Eata, Cuthbert, and other Celtic brethren were actually expelled from their residence, and their settlement given to others.[113] This eviction took place from Ripon, which was then handed over to Wilfrid (c. 661-2).

The story of the Council of Whitby (664) has often been told. Against the arguments submitted by the representative of the Celtic party, which Bede reported in a most fragmentary fashion, while he devoted much space to those of the Romanizer Wilfrid, the latter rudely replied to Colman: "The only people who are stupid enough to disagree with the whole world are these Scots and their obstinate adherents the Picts and Britons, who inhabit only a portion of these two islands in the remote ocean."[114] In his summing up, Wilfrid was reported as having spoken patronizingly of Columba and his pious successors. He declared that, were they living, they would immediately accept Roman usages. He then accused Colman and his friends of obstinate sin, adding:

> For although your Fathers were holy men, do not imagine that they, a few in a corner of a remote island, are to be preferred before the universal Church of Christ throughout the world. And even if your Columba—or, may I say, ours also if he was the servant of Christ—was a saint of potent virtues, can he take precedence before the most blessed Prince of Apostles, to whom our Lord said: "Thou art Peter ..."[115]

As a result of "Wilfrid's farago of fictitious tradition and fabricated testimony",[116] King Oswy was won over to the Roman side. But the Celtic ecclesiastics, loyal to their faith, were prepared to relinquish lands, homes, and positions, for what they regarded as their faith. "Colman, seeing his teachings rejected and his following discounted, took away with him all who still dissented from the Catholic Easter and tonsure—for there was no small argument about this as well—and returned to Ireland in order to consult his compatriots on their future course of action."[117] There is something very moving about Colman and his faithful companions, vanquished yet unconquered, leaving everything behind them and setting out for an unknown place in which they might worship as their consciences dictated. On the lonely island of Inishbofin, "The Isle of the White Calf", off the coast of Mayo, they established their new settlement. Fifty years after the event Bede characterized the accomplishment of the Synod of Whitby as "the exposure and banishment of the Scottish sect".[118] There was apparently no doubt in the historian's mind of the schismatical nature of the Celtic Church.

Following the council of Whitby the cause of the Roman mission prospered. Bede noted Wilfrid's achievement thus: "He introduced into the English churches many Catholic customs, with the result that the Catholic Rite daily gained support, and all the Scots remaining in England either conformed to it or returned to their own land."[119] But while the initial victory had been gained at Whitby and the Roman tradition accepted by King Oswy, it was not without centuries of struggle that the Celtic party was finally absorbed.

Aldhelm, abbot of Malmesbury, (+ 709) like Wilfrid a convert to the Roman party, was also an ardent advocate of his newly found faith. He complained in a letter to Geraint, king of Devon and Cornwall, that

> beyond the mouth of the Severn the priests of Cambria, proud of the purity of their morals, have such a horror of communication with us that they refuse to pray with us in their churches, or to seat themselves at the same table. More than this, what is left from our meals is thrown to dogs and swine; the dishes and bottles we have used have to be rubbed with sand or purified by fire before they will condescend to touch them.[120] The Britons give us neither the salutation nor the kiss of peace, . . . and if one of us went to live in their country, the natives would hold no communications with him till after he had been made to endure a penance for forty days.[121]

He added his estimate that the teachings of these heretics were not in accord with the Catholic faith.

Sometime about 768 the Celtic Christians of South Wales, that is, Somerset, Devon, and Cornwall, appear to have accepted the Roman usages.[122] Elbodus, bishop of Bangor, finally persuaded the people of

North Wales, that is modern Wales, to receive Roman traditions (*c.* 777). Long ago Ussher published a poem of Taliessyn, "chief of the bards" of the ancient Cymri, in which this conflict between Roman and Celtic Christians is poignantly put:

> Wo be to that priest yborn
> That will not cleanly weed his corn,
> And preach his charge among:
> Wo be to that sheperd (I say)
> That will not watch his fold alway,
> As to his office doth belong:
> Wo be to him that doth not keep
> From Romish wolves his sheep
> With staff and weapon strong.[123]

But scattered remnants of stubborn Celtic Christians persisted in their own ways until the eleventh century, when they were finally absorbed by the Roman party.

Having considered the relationship of the Celtic Christians in England and Wales with the See of Rome, it is necessary also to study the case of Ireland. Cardinal Baronius entitled one section of his Annals for the year 566: "The Bishops of Ireland, Schismatics".[124] He noted how the Irish Church, which had been apparently thriving well "made shipwreck in consequence of not following the bark of Peter which takes the lead of all".[125]

For the year 604 Baronius added the opinion which was evidently current in Rome:

> It is quite plain that the Scots were also just in like manner tinged with the same dark dye of schism as the Britons, and guilty like them of separating from the Church of Rome. And for this reason they were visited by God with the same vengeance as came upon the Britons in being given up for a prey to those inhuman savages, the Angles and the Saxons.[126]

There seems to be no reasonable doubt but that the cleavage between Roman and Celtic Christians was very wide, and could not be bridged without one party's giving way to the other.

The way southern Ireland was induced to conform with Rome came about something like this. About 629 a synod was held at Campus Lene (Magh Lene), near Tullamore, with Cummian the major advocate of conformity. He tells the story in a letter to his superior at Iona, listing the reasons why he left the Celtic traditions. He related how he had consulted "our ancient fathers, Bishop Ailbe, Kieran of Clonmacnoise, Brendan, Nessan, and Lugidus, what they thought of our excommunication decreed by the Apostolic Sees".[127] * This sentence is clear. Rome had evidently anathematized the Celtic Christians in Ireland sometime early in the seventh century, possibly following their rejection of the appeal to conform made by Laurentius. This would confirm the statement of Baronius that the Celtic Christians "were separate from the Church". Cummian sought to heal this hostility. The result of the Synod of Campus Lene was that the majority agreement "that the more worthy and approved practice, recommended to us from the source of our baptism and wisdom, and by the successors of the Apostles of the Lord",[128] should be adopted. But Cummian and the Roman party did not enjoy the success for thich they hoped. He complained bitterly that "a certain whited wall" arose who caused a revulsion of feeling, "who did not make both one, but caused a separation and partly rendered void what had been agreed to; whom the Lord, as I hope, will smite as seemeth him good".[129]

To mend this further rift, Cummian persuaded some Celtic representatives to journey to Rome to study the matter further. The delegates returned about three years later when there was another

> great Council of the people of Ireland in the White Field (near Carlow), among whom there was contention about the order of Pasch. For Laserian, abbot of the monastery of Leighlin, to whom were subject one thousand and fifty monks, defended the new order which came recently from Rome, but others defended the old.[130]

Fintan Manu, the venerable representative of the Celtic party, urged the assembly to stay by the old order. "The people therefore decided according to the opinion of the holy man and returned home with joy."[131] But even this decision was short-lived. Pilgrimages to Rome had become common, and more and more Celtic

---

* Note Cummian's reference to "Apostolic Sees", *sedibus apostolicis*. Later in his letter he mentions "the fourfold Apostolic See, namely of Rome, Jerusalem, Antioch, and Alexandria, in which there exists a perfect unanimity on the subject of Easter". He was evidently unaware of any dominance on the part of the Roman See.

Christians were influenced by Roman usages.[132] That the union party under Cummian achieved its aims is suggested by Bede, who wrote of the year 635: "The Scots in the south of Ireland had already conformed to the injunctions of the Bishop of the apostolic see, and observed Easter at the canonical time."[133]

The swing to Rome was precipiated by arguments similar to the well-known one made by Cummian: "What more harmful ideas can be held concerning our Mother the Church than if we are to say Rome errs, Jerusalem errs, Alexandria errs, Antioch errs, the whole word errs, but the Britons and the Scots are the only people who think right?"[134] A letter from the Bishop of Rome himself also probably helped. Bede has preserved the information that

> Pope Honorius also wrote to the Scots whom he learned to be in error about the observance of Easter, as I mentioned earlier. He earnestly warned them not to imagine that their little company, isolated at the uttermost ends of the earth, had a monopoly of wisdom ever all the ancient and new churches throughout the world, and he asked them not to keep a different Easter, contrary to the paschal calculations and synodical decrees of all the bishops of the world.[135]

John, who had just been elected pope, followed this up with an earnest appeal:

> [We] learned that certain persons in your province are attempting to revive a new heresy from an old one, contrary to the orthodox faith, and that they ignorantly refuse to observe our Easter on which Christ was sacrificed, arguing that it should be observed with the Hebrew Passover on the fourteenth of the moon.[136]

The Pope concluded: "We therefore beg you not to rake up the ashes of controversies long since burned out."[137] And so the Celtic Christians of southern Ireland capitulated and joined in communion with Rome.

But for more than half a century northern Ireland continued to hold out. Adamnan of Iona was the apostle of union. Recommended by his brethren to study abroad, Adamnan left his island retreat and travelled to England. At the court of his friend Alfred he learned the Roman way of "keeping Easter and many other

observances".[138] On his return to Iona, "seeing that his own following was very small",[139] Adamnan

> tried to lead his own people in Iona and those who were under
> the jurisdiction of that monastery into the correct ways that he
> had himself learned and whole-heartedly accepted, but in this
> field he failed. Then he sailed over to preach in Ireland, and by
> his simple teaching showed its people the proper time of Easter.
> He corrected their ancient error and restored nearly all who were
> not under the jurisdiction of Iona to Catholic unity, teaching them
> to observe Easter at the proper time. Having observed the
> canonical Easter in Ireland, he returned to his own island, where
> he vigorously pressed his own monastery to conform to the
> Catholic observance of Easter, but had no success in his attempts,
> and before the close of the next year he departed this life.[140]

It was probably at the Synod of Tars (697)[141] that northern
Ireland capitulated. But a further meeting was held in 704 to
confirm the decision. The ancient annalist recorded that:

> In this year the men of Erin consented to receive one jurisdiction
> and one rule from Adamnan, respecting the celebration of Easter,
> on Sunday, the fourteenth of the moon of April, and respecting
> the tonsuring of all the clerks of Erin after the manner of St
> Peter, for there had been great dissension in Erin up to that
> time; i.e. some of the clergy of Erin celebrated Easter on the
> Sunday [next after] the fourteenth of the moon of April, and
> had the tonsure of Peter the Apostle, after the example of
> Patrick; but others, following the example of Columbkille, cele-
> brated Easter on the fourteenth of the moon of April, on what-
> ever day of the week the fourteenth should happen to fall, and
> had the tonsure of Simon Magus. A third party did not agree
> with the followers of Patrick, or with the followers of Columbkille;
> so that the clergy of Erin used to hold many synods, and these
> clergy used to come to the synods accompanied by the laity, so
> that battles and deaths occurred between them; and many evils
> resulted in Erin in consequence of this, viz., a great murrain of
> cows, and a very great famine, and many diseases, and the
> devastation of Erin by foreign hordes. They were thus for a long
> time, i.e. to the time of Adamnan, who was the ninth abbot that
> took [the government of] Ia after Columbkille.[142]

But while the majority of Irish Celtic Christians accepted the Roman traditions, there was apparently a sizeable minority that continued to exercise independence. Even four centuries later, in the time of Malachy O'Morgair, the Bishop of Rome had grave misgivings about the way things were being carried on in Ireland.

In 1142 Malachy became abbot of Bangor and coarb of Comgal. His great biographer, Bernard of Clairvaux, called him

> an axe or a mattock casting down evil plantings. He extirpated barbaric rites, he planted those of the church. All outworn superstitions (for not a few of them were discovered) he abolished, and wheresoever he found it, every sort of malign influences sent by evil angels ... Moreover in all Churches he ordained the apostolic sanctions and the decrees of the holy fathers, and especially the customs of the holy Roman Church.[143]

This reform entered into all phases of the surviving practices of the Celtic Christians. Malachy introduced the "canonical hours after the fashion of the whole world ... For there was not such thing before, not even in the city" of Armagh.[144]

Some Celtic usages had evidently persisted long after outward conformity to Rome had been achieved at the end of the seventh century.

But the monks of Iona, and the other Christian settlements owing allegiance to it, remained firm to their ancient traditions in spite of Adamnan's persuasion. It was left to Egbert to bring about the union of Iona with Rome. Egbert was an Englishman who had been educated in Ireland. He vowed to become a pilgrim away from his homeland,[145] and resolved on a missionary journey into what would today be called Germany. He was persuaded to change his plans because of a vision granted to Boisil, to whom an angel gave this directive: "Now go and tell him that, whether he wishes it or not, he is to visit the monastery of Columba, because their ploughs do not run straight, and it is his duty to recall them to the right way."[146] Egbert's mission was a success, for not long afterwards the Scottish brethren who lived in the Isle of Iona, and also the monastic settlements under their jurisdiction, were induced to adopt Roman usages.[147]

But while this might be the decision of the majority at Iona, the matter was by no means settled. Rival abbots ruled side by side

for some time in the island. King Nectan was disturbed by these
divisons, and, having received a reply to a letter he had written (*c.*
710) to Ceolfrid, abbot of Jarrow, explaining the Roman traditions,
he resolved to act. And so in 717 "the family of Iona were expelled
across the mountains of Britain by Nectan".[148] To those who had
refused to comply exile beyond the Grampians was decreed. Having
brought about a clean sweep of the schismatical element, the Roman
cleric Egbert "consecrated the island anew to Christ".[149] But as in
Ireland, so in Scotland, remnants of Celtic Christians persisted until
the coming of Margaret, the bride of Malcolm, king of Scotland. This
energetic queen soon set about eradicating "wholly the illegalities
that had sprung up in (the church). For when she saw that many
things were done in that nation contrary to the rule of the true
faith and the holy custom of the universal church",[150] she worked
with the Celtic church leaders to reform them. The queen finally
offered the remnants of these Christians, in Ninian Hill's terse
phrase, "conformity or Canossa".[151] They prudently accepted the
former, and eventually disappeared from the British scene. By the
Council of Windsor (1072), Scotland was placed under the Archbishop of York,[152] and Lanfranc was as triumphant in Scotland as
he had been in Ireland.

The weight of the arguments from the sources irrefutably show
that there existed fundamental and far-reaching differences between
the Celtic Christians and the Roman Church, which held them as
schismatics and heretics.[153] Rome was ignorant of these differences
until the opening decade of the seventh century. It seems reasonable
that the Celts were also ignorant of the usages and beliefs of Roman
Christians. The rights and wrongs of the situation are no concern of
the historian. His purpose is to discover what these differences were.
These divergencies will aid in shedding light on the actual beliefs
and practices of the Celtic Christians.

CHAPTER 1 the Role of the scriptures

By far the most influential book in the development of the Celtic Church was the Bible. It moulded the theology and guided the worship of the early Christians. It suggested rules of conduct and transformed the ancient laws of Irish and Welsh pagans into Christian statutes. It lay at the foundation of the education of children and youth, and sparked the genius of poets and song writers. It provided inspiration for the scribes of history and hagiography and affected the language of the common people, becoming the dynamic for the production of the most beautiful hand-written books ever made. A study of the beliefs and practices of the Celtic Church compels the historian to consider the role played by the Bible in their development.

Let us begin with Patrick and the Bible. One of the most arresting characteristics of the writings of Patrick is the number of biblical citations they contain. Besides direct quotations there are many phrases filled with imagery borrowed directly from the Scriptures. In the short *Confession* and the shorter *Letter to Coroticus*, N. J. White has counted three hundred and forty examples from forty-six books of the Bible.[1] Because of this Patrick was styled "the man of the lasting language, i.e., the holy Canon".[2] There is nothing in

Patrick's works which indicates his acceptance of the teachings of church fathers or the canons of councils. He appealed solely to the Scriptures in support of what he believed, practised, and propagated: "The words are not mine, but of God and the apostles and prophets, who have never lied, which I have set forth in Latin. He that believeth shall be saved, but he that believeth not shall be damned. God hath spoken."[3] This attitude, as will be noted in the next chapter, is typical of the Celtic teacher. He took for granted that the Bible was God's Word and could and should be understood by all, and carefully obeyed. The Hymn of Secundus eulogized Patrick's regard for the Bible as the basis for his theology:

> He finds in the sacred volume the sacred treasure ...
> Whose words are seasoned with the divine oracles ...
> Whose seeds are seen to be the Gospel of Christ. ...
> He sings Hymns with the Apocalypse, and the Psalms of God,
> On which also he discourses, for the edification of the people
>   of God;
> Which Scripture he believes, in the Trinity of the sacred name,
> And teaches the One substance in Three Persons.[4]

Gildas the Briton, possibly from Bangor-on-Dee, apparently referred to no book but the Bible in *De Excidio*, which, like Patrick's works, is replete with quotations from the Scriptures only.[5] His citations show a thorough grasp of its meaning, and his use of its imagery suggests that he was completely saturated with its language Gildas' copy of the Scriptures appears to have been the Itala.

Bede's testimony to Celtic missionaries was that they "diligently followed whatever pure and devout customs that they learned in the prophets, the Gospels, and the writings of the Apostles".[6] And of Aidan and his friends he added: "His life is in marked contrast with the apathy of our own times, for all who accompanied him, whether monks or lay-folk, were required to meditate, that is, either to read the Scriptures or to learn the Psalms. This was their daily occupation wherever they went."[7] Following the example of Patrick, Columba and Celtic Christians for centuries made the Scriptures the foundation of their studies. The *Lives* of the saints often vouch for the fact that the Bible, and especially the Psalter, lay at the basis of their teachings. St Samson, for example, was "very often immersed (*sensatus*) in searching and in learning the Holy Scriptures".[8]

A conclusion as to which biblical books were to be regarded as canonical was evidently reached early in the story of Celtic Christians, but it is not known when and by whom this decision was made. The Old-Irish glossator observed that certain unnamed heretics had read the canon of the Old and New Testaments but had perverted them.[9] The Muratorian Fragment from the ancient Celtic settlement at Bobbio, compiled about 800 from a much earlier document, points to the interest of Celtic scholars in what were inspired Scriptures. Jerome's list of the canonical books of the Bible could hardly have reached Ireland before his Vulgate, which was believed to have arrived there towards the end of the sixth century.*

The Bible most popular with Christians of Celtic lands was the Old Latin. It is called the Itala. This version was pre-Hieronymian,[10] and similar to the recension known in Africa and Gaul before 383.[11] Patrick's New Testament citations may possibly include two from the Vulgate,[12] but it is probable that either Jerome himself followed the Old Latin, or that the scribe, when later copying Patrick's works, inadvertently inserted the version he knew from memory.[13] N. J. White called attention to the fact that: "It is noteworthy that some of the readings found in St Patrick's Latin writings suggest that he used manuscripts emanating from south Gaul. In particular, there are several remarkable readings common to him and the Latin translation of Irenaeus."[14] J. F. Kenney observed that, even though many of these Gallican and African versions have perished, "the Irish were the most important of the agents who have transmitted to us Old Latin texts. . . ."[15] In the copy of the Pauline Epistles used by the Würtzburg glossator, Colossians occurs between 2 Thessalonians and 1 Timothy. A careful study of the sequence of the New Testament books cited by Gildas shows that in his Bible Colossians had this position too.[16] This is also the case in the New Testament in the Book of Armagh, and would seem to be characteristic of the Scriptures used by the Celts. It is interesting to discover that this is also a feature of the African version employed by Augustine, Primasius, and Isidore of Seville.[17]

It is very likely that the copy of the version of the Hermit of Bethlehem was first brought to Ireland by Finnian (+ 579), who

* See p. 49 below.

crossed the sea with "the law", for "it was Findia that first brought the whole Gospel to Ireland",[18] where its arrival caused great rejoicing.

The desire to use the purest version of the Bible, and to make sense of it free from all speculation, is underlined by the comminatory legend of Maelsuthain O'Carrol, "chief doctor of the western world in his time".[19] He was accused of interpolating biblical passages with his own words and theories. Michael summoned three of Maelsuthain's pupils and announced that he would be "sent to hell for ever for this and other sins". The three students flew to earth in the form of doves and warned their unfortunate master of his impending fate. Maelsuthain repented, vowing, "I will put no sense of my own into the canons, but such as I shall find in the divine books."[20] This is an illustration of Celtic expositors' constant attempts to make the Bible its own interpreter, without recourse to the commentaries of others, either of the fathers of the Church or of their contemporaries.

But with the Romanizing of the Celtic Christians the Old Latin was gradually modified with phrases from the Vulgate. Of the Gospels[21] a well-developed "Irish version" finally evolved, in which are readings not found in any surviving copy of the Old Latin.[22] These variant "versions" point to the individuality and eclecticism of both scribe and exegete. When compared with the deep regard for the sanctity of the holy Scriptures shown by the early Celtic Christians, writers after the time of the Danish invasions placed less and less stress upon the Bible and more on tradition, eventually appealing to the fabulous and foolish. But, before this interest in the authority of the divine oracles had waned, the Old-Irish glossator emphasized that "the authority of the word of God . . . is greater than the word of men",[23] adding: "It is not possible to doubt God's words, i.e., to say that what the word of God may say should not be true. It will effectively accomplish the work to which it is put. As pure silver is used for some purpose, so with the words of the Lord, a deed is effected from them at once after they have been spoken."[24] The Scriptures were accorded paramount authority, and were listened to as the voice of the Holy Ghost addressing his people in the character of a king upon his throne.[25] An admonition which grew from this view is voiced by Cummean in his penitential: "He who takes up any novelty outside the Scriptures, such as might lead to heresy, shall be sent away."[26]

Even during the twelfth century, when the views of Celtic Christianity had all but disappeared, the Bible was remembered in eulogy:

> One of the noble gifts of the Holy Spirit is the Holy Scripture, by which all ignorance is enlightened, and all worldly affliction comforted, by which all spiritual light is kindled, by which all debility is made strong. For it is through the Holy Scripture that heresy and schism are banished from the Church, and all contentions and divisions reconciled. In it is well-tried counsel and appropriate instruction for every degree in the Church. It is through it the snares of demons and vices are banished from every faithful member in the Church. For the Divine Scripture is the mother and the benign nurse of all the faithful who meditate and contemplate it, and who are nurtured by it, until they are chosen children of God by its advice.[27]

Whence did the ancient Celtic Christians receive such a veneration for the Scriptures? It probably came with their ideas regarding the religious life. Cassian's (+ 435) influence in Western monachism shows the pervasive effects of his *Collations* and *Institutions*. In a conversation which Germanus had with his friend the Abbot Nestorus, Germanus inquired as to the best way of expelling from the mind the notions of pagan authors. The Abbot replied in effect: "Read the sacred books with the same zeal that you read heathen writers and your thoughts will be pure." And so the pious Christian bent his energies to mastering the Bible. Cassian set aside the commentators and advised his disciples to do the same, devoting their time to prayer, fasting, and meditation, so as to reach an understanding of the Scriptures,[28] promising that God would reveal to them in their dreams the sense of the passages which they thus considered.[29]

Cassian also stressed the need for active labour of all kinds, to be combined with a study of the Scriptures, as the best education for life and eternity. So there developed schools attached to his communities. The pupils were taught to read the Bible. They practised writing by multiplying copies of parts of the Scriptures. With this increasing stress on biblical studies devotion to philosophy and pagan authors, and even the commentaries of the early church leaders, diminished. As there were no fixed criteria of criticism or interpretation, each preacher and teacher was a law to himself in his expounding of the Bible.

Of all Celtic lands Ireland became the cradle of this movement towards this deeper study of the Scriptures. Many came from Britain and the Continent to sit at the feet of the great Irish teachers. A seventeenth-century poem by a Continental scholar, B. Moronus, published by Ussher, eloquently pictures this trend:

> Now haste Sciambri from the marshy Rhine;
> Bohemians now desert their cold north lands;
> Auvergne and Holland, too, add to the tide.
> Forth from Geneva's frowning cliffs they throng;
> Helvetia's youth by Rhone and Säone
> Are few: the Western Isle is now their home.
> All these from many lands, by many diverse paths
> Rivals in pious zeal, seek Lismore's famous seat.[30]

Finnian founded the school at Clonard which earned this great renown, and was said on occasion to have had three thousand students. These Irish colleges trained ministers not only for Celtic churches but also for some adhering to the Anglo-Saxons. Agilbert, successor of the Roman missionary Birinus and evangelist to the West Saxons, had fitted himself for more proficient service by "studying the Scriptures in Ireland for many years".[31] Even Anglo-Saxon noblemen pursued their education in Ireland in preparation for careers in their own church.[32] In 664 Britain was stricken by the plague. While Ireland was also afflicted, some regarded it as a safer place, and, arriving there, devoted their time to "studying under various teachers in turn. The Scots welcomed them all kindly, and, without asking for any payment, provided them with books and instruction."[33] And so a love for the Scriptures was fostered and extended.

It is significant that from Irish schools comes the earliest surviving commentary produced in the British Isles, the Würtzburg glosses on the Epistles of St Paul. Bede's commentaries are lost; Alcuin wrote only on Titus, Philemon, and Hebrews. M. L. W. Laistner thus succinctly noted the contribution of Ireland:

The preoccupation of Irish scholars with Biblical exegesis, which has sometimes been assumed without adequate proof, has very recently been placed beyond doubt and shown to have been intense and widespread ... Many of these productions of the Irish show certain traits in common. Characteristic phrases recur, there is a fondness for displaying erudition by explaining the sense of words or names in Latin, Greek or Hebrew. Above all, *many stress the literal interpretation of the Bible*, a fact which to a great extent explains their ultimate disappearance, because by the ninth century the predominant trend in exegesis was to follow Gregory and Bede and to lay the chief emphasis on the allegorical and moral sense of Scripture.[34]

This literalistic attitude toward the Bible must never be lost sight of in any study of Celtic Christian beliefs and practices.

While the earliest writers of the Celtic Church, Patrick, Gildas, Adamnan, to mention three, made practically no use of non-canonical books of Scripture, hagiographers and homilists after the tenth century used the stories and imagery in them freely. The Book of Enoch provided frequent inspiration: for example, prayers were addressed to the seven archangels for each day of the week,[35] and reference was made to the seven heavens.[36] But there is no evidence that the writer has direct access to the Apocrypha. R. E. McNally rightly summarized its role in Celtic theology: "A careful study of the occurrence of the apocryphal literature as source material seems to indicate that the Bible commentators used it mainly to supply inconsequential, imaginative details and almost never to displace the traditionally Christian sense of Scripture."[37] But while the early Celtic writers quoted from neither councils nor church fathers, during the seventh and succeeding centuries more and more books must have reached the British Isles in the satchels of *peregrini*.[38] References from the following writers are found in Celtic commentaries subsequent to the second half of the eighth century, without, however, any acknowledgement of the source being made, either to the author or to his work:

Ambrose	Commentary on St Luke and Hexaëmeron.[39]
Aquila	Commentary on the Psalms.[40]
Augustine	City of God and De Genesi ad Litteram.[41]
Cassian	Institutiones.[42]

Gregory	Magna Moralia on John and Homilies on Ezekiel and the Gospels.[43]
Hilary	"Ambrosiaster", on St Paul's Epistles.[44]
Isidore	Etymologiae and Sententiae.[45]
Jerome	Commentaries, letters, De Viris Illustribus, and translation of Origen.[46]
Origen	in translation by Jerome and Rufinius.[47]
Pelagius	Commentary on St Paul's Epistles.[48]
Primasius	Commentary on St Paul's Epistles (?)[49]
Prisian	Commentaries.[50]
Symmachus	Commentary on the Psalms.[51]
Theodore of Mopsuestia	Commentary on the Psalms.[52]

There are also allusions to the Irish commentators Mailgairmrid[53] and Coirbre[54] by the glossators.

The later Celtic commentator borrowed indiscriminately. In that gold-mine of his opinion, the Würtzberg glosses in Old-Irish on the Pauline Epistles, this is clearly manifest. Augustine was quoted eleven times; Isidore five; Origen twenty-one; Hilary or "Ambrosiaster" twenty-nine; Jerome one hundred and sixteen; while there are one thousand three hundred and sixteen citations taken directly from the arch-heretic Pelagius himself.[55] * Attacked by Jerome, anathematized by the Bishop of Rome, preached against by Germanus and Lupus, hounded from pillar to post, Pelagius was strongly entrenched in the hearts of his own Celtic friends, who ignored the prohibitions of councils and the proscriptions of the fathers. His writings were used for centuries in Ireland, on occasion, however, modified when not acceptable to the eclectic theologians. Here is another instance of the independence of Irish expositors, and a

---

* For discussion of the position of the Pelagian writings in the Celtic Church see H. Zimmer, Pelagius in Irland, where all the references are printed in full (pp. 40–112). H. Williams argues rightly that Pelagius was not held to be a heretic (if the Irish even knew of his condemnation as such) in the Celtic Church; see "A review of Heinrich Zimmer's Pelagius in Irland and The Celtic Church in Britain and Ireland", ZCP IV. 3 (1903); cf. F. W. Wasserschleben, Die irische Kanonensammlung, where the Irish canons xviii, xix, quote Pelagius. This is further evidence that Pelagius was regarded as valid authority by Irish Christians. Pope-elect John (c. 640) appealed to the North Irish to give up their allegiance to Pelagius. Some of them were evidently quoting Pelagius freely.

defiance of the opinions of the broad stream of Western Christianity.

The remarkable thing, however, about all these citations from the fathers is that not one is used for defining doctrine, or as authority for practice. They were employed because they aptly expressed the thought which the commentator desired. As will be noted, statements by various fathers are placed side by side. Occasionally as many as five different views were presented, and the reader or homilist is left to choose the one which he thinks the best.

The decrees of ecclesiastical councils were also treated with caution or indifference. When the canons of the Frankish synods were quoted against Columbanus, he met argument with argument, and cited in response the canon of the Council of Constantinople which recognized the liberty of "the churches of God planted in pagan nations, [to] live by their own laws, as they have been instructed by their fathers".[56] More than a century later Boniface (+ 754) complained to Pope Zachary against Irish missionaries, certifying that their leader Clement ignored the canons of the Church, rejected the writings of the fathers, and despised the authority of the synods.[57] Ussher pointed out that Alcuin (+ 804) had noted that some Irish theologians of his day put little weight on authority and custom "unless some reason was added to authority".[58] This helps to tell us why the represenatives of the Roman mission of Augustine were surprised that the Britons differed from them in so many respects.

It would be well at this juncture to consider the methods used by the Celts in biblical interpretation. It took many centuries of trial and error before Western Christianity devised techniques, and so it is not surprising to find among the Celts several different ways of explaining the Bible. Cassian, whose influence has been noted, declared that the narrative of the Scripture, usually easily understandable in its historical sense, ranked lowest. To the questing student the allegorical meaning lay beneath the surface, and finally, deeper still, the anagogical significance was the richest.[59] But among Celtic commentators there is discernible no systematized form of exegesis.

Most often the simple historical sense alone was taken. On the psalmist's reference to "enemies" the comment was, "These are the Moabites, Ammonites and Idumeans".[60] The commentator read Psalm 108 and applied it to the days of Hezekiah, noting that the "fool" referred to Sennacherib.[61] St Paul's prediction of the "falling away",[62] was taken to refer to the departure of the Empire from the Romans. The Celtic expositor was evidently unaware that this had already taken place when he penned his comment in the seventh or eighth century. "Thorn in the flesh" was explained as "headaches".[63] In these examples, which are part of hundreds which might be cited, what was considered to be the simple historical purport of the text was drawn from the biblical terms.

The historical meaning was occasionally used in combination with the allegorical. On the Apostle's allusion to the different calls played on a trumpet, the homilist noted that this referred to speaking, for "unless the foreign language is distinguished and translated, no one who hears it understands".[64] Does this comment indicate that in parts of Ireland worship, or perhaps preaching, was carried on in the vernacular?* One more instance of the allegorical method will suffice. On St Paul's reference to "leaven" the glossator remarked: "As it was forbidden to put leaven in bread at the feast of the lamb, so it is not right that there should be any of the leaven of sin in the feast of the Lamb, i.e. Christ."[65] The literal meaning or story (*stoir*) is contrasted with the allegorical (*sens*),[66] or sometimes with the secret or mystical significance (*ruin* or *run*).[67]

Very rarely a threefold system of interpretation was used, namely, the literal meaning (*stoir*), the mystical or allegorical meaning (*sians* or *sens*), and the moral or tropological significance (*morolus*). Sometimes a fourfold system was employed, but this was rare. The commentator applied the narrative twice. There was a first application to the time of the biblical writer, and a second was made to later Hebrew history. Here is the Old-Irish expositor's philosophy of hermeneutics:

> There are four things that are necessary in the Psalms, to wit, the first story (*stoir*), and the second story, the sense (*siens*) and the morality (*morolus*). The first story refers to David and to Solomon and to the above-mentioned persons, to Saul, to Absalom, to the persecutors besides. The second story to Hezekiah, to the Maccabees. The meaning (*siens*) to Christ, to the earthly and the heavenly church. The morality (morolus) to every saint.[68]

* See ch. 8 below.

While there existed a Western Christian fourfold method of interpretation, this Celtic system was different, perhaps evolved from that of Theodore of Mopsuestia.[69] Columba was believed by his biographer to have had a system somewhat akin to this:

> He divided a division with figures,[70] between the books of the law, i.e. he divided a division with allegorizing between the books of reading or of Lex. i.e. of the Law of each, the Old Law and the New Testament, i.e. he used to distinguish history (*stair*) and sense (*sians*), morality (*morail*) and mystical interpretation (*anogaig*).[71]

That this Celtic technique was regarded as a good one is suggested by the poem attributed to Airbhertach (+ 1016):

> Four things in the Psalms (pure counsel), the first story, the second story (*stair*),
> There are found in them (it is not falsehood!) noble sense (*sians*) and morality (*moralus*),
> It is with these that the first story is concerned: with David, with Solomon.
> With the persecutors of the hosts, with Saul, with Absalom.
> The second story which is here declared refers to Hezekiah, to the People,
> To the Kings (excellent the fame!), to Moses, to the Maccabees.
> The meaning (*siansa*) of the Psalms, with their divisions, to Holy Christ, to the Church;
> The morality after that severally to every just one, blessed vigil-keeping.[72]

The Celtic expositior was seeking a method of construing the meaning of the Scriptures in a practical way. "The second story" points to the application of the original biblical message to a later generation, that is, the message of the Pentateuch, the Books of Joshua and Judges, and even the writings of 1 and 2 Samuel, point to later periods and persons, such as Hezekiah and the people of Israel. The third stage of significance, called the meaning (*siansa*) drew attention to Christ and his Church. The fourth and final application was "to every just one". This Celtic fourfold division, quite different from the quadriform system which developed in the

Western Church, was concerned with pragmatic issues. How the message of the Scriptures could be applied to the needs of the Christian was the concern of the Celtic homilete.

A careful study of the glosses in the Würtzberg commentary demonstrates that biblical exegesis shows a great reverence for the antiquity and authority of the Scriptures. No desire is anywhere detectable in the Celtic expositions to formulate a system of dogmatic theology. There is little or no curiosity or speculation regarding obscure passages. But there is a tranquillity, a complete absence of controversy pervading the study of the oracles of God. The interpreter was preoccupied with the spiritual and the practical, and sought to make this plain.

There is little evidence that Celtic theologians, as a whole, had any great knowledge of the original languages of the Bible, but there are indications that a few readings from the Hebrew and Septuagint were known. The eighth-century old-Irish glossator occasionally observed: "so far the text of the Hebrew version",[73] and, "this is the translation of Jerome, and he is commenting on ... the version of the Septuagint".[74] But these readings probably reached Celtic scholars through the writings of commentators after the seventh century, since, as has already been noticed, it does not appear probable that these works would have preceded the arrival of the Vulgate.

Greek and Hebrew words are sprinkled over the commentaries. The Celt was interested in etymology.* Often, apparently with several works before him, he selected what appealed to him from each: "This is the etymology which Isidore says ..." He then added, "Sergius, however, gives another sense ..." And still farther, "Cassiodorus, however, gives another sense, to wit ..." And then, "Ambrose, however, says ..."[75] The glossator gave his readers this warning on semantics: "It does not behove us to add to the Holy

---

* KM, *Hibernica Minora*, 31: "Question. How is their meaning arrived at? Not difficult. There is found a Greek neuter noun, ψάλμα, ψάλματος. *Iunctio* is its interpretation. It receives the Greek Preposition διά, with a sense of separating, so that it makes διάψαλμα, and *disiunctio* is its interpretation, to wit, separation of the sense and the purport and the author and the form that are in the psalms. *Diapsalma* is put to separate anything that has been joined together by misreading. The same noun also receives the Greek preposition σύν, which, interpreted, is *con*, so that it makes σ νψαλμα which, interpreted, is *coniunctio*. *Sympsalma* is put, to join together anything that has been separated by misreading."

Scriptures from without, for whenever the author lets out a word on his mouth, there is a word in his mind that answers to it."[76]

Sometimes the commentator was working either with a poor copy or with a limited knowledge of Greek, as illustrated by his note on St Paul's "labouring, i.e. making ropes". His mistook σκηναί, tents, for σχοῖνοι, ropes.[77] That he was more intent on applying the passage under discussion to the spiritual needs of his hearers is demonstrated by the gloss on the Apostle's statement in 1 Cor. 15.53: "Whether in the active or the passive it should be done. Whether the verb *induo* ends in 'o' for the active, or in 'r', *induor*, for the passive, there is passivity on the part of the one who submits to God."[78] His interest in grammar is shown by the comments on "wicked": "i.e. to the adjective, i.e. a substantive, i.e. a substantive is not added to them, because the Psalms were sung in metre. The sense demands it, though the metre does not allow the substantive to be added to the adjective".[79] There is a slight indication that the expositor on Ps. 30.9 had some knowledge of the Hebrew (*kāphār*) in his explanation: 'he covered up and forgave their sin, and reckoned it not as a reproach unto him".[80] From these illustrations, and very many more might be added, the conclusion seems inescapable that the Old-Irish commentators had only a limited knowledge of Greek and Hebrew words, and that they probably gained this from the writings of others.

Preaching, in harmony with the divine command, was an important means by which the Celtic missionaries, Patrick and Columba, Columbanus and Aidan, spread the gospel. There are scores of allusions to preaching in the Old-Irish glosses, and even in biblical passages in which there are not any apparent suggestions of preaching, the Celtic homilete saw some.* Illustrations might be multiplied. It seems reasonable to suppose that these notes represent the views of preachers, as they prepared to address their congregations or to teach their theological students or catechumens.

* "Preach" – Whether any one likes it or dislikes it, preach to him. 2 Tim. 4.2, TP I, 696.

"Speak we" – It is Christ we preach. 2 Cor. 2.17, TP I, 597.

"Sentence or answer" – We had the death of Christ for a subject of preaching. 2 Cor. 1.9, TP I, 592.

"Grace" – The grace of teaching or preaching; for it was to preach to all that I received this grace. Rom. 15.15, TP I, 539.

"Keep under" – Through preaching, and not accepting pay. 1 Cor. 9.27, TP I, 556.

That the cleric strove to make his discourse as pleasant as possible is indicated by his ideal of preaching as "a stream of eloquence of speaking with the grace of sweetness upon it".[81]

The thousands of Irish glosses written between the lines of biblical manuscripts or commentaries on books of the Bible were a sort of *midrash* on the text. In his introduction to Psalm 9 the glossator has left a record of his methodology: "It is customary, then, in this book to say the words of the psalms, and then words are brought in from this commentary to complete the psalms."[82] The fact that these twelve thousand comments are written in Old-Irish would point to preaching in the vernacular. The expositor or preacher used these notes as reminders of the thoughts he wished to convey when he was actually before his listeners. The comments are, for the most part, very short; their ideas greatly condensed. The teacher was free, then, to discourse as he pleased. Sometimes as many as five different interpretations are found on a single passage.* The remarkable point about this is the complete absence of anything fixed or dogmatic. There is nothing partisan. A. W. Haddan long ago noted that "The difference between [Ireland] and other parts of the Church, lay chiefly in her possessing a wider and more self-grown learning, and in the consequent boldness and independence of her speculations".[83]

An unknown Irish teacher has left a brief treatise on what he considered were the steps in sermon construction.† It is embedded in a fragment of an Old-Irish work on the book of Psalms. The homilete desired his students to concentrate on clarity above all, and to couch his thought in short words.‡ Topics should be chosen

---

* On Ps. 68.29 the glosses are: "He is here commenting on the text of Symmachus. Mailgaimrid cecinit:...of the birth whereby he was born of the Father before every element, though it is not easy to get that out of the commentary; for as the sun is prior to the day, and it is the day that makes clear everything, so the birth of the Son from the Father is prior to every element; i.e. he considers *Oriens* here as a name of God. He was here a commentary on *ad orientem*. Mailgaimrid: *ab initio*, i.e. of the generation of the Son by the Father." *TP* I, 285.

† "Question. What is *argumentum*? Not difficult. *Acute mentis inventum*, 'a sharp invention of the mind', or *acutum inventum*, or 'a sharp invention'. There is a word *arguo*, that is *ostendo*. *Argumentum*, then, *ostendio* 'showing'.

"Question. For what use were arguments invented? Not difficult.

‡ To set forth through stout words the sense which follows, *ut dixit Isidorus*: *Argumenta sunt quae causas rerum ostendunt. Ex brevitate sermonum longum sensum habent.*

to rivet attention and divisions of the theme should enable the hearers to pursue the subject, without distracting digressions. Diligent and acute thought was to be employed to gain new insights. This is certainly an excellent piece of homiletic instruction! It is endorsed by the glossator, of about the same period, in his explication of the Pauline use of the word "tongues": "Translating from one language into another, like Jerome and the seventy interpreters: or, to draw forth hidden meanings from single words, and then to preach from them afterwards, as is the custom of preachers."[84] Most of the surviving sermons, however, simply consist of an elucidation of the text of Scripture. A passage might be read from the Gospels, or the Epistles, or the Psalms. The homilete would then make a few germane remarks. His purpose was twofold: firstly, he wished to convey the intent of the author of the biblical passage; secondly, he desired to make its application helpful in the daily lives of his hearers. An example is found in the second of the three lives of Patrick. The speaker opened his homily by reading, in Latin, the directive of our Lord to the Apostles, "Go ye therefore, and teach all nations, baptizing ..."[85] On this text he expatiated as follows:

Meet is the order, teaching before baptism. For it cannot be that the body should receive the sacrament of baptism before the soul receives the verity of faith.

"All nations", that is, without acceptance of persons.

"Baptizing them", that is, men of the Gentiles. "In the name of the Father, and the Son, and the Holy Ghost." "In the name", he saith, not "in the names". Here is set forth the Unity and Trinity of Persons. For the singularity of "name" expresses Unity. But the diversity of appellations indicates the Trinity.

"Teaching them to observe all that I have commanded you." An especial order: He directed the apostles first, to teach all nations, and then to baptize them with the sacrament of faith, and in favour of faith and baptism, to enjoin all things that were to be heeded. And lest we should think that the things

---

"Question. For what use were divisions invented? Not difficult. To distinguish the sense which follows."

"Question. What then is the difference between the argument and the title? Not difficult. The arguments were invented to set forth the sense that follows, ut diximus: Titulus to illustrate the cause and occasion at which the psalm was sung." KM, op. cit., 29.

ordered were few and trifling, he added: "All that I have commanded to you", so that they who have believed and been baptized in the Trinity may do all that hath been enjoined. "And
lo, I am with you alway even unto the end of the world", as if
he would say, "This is your reward", and as if he had said, "Fear
not to go into the world and to be harassed with tribulations,
for my help will be present to you therein, even to the end of
life, in doing signs and miracles." The apostles fulfilled [this],
and so forth.[86]

This is not profound exposition, but it is preaching in slow motion.
The thought, as some precious stone, is held up before the listeners,
and slowly turned around in the hands of the speaker as he des-
cribes its various facets. There is little movement, no rush of ideas.
There is, however, a devotional study of the implications of Scripture to aid practical piety.

J. Strachan long ago published one of the very few genuine Old-
Irish homilies which have survived.[87] It was evidently addressed to
a group of Christians as an encouragement to more joyous adoration of God and a deeper devotion to the virtues of Christian living.
It begins with a short, direct introduction in the form of a statement of purpose. This would be natural before a congregation as-
sembled for their regular service of worship. Here is what an outline
of this sermon might have looked like as it lay on the lectern before
the Celtic preacher:

Introduction: The Christian must be thankful to God.

I. It is REASONABLE to be thankful for all God's blessings.
    i. Creation praises its Creator.
    ii. Sinners have cause to praise their Saviour.
    iii. Christians naturally praise God.
II. It is a DUTY to be thankful for all God's blessings.
    i. God abides with the righteous, and expels the devil, who
    dwells in the wicked world.
    ii. The emancipated Christian will praise God from his heart.
III. Upon WHAT may he expect God's Blessing?
    i. Upon all he possesses—animate and inanimate, for without
    God life is hell, with him, heaven.
    (a) What is hell like?
    (b) What is heaven like?

EGO ENIMSV

dñs ds̄ tuus quieduxitedeterraaegypti

etdedomo feruituuf. Nonhabebisdeos
                                      ·i· idola

alienos coramme · Nonfaciestibifculp
                                 ·i· idola

tile · neq; omnē fimilitudinē quē eft in

ignemælignia caelo defuper · &quēinterradeorfum .
&lapidef·
                              ·i· animalia marif·

Nequeeorum quēfunt inaquiffubterra
  ·i· flectendo genua·   ·i· donef·

Nonadorabifea nequecolef· K

E gofumdñfdf̄ tuuf fortif · etzelotif· K·

U ifitanf iniquitatem patrum infiliof· in

tertiā etquartā generationē eorumqui

oderuntme· Et facienfmifericordiaf

intmilibuʃhif quidiligunt mea pcepta · K

N onadfumernomendñdi̇tuuf inuanū ·

N eque eñ infontē habebitdñf eum· quiad

fumerit nomendñidifui fruftra iuramento K

M ementodiem fabbati fctificef· fexdiebuf

operabirif· etfaciefomnia operatua·

iubeluuʃuṇannox·   VII· autē diem fabbatum dñidi̇ tui·

ii. What will be the RESULT of abiding in
   (a) the atmosphere of hell?
   (b) the atmosphere of heaven?

Conclusion: Let all enter into a relationship with God in which blessings—now and ever—will result.

Imagination and extempore speaking filled in the details.

The way in which the Irish preacher went about developing his theme was simple and direct. Following his opening statement, which was an unadorned declaration: "We give thanks to Almighty God, Lord of heaven and of earth, for his mercy and for his forgiveness, for his charity, and for his benefits which he has bestowed upon us in heaven and on earth", the preacher read Ps. 145.10 in a Latin version which differed from that of Jerome. This he immediately translated into Old-Irish for the benefit of those of his hearers who did not understand Latin. He took up the first idea, "All Thy works ..." and went on to demonstrate how all creation praises the Creator. He then cited Ps. 103.22, and translated it, developing the thought that even sinners are not without divine blessings, and quoting what appears to be a paraphrase of Acts 17.25, which he translated into Old-Irish. Since God is good and distributes his benefits to righteous and wicked alike, he is worthy of praise. There follows a list of the attributes of God. He is eternal, omnipotent, the creator and sustainer, the nourisher and gladdener, the illuminator, ruler, teacher, giver of the law, and judge of the world.

His second main point demonstrated that it was a duty for the Christian to praise God. He quoted from St Peter[88] and then paraphrased the apostle's words, "the man who thanks God for his grace and benefits is a fee simple estate to the King of all". God abides in him while the devil dwells in the ungrateful. The speaker then underlined the latter thought by a further citation from St Peter,[89] and remarked that the devil possesses the ungrateful. It is for this reason that we should "give thanks to God for his innumerable benefits". This Latin passage is translated, or rather paraphrased.

His third point is a discussion of the objects upon which God bestows his benefits. He listed the blessings of nature, the sun, rain, and ripening grains. He then moved without a pause into: "For he who receives Christ's folk, it is Christ whom he receives

c

therein; as He himself says, *Qui vos recipit me recipit, qui vos spernit me spernit*", which he translated into Old-Irish. In three ways he repeated this thought without any amplification or exegesis, which is almost completely absent from his discourse. He then dilated on the "likeness of the kingdom of heaven and of hell in this world". Hell he illustrated by winter and snow, tempest, cold, age, decay, disease, and death. Heaven he pictured by fair weather, summer, blossom, leaf, beauty, feasts, feats, prosperity. But there was an even severer form of hell to which sinners will be condemned on the day of doom when Christ bids them "Depart ..." This, too, was said in Latin and Irish. The preacher was moved by his theme into giving a terrifying description of hell:

> Its site is low, its surrounding is strong, its maw is dark, its dwelling is sorrowful, its stench is great, its monsters are everlasting, its surface is [rough], its soil is unfruitful, it is a cliff to restrain, it is a prison to keep, it is a flame to burn, it is a net to hold fast, it is a scourge to lash, it is an edge to wound, it is night to blind, it is smoke to stifle, it is a cross to torture, it is a sword to punish.

There is no attempt to present a biblical view of Hades. He allowed his imagination to carry him away. He next presented a list of things the Christian might do to avoid hell: "Labour and study, fasting and prayer, righteousness and mercy, faith and charity," were his prescriptions. To those who are faithful in all these things Christ will one day say, "Come ye blessed ..." This statement he gave first in Latin and then in translation. The speaker then came to his final paragraph, which was an appeal: "One should, then, strive after the kingdom of heaven." This was unlike the present world, which he then went on to describe in the most lurid language:

> It blinds like mist, it slays like sleep, it wounds like a point, it destroys like an edge, it burns like fire, it drowns like a sea, it swallows like a pit, it devours like a monster. Not such, however, is the kingdom which the saints and the righteous strive after. It is a fair blossom for its great purity, it is a course of an ocean for its great beauty, it is a heaven full of candles[?] for its exceeding brightness, it is a flame for its beauty, it is a harp for its melodiousness, it is a banquet for its abundance of wine.

He finally reached his peroration which consisted of an ascription of praise to God for his goodness and mercy to all mankind.

> Blessed is he who shall reach the Kingdom where is God Himself, a King, great, fair, powerful, strong, holy, pure, righteous, keen, ... merciful, charitable, beneficent, old, young, wise, noble, glorious, without beginning, without end, without age, without decay. May we arrive at the Kingdom of that King, may we merit it, may we inhabit it *in saecula saeculorum*. Amen.

No analysis of Celtic preaching has been attempted before. If this is typical it reveals several interesting qualities. The portions taken from the Scriptures were either read or cited from memory from the Old Latin version, which, as is usual, contained texts differing from the Vulgate. The quotations in this short homily, nine in number, form a considerable part of the discourse, since they were cited, and then translated, and finally paraphrased. The preacher was ready to indulge in vivid descriptions, allowing his imagination to suggest the qualities of heaven and hell usually supplied in the Bible, and also the attributes and activities of God; the items upon which the blessings of God rested and the snares of the kingdom of this world and the wonders of the kingdom of heaven. His introduction was brief to the point of abruptness. His conclusion consisted of both ascription to God and appeal to his fellows. The atmosphere of the homily is quiet, simple, meditative, sincere, and practical. It is easy to follow. It displays no interest in theology as such, and is purely devotional.

Besides the homily, a question-and-answer method was common with Celtic teachers, as even a cursory perusal of the sources will reveal. The Irish catechist, as well as the hagiographer and compiler of annals, would often, and abruptly, ask a question, to which the response, psychologically suggestive, was generally "the answer is not difficult".* Simple biblical tests were also employed. An eighth-century text, found in the monastery of St Gall, is an

---

* Col. 2.11, TP I, 672: "Circumcision – Question: What is the circumcision of Christ? The answer is not difficult: It means his death and burial; it is these that effect a circumcision from vices."

ALI IV, 365: "Question: What is the penalty of wounding a virgin bishop? Answer: Three victims to be hanged from every hand that wounded him; half the debt of wounding is paid for insulting him."

"example of medieval Bible study undertaken independently of the Fathers:"[90]

Who died but was never born? (Adam)
Who gave but did not receive? (Eve, milk)
Who was born but did not die? (Elias and Enoch)
Who was born twice and died once? (Jonas the prophet, who for three days and three nights prayed in the belly of the whale. He neither saw the heavens nor touched the earth)
How many languages are there? (Seventy-two)
Who spoke with a dog? (St Peter)
Who spoke with an ass? (Balaam the prophet)
Who was the first woman to commit adultery? (Eve with the serpent)
How were the Apostles baptized? (The Saviour washed their feet)

This series of questions might reflect "the academic method of the day, though it may be nothing more than a parody on the *disputatio* of the early medieval Bible schools".[91] It obviously reflects a time when precise knowledge of the facts of the Bible was becoming blurred!

But while the Celtic theologian was keenly interested in the whole of the Scriptures, his preoccupation with the Ten Commandments was even deeper. The earliest Christian service included a recitation of the Decalogue.[92] It might well be that Pliny's statement that Christians bound themselves by an oath not to kill or steal reflected his understanding of the meaning of the repetition of the Ten Commandments in the Christian liturgy.[93] If this be granted, then "this will explain both the sudden decision of the Jewish authorities to omit the Decalogue from their daily service and the great prominence accorded to it in early Christian literature".[94] The Christianity practised by Patrick's parents and introduced by him into Ireland was characterized by a profound respect for the Ten Commandments. Antinomianism and anti-Semitism had not succeeded in banishing the Decalogue from Britain. In his comment on the word "teachers" the Old-Irish glossator observed: "That they might be engaged in framing laws with kings".[95] This was an allusion to the tradition that the Brehon code of Ireland was revised under the direction of Patrick.[96] The introduction of the *Senchus Mor* contains a prophecy of an early Irish sage which underlines the point of view of Celtic Christians that the Decalogue was part of what they regarded as their code of conduct:

> They had foretold that the bright word of blessing would come, i.e. the law of the letter; for it was the Holy Spirit that spoke and prophesied through the mouths of the just men who were formerly in the island of Erin, as he had prophesied through the mouths of the chief prophets and noble fathers in the patriarchal law; for the law of nature had prevailed where the written law did not reach.[97]

This introduction also contained the delightful statement that Patrick was helped by Dubhthach Mac ua Lugair, who put "a thread of poetry around" the laws.[98] It would be a joy to the student of all legal enactments were a Patrick to insist that in every legislative assembly a poet do the same! The Brehon laws, at least in their Christian aspects, were based on the Decalogue and other parts of the Mosaic legislation,[99] for the tradition is preserved that

> What did not clash with the Word of God in the written law and in the New Testament, and with the consciences of the believers, was confirmed in the laws of the Brehons by Patrick and by the ecclesiastics and the chieftains of Erin; for the law of nature had been quite right, except the faith, and its obligations and the harmony of the church and the people. And this is the *Senchus Mor*.[100]

Another clue to the pervasive influence of the Bible on the Old-Irish legislation is the echo of St Paul's declaration that "the scripture hath concluded all under sin", and "now we know that what things so-ever the law saith, it saith to them who are under the law: that every mouth may be stopped, and all the world may become guilty before God,"[101] which lie behind this explanation in the *Senchus Mor*:

> For all the world was at an equality, i.e. for all the world was at an equality of ignorance or injustice until the great "cas" of the seniors came to be established, i.e. "hand for a hand, foot for a foot"; or, each person's right was according to his might.[102]

This synthesis, of the old Brehon Laws and the regulations of the

Old Testament, throws light on the practices of the ancient Irish Christians, and hence of the Celtic Church. It probably goes back for its inspiration to the old law book, *Liber ex Lege Moisi*. Wherever Patrick established a church he was believed to have left a copy of "the books of the Law and the Books of the Gospel".[103] The *Liber ex Lege Moisi* is the only work surviving from Celtic sources which answers to the description, "books of the Law". Each of the four extant manuscripts of this work has an Irish provenance.[104] The earliest has been dated about 800, and had apparently been copied from an earlier manuscript. It commences with the Decalogue and contains selections from the Books of Exodus, Leviticus, Numbers, and Deuteronomy,* which are filled with citations from the Old Latin. Its interest lies not only in the texts it contains, but also in the parts of the Mosaic legislation it omits. In the Corpus Christi College Ms. 279 it forms part of the *Canones Hibernenses*, which end with the following sentences:

> The people of Israel ought to have been ruled by the Ten Commandments of the law, since for the sake of these God smote the Egyptians with the ten plagues; therefore are there ten commandments; while there are precepts in the law which God did not command, but (for example) Jethro the kinsman of Moses told Moses to choose seventy leading men who would judge the people with Moses; and this is the judgment, that if we find judgments of the heathen good, which good Nature teaches them, and it is not displeasing to God, let us keep them.[105]

Not only were Patrick and the framers of the *Senchus Mor* interested in the Decalogue, Brigit was also "a keeper of God's commandments",[106] and Columba was likewise credited with teaching "the books of the Law completely",[107] for "Christ's law they used to chant, with mysteries they used to search it out, with their host no heedlessness was found".[108] As Fournier long ago pointed out, this little book apparently played an important part in the framing of the laws of Ina, and hence of those of Alfred the Great and later legislators.

The significance of the *Liber ex Lege Moisi* has been overlooked in studies of Celtic beliefs and practices. Not only were laws modified by it, but also theological concepts and many practices show direct

---

* For a description see Appendix, pp. 209–16 below.

dependence upon its regulations. The following pages will demonstrate this relationship. The Celtic Church cherished a deep love of the Bible, and from the Epistles of St Paul developed their theology. The Psalms were used in worship, and were the inspiration of poets and preachers. Without the influence of the views of church fathers Celtic theologians set about discovering what the Scriptures meant. Their tenets and practices, based on this understanding, show the eclecticism and pragmatism of exegete and layman. The legislation of Moses pervaded social, economic, and legal relationships to an extent seldom seen in the history of other branches of the Church. Unlike the theologians of Roman Christianity who appealed more and more to the teachings of Church and councils, Celtic teachers stressed the Bible. The role of the Scriptures in Celtic Christianity was indeed a vital one, so much so that no thorough study of the beliefs and practices of the Christians of Celtic lands is possible without bearing this fact in mind.

CHAPTER 2 **majoR doctRines**

The object of this chapter* is to sketch the principal doctrines of the Celts, beginning with the time of Patrick and ending at the period when the last segment of the Celtic Church conformed to Roman usages.

The Celtic Christian's devotion to the Scriptures has been demonstrated from his writings and from the records of his contemporaries. From the Bible Patrick derived his understanding of what should be believed and practised. He took his duties as the apostle of Ireland very seriously, affirming "that according to the rule of faith in the Trinity, I should *define* doctrine, and make known the gift of God and everlasting consolation, without being held back by danger, and spread everywhere the name of God without fear, confidently".[1] And so he later came to be regarded as "the father of teaching and faith for Irishmen".[2]

Irish missionaries disseminated Patrick's teachings across Britain and into the Continent. This chapter is partly based on passages in the *Lives* and ancient laws and penitentials which bear on theology, but its conclusions are derived mainly from the almost twelve-

---

* No systematic study of Celtic doctrines has been carried out from the sources. Since the topics covered in this chapter are so wide, discussion of each doctrine is kept very brief in this initial investigation.

thousand Old-Irish glosses on passages from the Psalms, part of the Gospels, and the Epistles of St Paul.* These constitute a remarkable window into the Celt's mind. J. F. Kenney assigns the earliest comments to the seventh century, and the major portion to the eighth.[3] They seemingly reflect the views of the Irish scholars uninfluenced by the dogmas of the Roman party, and, although written by two or three hands, form a homogeneous body of Celtic Christian thought.

DOCTRINE OF GOD

The Celtic view of Deity was trinitarian, but there was no speculation, for as the commentator remarked, "we know little of the mysteries of God".[4] God was eternal, without beginning[5] and omniscient. He upheld the universe[6] and might predict events,[7] thus revealing his omnipotence,[8] and worthiness to be adored.[9]

Arianism was believed to have made inroads among early British Christians.[10] Evidence for this has been drawn from the fact that mention of the names of the Father, Son, and Spirit were omitted from the baptismal formula.[11] But arguments based on silence form a perilous platform.† That the Celtic Christians were aware of Arianism appears from the attempt to extract trinitarian meanings from less obvious texts. Commenting on St Paul's statement: "Now our Lord Jesus Christ, himself, and God, even our Father, ... comfort your hearts", the Old-Irish theologian noted: "He indicates the Trinity here: the Son, when he says, 'our Lord'; the Father, when he says, 'God'; and the Holy Ghost when he speaks of 'a Comforter'."[12] He evidently was on the lookout for trinitarian passages!

Columba, so the tradition goes, was reproved by Pope Gregory, to whom he had sent a copy of "Altus Prosator", because it failed to stress belief in the Trinity.[13] But this is probably a comminatory story to establish Roman connections. Disbelief in the Trinity, however, is certainly not discernible from the sources. The gloss on St Mark corrects a quaint view, mooted by some unknown student:

The quaternity, i.e. that our belief should not be thus, that we

---

* These have been conveniently collected and translated by W. Stokes and J. Strachan in *Thesaurus Palaeohibernicus*. In the references which will be given the relevant Scripture will be noted first, as the essential root from which the comment sprang.

† For the Celtic baptismal practices see chapter 4 below.

should deem different the Person of the Son of God and [that of] the Son of Man, i.e. so that it should be a belief in four persons with us, i.e. a Person of the Father, and of the Son of God, and of the Son of Man, and of the Holy Ghost.[14]

The supreme governmental authority of God, exhibited in disciplining his people, was often noted. Punishment, it was believed, was always administered in order to correct sin, and never in spite or anger,[15] because God gave his Son to justify and not to condemn fallen man.

The Celt was absorbed in Christ's character and ministry and produced a large and beautiful devotional literature on this theme, but made no attempt to deal with the mystery of his nature. Patrick affirmed that while Christ "always existed with the Father",[16] He was also "begotten before the beginning of anything",[17] suggesting that the saint had slight Arian leanings. This tendency is also indicated by the gloss on St Paul's statement, "Today have I begotten thee", that this referred to "the day of the existence of God".[18] Christ's coming into being was thus definitely stated as following God's, and hence would fit in with semi-Arian arguments. Yet the Deity "gives equal honour with himself and with the Godhead of the Son to the Manhood of the Son",[19] for Christ was equal with the Father in might and majesty.[20] But with uncritical statements such as these the Celt ceased to discuss the matter, terming it a "mystery",[21] and leaving it at that.

Christ's equality with God was unaffected by his humanity. There evidently arose some discussion as to whether our Lord maintained his own divine status as a man, or whether he received divinity as a gift from his Father. The commentator sighed: "Whether it be from the Godhead of the Son or from the Godhead of the Father that the Manhood of the Son assumed that which he hath assumed, it matters not."[22] But then he noted tensions caused by wisps of Arian heresy:

> It is from the Father that the Son hath received power, i.e. this is what the heretics say, that the Godhead of the Son is less than the Godhead of the Father, for it is from the Father that the Son hath received power; he then who receives is less than he from whom it is received, and he who is endowed than he who bestows it.[23]

He was certain, however, that the Godhead was never subject to the manhood of Christ.[24] Christ was the true image of God,[25] and held to be eternal,[26] manifesting fully the nature of God,[27] having "the same form and substance"[28] as the Father. Regarding Christ as very God, the glossator warned against those who maintain "that the Godhead of the Son is less than the Godhead of the Father, which, however, is a heresy".[29] He failed to note that, when he acknowledged that the Son's being followed that of the Father, he was in a measure denying the strict coeternity of the two Persons. However, he might counter in the words, God granted his Son equality of honour with himself.[30]

Appreciation for the great love Christ manifested in taking human nature in order to die for the fallen race is often noted.[31] His advent and his entire ministry of reconciliation fulfilled the Old Testament predictions and types.[32] But in the works of Patrick and other Celtic writers, including the glossators, there is no mention of the virgin birth, nor is there any conscious effort to suppress the fact. Faith is simply expressed in his birth.[33] But in the *Lives*, written after union with the Roman party had been achieved, there are many allusions to the virgin birth, and some strangely superstitious notions: he was born through the crown of the Virgin,[34] while Mary was impregnated by the breath of the Third Person.[35]

Because man's sin resulted in his condemnation and separation from God, Christ went "to foreign parts" to help the human race,[36] and to rescue lost mankind by striking it from the grasp in which the Devil held it,[37] who was ready to mete "penal death" to the finally unrepentant. This death, the Celt believed with Pelagius, was different from the common death of mankind, which later, in the context, seems to suggest final annihilation. There would evidently be no eternally burning hell. Eternal life, lost to the human race by Adam, could be restored to the victorious sinner only through Christ,[38] who suffered, not for one or two persons only, but for all.[39] This salvation was accomplished through Christ's "material blood"[40] which poured from his side as he hung on Calvary, and became effective in the case of the individual sinner through his faith.[41]

The resurrection of Christ is often alluded to in the glosses.[42] When he ascended to glory he was immortal and in the fullness of Deity.[43] A belief in this truth was regarded as of vital consequence, for the commentator remarked: "It is manifest that unless you believe the resurrection of Christ from among the dead, your faith will not sanctify you in that wise, and will not save you from your sins."[44] Man's existence in that case would be confined to this present world.[45] When Christ was "received up"[46] to his Father, he was enthroned above all powers in heaven and earth,[47] and began his ministry as the mediator between "himself and man".[48] This was possible because Christ had procured the atonement, which the glossator pleasantly defined as "peace with God through faith in Christ".[49] This relationship came about as the result of no after-thought on the part of God, but sprang from "the secret counsels of Deity",[50] which brought about the forgiveness of sins[51] and the restoration of the broken communion between God and the sinner. There is no hint of any other intermediary—angel, saint, or priest—between God and fallen man in the writings of Patrick and for three centuries after his day. Christ alone was regarded as making "intercession—he mediates, i.e. the manhood which he received from us makes supplication to the Deity that we may not die".[52] For the Celt faith laid hold on his resurrected Lord with the petition, "May Christ prepare my pleadings".[53] This view must be set against that held in Roman Christianity with its many intercessors.

Celtic literature is pervaded by devotional expressions of adoration. But perhaps the most beautiful invocation of the Lord Jesus Christ, in all his attributes, is the magnificent prayer, part of which now follows:

> Be Thou my Vision, O Lord of my heart;
> Naught is all else to me, save that Thou art,
> Thou my best thought, by day and by night,
> Waking or sleeping, Thy presence my light.

> Be Thou my Wisdom, Thou my true Word;
> I ever with Thee, Thou with me, Lord.
> Thou my great Father, I Thy dear son;
> Thou in me dwelling, I with Thee one. . . .

> With the High King of heaven, after victory won,
> May I reach heaven's joys, O bright heaven's Sun!
> Heart of my own heart, whatever befall,
> Still be my Vision, O Ruler of all.[54]

The attitude of Celtic theologians to the problems connected with the conflicts and tensions of Christology is reflected by the terms in which they described aspects of the ministry of Christ: the salvation of man was a mystery,[55] as was the incarnation and birth of Christ,[56] and the cross on which he suffered.[57] The theme of Calvary, the glossator warned, would be obscured were the preacher to indulge his eloquence; simplicity must be the way of its presentation.[58] Even then, the preacher should never forget that he is proclaiming a mystery.[59] The spirit of the glosses is simple and sincere, with the purpose of stressing the practical force of Christian teaching with no attempt at defining its mysteries.

No question arose regarding the deity of the Spirit. Patrick and the commentator both regarded him as one of the Trinity.[60] But while he breathes in the Father and the Son,[61] Patrick noted that it was Christ alone who shed on the believer the gift of the Spirit as the earnest of salvation.[62] The Nicene Creed, on the other hand, affirmed that the Spirit proceeds from both the Father and the Son. Patrick apparently did not know this formula, or chose not to adhere to it.

The Holy Spirit was believed to have spoken through the prophets of the Old Testament and the writers of the New. This would, of course, account for the veneration with which the two Testaments were regarded in the Celtic Church. Not only did the Spirit manifest himself by inspiring the writers of the Bible, he also poured "gifts" upon the faithful.[63] Among these the glossator mentioned the gift of healing, explaining this as power bestowed upon the missioner to attend the sick as physicians do.[64] This was the notion of Pelagius also, and has nothing of the miraculous in it.[65] Another gift of the Spirit was teaching, a ministry carried out amazingly well by Celtic evangelists for many centuries.[66]

The Spirit was also believed to inspire belief which resulted in salvation,[67] inducing men to obey the divine laws, and enabling them to become sons of God and joint heirs with Christ.[68] The Spirit placed his sign[69] on the faithful so that they might be recorded as being in unity with Christ,[70] through their drinking great draughts of the grace of the Spirit.[71] Thus the Spirit helped to restore in man's fallen nature the divine ideal which he had lost at the fall.[72] Patrick noted the same thought, remarking that it was the Spirit who dwelt in his heart and who had brought about the change in his character.[73] The Christian's mind was termed "the guest-house of the Spirit",[74] and with him abiding within it was easy for the disciple to do what was good.[75]

The Spirit also enables man to discover truth[76] by illuminating his mind through grace,[77] and directing his prayers,[78] which were held to be ineffectual without the inspiration of the Spirit. This illumination will bring about "the resurrection" or new birth through baptism,[79] which results in the believer's possessing "the mind or desires of the Spirit",[80] for it is the Spirit who places holy aspirations in the soul of man. An Old-Irish poem epitomized the longing for the in-dwelling of the Holy Spirit:

> The Holy Spirit to inhabit
> our body and our souls,
> to protect us speedily ...
>
> O Jesus, may it sanctify us,
> May Thy Spirit free us![81]

From the fragmentary evidence which comes from the Old-Irish period the semi-Arian view of Christ's birth and the single procession of the Spirit from Christ alone are the peculiar emphases of the Celtic doctrine of the Trinity.

DOCTRINE OF CREATIONISM

Celtic cosmological views were based on a literal interpretation of the story of Genesis. The elements which make up the material universe came into being as the result of a fiat creation,[82] through the agency of Jesus Christ and by his power.[83] One of the purposes, stressed by the commentators, for which the world was brought into being, was that the character of God might be learned through a study of it.[84] For instance: "Not less does the disposition of the elements set forth concerning God and manifest Him than though it were a teacher who set forth and preached it with his lips."[85] While it is true that there was no spoken language through which nature communicated with men, the Celtic mystic felt that "without art of learning and practice by anyone, it is understood in every nation the way in which the elements sound and show forth the knowledge of God through the work that they do and the alteration that is on them".[86] It was probably this appreciation of nature's revelation of the character of God that led to the production of so much beautiful mystic nature poetry.[87]

But following the time of the Danish invasions Celtic writers more and more formulated running stories of Creation, the Fall, and the working out of the plan of salvation based on speculation. The *Salthair na Rann* appears to have anticipated the plan of *Paradise Lost* and *Paradise Regained*. In this ancient poem the universe was pictured as consisting of seven heavens surrounded by coloured and fettered winds, with the sun passing rhough the open windows of the twelve divisions of the heavens. This curious concept of the heavens was matched by an equally interesting concept of the earth surrounded by a firmament, "like a shell around an egg", and constituting the centre of the universe.[88] These views are in marked contrast with the Old-Irish records which hold to a literal interpretation of the scriptural narrative. The later views were themselves modified into highly speculative, poetic fantasies such as are contained in the *Ever New Tongue*.[89]

DOCTRINE OF MAN

As already noted, Celtic Christians accepted the story of the beginnings of the human race as recorded in Genesis. Formed by God, from whom all things have their origin,[90] first created Adam was put as ruler over birds, fish, and all beasts.[91] Man himself was understood to be constituted in the threefold designation of the Apostle, body, soul, and spirit.[92] The commentator has left these two definitions: "The soul and spirit are one part, and the flesh is another, but the division of them is understood by the Word of God ... The soul itself is the animal life; the spirit is the spiritual reason in the soul.[93] Spirit—the primary part of the soul, by which we understand."[94] But by the term spirit he appears to have understood the mind of man, while "it is the soul that is ready to fulfil the law of God, and not the body".[95]

Although created perfect, man's first parents, having been attacked by the Devil and seduced, fell into sin.[96] It is in his body that man "sinned from Adam".[97] His immortality, the Celt felt, was contingent on his obedience to the law of God. This should be stressed. Man was mortal and after punishment the sinner would be annihilated. If he lived merely for pleasure, he resembled the quadruped,[98] but should he overcome, an immortal dwelling would be set down around him from heaven,[99] and the victor would be granted eternal life when the deeds of the flesh had been mortified.[100] Here again stress upon the divine requirements should be noted, as another instance in which Pelagius was followed. Man's nature is immortal only on condition of his obedience to God's law.

The Celtic Christian seems to have regarded himself as a part of the divine scheme of things; his life was under the guidance of God. Patrick, for instance, was confident that he had been fore-ordained by providence: "I make no false claim. I have part with those whom he called and predestinated to preach the Gospel amidst no small persecutions, even unto the end of the earth."[101] The glossator attempted to explain this doctrine of predestination in the context of God's dealings with the Jews and the Gentiles: "God's purpose was the election of one [the Jew] through mercy, and the condemnation of the other [the Gentile] by a just judgment",[102] but notwithstanding, being the one God over all, he desires the salvation of all mankind.[103] The commentator equated adoption and election in his estimate of the meaning of the Apostle's state-ment that God has predestinated man to be his children, "sons by election, not by nature".[104]

The Celt set out to find the solution of the age-old question, Why, if God desires the salvation of all men, are not all men saved?

> The answer is not difficult: Because no one is constrained against his will; or, a part is put for the whole, for there is no race or language in the world, of which some one was not saved; or, it was those only whom he desired to save that he did save, i.e., "who will have all men to be saved", that is, Augustine says, as much as to say, no one can be saved except him whom he wills.[105]

While he remarked that the answer was not difficult, the presence of no fewer than five different explanations reflects the existence of the grave difficulty which has confronted all theologians in their discussions of the dealings of God with man. The first answer was by Pelagius, who stressed man's free choice. Later comments, show-ing dissatisfaction with this answer, indicate a quest for others. In God's plan, the glossator noted, all men were in the same state through their unbelief. This was not because God arbitrarily decided to condemn mankind, but is perfectly reasonable, since all men have sinned. No one has any advantage over another, and "to boast of one's merits is of no avail here, so that it was by God's mercy that they were saved".[106] The expression "a law of providence" recurs in the glosses. It seems to mean an overruling divine purpose. Some argued that there was no such providence, and that "might was right".[107] Others contended that, when the poor or weak were under the rich or powerful, God was carrying out his plan to help them. Eventually God will vindicate all who trust in him,[108] for those who are disciplined by tribulation are often much more ready to be grateful for God's help, and become eager to pray for it. The Pelagian point of view is here manifest. Man's freedom of will, modified by trials, should be exercised in choosing God's way. Thus the operation of grace would bring about man's ultimate well-being. But nowhere was there any peculiarly Celtic view stated.

Secundus' concept of man's human nature was an exalted one. Nowhere in the commentaries of Old-Irish writers was there any stress on the worthlessness of the body. Secundus sang of Patrick: His "flesh he hath prepared as a temple for the Holy Spirit; by whom, in pure activities, it is continually possessed; and he doth offer it to God as a living and acceptable sacrifice".[109] But Patrick himself was all too aware of his own human weaknesses:

> I do not trust myself as long as I am in the body of this death, because he is strong who daily endeavours to turn me away from the faith, and from that chastity of unfeigned religion which I have purposed to keep to the end of my life for Christ my Lord. But the flesh, the enemy, is ever dragging us unto death, that is, to do that which is forbidden.[110]

Only God's empowering grace, he felt, would turn this impotence into victory, but final glorification of man would be attained only after the resurrection at the last day:

> Most surely I deem that if this should happen to me, I have gained my soul as well as my body, because without any doubt we shall rise on that day, in the clear shining of the sun, that is, in the glory of Christ Jesus our Redeemer, as sons of the living God, and joint heirs with Christ, and conformed to his

image, that will be; since of him and through him and in him we shall reign.[111]

But besides this notion of the resurrection of the body in the last days, other views were also mooted. Some wondered whether by the idea of the resurrection was meant "sons succeeding their fathers", or even the coming out of bondage and tribulation of God's people.[112]

But whatever the road, the goal of godly living was eternal life in future glory,[113] to the attaining of which the Celtic preacher constantly urged his hearers.[114] Patrick, too, looked forward to this ultimate consummation of life's hopes: "We, on the other hand, who believe in and worship the true sun, Christ—who will never perish, nor will any one who doeth his will; but he will abide for ever, as Christ will abide for ever, who reigneth with God the Father Almighty, and with the Holy Spirit, before the worlds, and now, and for ever and ever."[115] While the belief was held that the righteous will be resurrected on the last day, the wicked would then be destroyed in hell. Patrick's declaration illustrated this point regarding "those whom the devil grievously ensnared. In everlasting punishment they will become slaves of hell along with him; for verily whosoever committeth sin is a bondservant of sin, and is called a son of the devil."[116] The crux of the relationship between fallen man and God's grace was human choice. Placed on the side of divine providence it made possible the outworking of God's purpose on behalf of the sinner. In the emphasis placed on the need for man to exercise his will to do right Pelagian overtones are detectable.

DOCTRINE OF DUTY

Celtic interest in the Decalogue has been noted. This section considers the theological implications of this attitude. The term law, loosely applied by Celtic writers to the entire message of God, meant:

These four laws are recognized in judicature. The law of nature, i.e. the rule which Adam had. The patriarchal law, i.e. this was the rule which his Pater, his Father, spoke to Moses. Law of the prophets, i.e. Isaias, &c. The law of the New Testament, i.e. this is the rule of the testament from the birth of Christ to the present day.[117]

But more specifically the word law pointed to the Decalogue.

Through the law of Moses sin was defined to the believer, who discovered that it ultimately brought about death.[118] Sin cannot be discerned without law,[119] and the very Decalogue is called the "law of sin because it makes sins manifest".[120] To those who see sin through the ministry of law, and who then purpose to carry out its requirements, all the rewards which God has promised will be granted,[121] and the very law itself will prove to be a delight. This enjoyment of the commandments by the Christian himself constitutes a proof that it is good.[122] In these emphases on the function of law further Pelagian overtones are to be seen.[123]

All who disobey will be condemned by the Decalogue which they have outraged, and suffer the vengeance which has been threatened.[124] Those, on the other hand, who fulfil all its requirements[125] will attain to all the blessedness promised in the Bible.[126] In none of the writings of Celtic theologians is any antinomian view to be found. But there is indication that this enthusiasm for the Decalogue was deprecated by detractors who "used to count as a reproach to us that we should be subject to Law".[127] But in spite of a high regard for the law the commentator was well aware of its limitation in not being able to "completely accomplish justification",[128] since it was obvious the law could make no one perfect.[129] Its weaknesses were shadowed forth by the ritual of the ancient Hebrews, and yet these very transitory ceremonies of the law adumbrated Christ's sacrifice and mediation: "for it is he that hath been figured in the Law and declared in the Gospel; to bring you from the gospel into the ten commandments of the Law".[130] This is an interesting point of view: the Old Testament laws with their ritual and sacrifices pointed to Christ as the fulfilment of their hopes; Christ and the gospel turned the Christian back to the Old Testament Decalogue to find out why his Lord needed to die. Having discovered this the Christian is more ready to accept what his Saviour has done for him. In exposing sin the law drives the penitent to Christ, who empowers him to live according to the divine standard, and then the Christian comes back to the Ten Commandments to check his own progress in righteousness. Prohibition clarifies sin[131] and underlines guilt.[132] The knowledge of the law then increases responsibility.

The role of the Decalogue in the life of the Celtic Christian was of great importance. It modified the old tribal regulations and made the sentences for crimes less barbarous. It was reflected in the observances of many of the Old Testament regulations, and moulded theological attitudes towards sin and righteousness.

DOCTRINE OF SALVATION

Since the human race was ungodly[133] because of the Fall, man was believed to be helpless until he became a follower of Christ.[134] Left to his own resources he could not serve God. Only by the empowering of divine grace could man accomplish any good. Patrick was conscious of the working of this heavenly impulse in his life: "The Lord opened the understanding of my unbelief that, even though late, I might call my faults to remembrance, and that I might turn with all my heart to the Lord my God",[135] and it is thus that God "makes those who believe and obey to become children of God the Father and joint heirs with Christ".[136] So man is saved, not by the merits of his deeds, "but by God and His grace."[137] This Celtic viewpoint was again stressed by the Reformers.

The merits of Christ were felt by Celtic theologians to be vital to salvation. Imputed by the Saviour to the believer,[138] they procured his acceptance by God. The sinner could claim no other goodness, his own or the works of the law,[139] as the basis of his salvation. Through belief in his heart the sinner was regarded as righteous. By his confession of faith he was made "safe". "Through these two means a man becomes righteous, and is saved, so that he may be so forever."[140] By an act of will the penitent places himself on the side of Christ and righteousness. The sin he served he regards as dead.[141] He then is about to cry exultantly, "I am only alive because Christ is in me."[142] So man is justified, the glossator noted, "by faith only, i.e. by faith on belief in Jesus Christ".[143]

The question evidently arose, Does grace abrogate law? To this the commentator responded, "We establish it [the law] while we prove the truth of God's promise."[144] The Christian must rest his faith in God in the same way in which Abraham did, for even in the Christian era "it is the righteousness of Christ that justifies, and not the righteousness of the law".[145] Not only did faith justify, it was the sole basis for sanctification of the Christian's life which followed his justification. As the repentant sinner day by day seeks to carry out the will of God as revealed in his law, he becomes sanctified through empowering grace.[146] So Patrick affirmed, "Most surely I deem that from God I have received what I am",[147] adding, "I am only worth what he himself has given to me."[148] There is no stress in the glosses, as there is none in the writings of Patrick and other writers of the Celtic period, on works of merit. The basis of salvation is the grace of Christ accepted by faith on the part of the Christian, and operating in his life to bring about conformity to the will of God as revealed in his law.

The commentator appears to have been confused regarding the nature of the sin inherited by man. St Paul's term, "the old man", he defined as "the mass of old sins: or, Adam with his deeds".[149] Explaining the Apostle's statement that humanity was "sold under sin", he noted that it is "Adam; or, my carnal will sold me so that I am under bondage to sin".[150] Then, on the implications of Adam's transgression, he observed, "I say it was not imputed."[151] This was the view of Pelagius, who understood that each man was condemned because of his personal sin, and not through any inherited guilt. There was no such thing as "original sin." But there was a question whether Adam's guilt was "imputed" to man. Some argued that if Adam's sin infected all men, then Christ's righteousness should benefit all men also.[152] But this view was regarded as heretical. The doctrine of sin was simply left with the remark that upon humanity "judgment is through one sin by Adam; grace of many offences, by Jesus Christ, unto me".[153] But there was an important proviso in the mind of the commentator, who declared that we have sinned not "from the nature of original creation, but it is from our sinful nature that we have transgressed since Adam".[154] This is significant as indicating that some felt that Adam's sinful nature had passed to his posterity, while others considered that each man sinned through his own volition without reference to any potential to sin through his heredity.

Because of Adam's transgression death passed on all. With Pelagius the Celt differentiated between two kinds of death. Natural death was "the separation of body and soul".[155] This was the common death[156] of all humanity. "Penal death",[157] on the other hand, would overtake the wicked only. It was this death which Christ suffered on Calvary, bearing the punishment which should have been meted to the sinner.[158] But the commentator was unable to decide whether the view of Pelagius was correct: that sin resulted in the individual by the exercise of his choice, and did not originate from Adam's sin through an hereditary succession. But of the fact that Celtic views on sin were affected by Pelagius there would seem little doubt.

Prayer was a marked and vital characteristic of the Celt. Patrick used to pray as many as one hundred prayers each night.[159] A spirit of reverent devotion breathes through the brief, epigrammatical petitions of the Old-Irish glossators:

> I dare to entreat thee that thou hear me. I bind my thoughts to thee, I pray that thou forgive me what I pray for to thee. I am compelled to pray for them to thee.[160]

> It is best grateful in thy eyes, O God, to offer to thee the service of well-doing, for it is that which thou deemest the best that is offered to thee.[161]

> Every praise wherewith I have been praised, O God, has been wrought through thee.[162]

> My purification is lacking, if thou purify me not, O God.[163]

Scores of these petitions exist. It was evidently a predilection of Celtic clerics to improvise prayers. Later they were accused of spoiling the Divine Office with too many![164] Petitions were addressed to God,[165] and to Christ,[166] with the understanding that what was contrary to salvation would be denied by God,[167] in spite of many prayers. The Christian was warned against a mere repetition of empty words. "Whosoever, therefore, merely prays with his lips and belies his prayers by his conduct, procures scorn for himself; nay, renders himself hateful rather than pleasing to the Lord. Therefore, they only are wont to be heard by the Lord who seek a thing by prayer and ensure it by good conduct."[168] To this careful intention to pray with sincerity must be added diligence, for prayers from "slothful and sleepy" petitioners are powerless.[169] Christians were also recommended to pray for each other, for "mutual intercession" is a necessary part of the life of piety.[170]

The ideas regarding prayer, held in the community in which the glossator lived at the end of the eighth century, are of considerable interest in showing his attitude towards the canonical hours:

> Question: What is prayer without ceasing? The answer is not difficult. Some say it is celebrating the canonical hours, but this

is not the true meaning. But it is when all the members (of the body) are inclined to good deeds, and evil deeds are put away from them. Then, when doing good, they are praying to God, that is, they incline their eyes to see what is good, as Job says, "I made a covenant with mine eyes".[171]

There are traces in the writings of Columbanus and Adamnan[172] that set hours for prayer were observed, but there is no evidence that the same practices were followed in other localities by all Celtic Christians. In fact, one of the reforms achieved by Malachy was the establishment of the regular canonical hours, "for there was not such thing before, not even in the city" of Armagh prior to the twelfth century.[173]

There is no indication that Patrick, or Celtic Christians for two centuries after him, invoked saints or angels. As was seen above, Christ was regarded as the only Mediator. But following the acceptance of the Roman Easter and other eighth-century Western Christian views, hagiographers recorded many petitions addressed to various saints,[174] angels, martyrs, and the Virgin.[175] Comminatory stories were told to establish this belief,[176] and later litanies were fathered on early Celtic saints, including Adamnan,[177] to gain authority for these changes. Some traces of petitions on behalf of the dead are found as early as the sixth century, but they consist of single invocations carved on grave-stones. Notwithstanding this, a canon attributed to Patrick sought to show the futility of prayer for the dead:

> Of offering for the dead: Hearken unto the Apostle when he saith: "There is a sin unto death, for that I say not that any man ask." And to the Lord: "Give not that which is holy to dogs." For he who did not in his life deserve to receive the sacrifice, how shall it be able to help him after death.[178]

But the Old-Irish Penitential (c. eighth century), reflecting a Roman influence, represents a modification of this point of view:

> Anyone who kills himself while insane, prayers are said for him, and alms are given for his soul, if he was previously pious. If he has killed himself in despair or for any other reason, he must be left to the judgement of God, for men dare not offer prayers for him — that is, a Mass — unless it be some other prayer, and alms-giving to the poor and miserable.[179]

This simple philosophy of prayer was later changed when the doctrine of an intermediary state between heaven and hell was accepted by Celtic Christians, and an involved technique for rescuing the dead devised.

DOCTRINE OF ANGELS

From Patrick's simple allusions to angels,[180] their position and function became more prominent and complex in later writers who accepted the views of the Romans. Every reference by Patrick to the functioning of angels was a biblical quotation. The Würtzburg glossator gave his view thus: "It is the angels of God who will be engaged in guarding the righteous man, and their substance is nobler, and their creation is prior to men, and therefore they guard him, that the trials of the Devil may not reach him."[181] The later hagiographers frequently refer to the nine orders of angels who did not rebel with the Devil,[182] and who constitute the quire of the household of heaven.[183] But some of the loyal angels, who make up the "household of heaven",[184] rebelled and became "fugitive".[185] The *Altus Prosator* paints a vivid picture of this concept:

From the summit of the kingdom of heaven, of angelic rank
From the brightness of effulgence, from the loveliness of beauty,
Lucifer, whom God had made, fell by being proud,
And the apostate angels, with the same mournful fall
Of the author of vain-glory, and of obstinate envy;
The rest remaining in their Principalities.

The Dragon, great, most foul, terrible and old, . . .
Drew with him the third part of the stars,
Into the pit of infernal places, and of diverse prisons,
Deserters of the true Light, cast headlong by the parasite.[186]

These evil angels were believed to be able even to "preach another gospel" to the unwary.[187] Fantastic stories were invented after the tenth century to prove the prowess of angels. One helped Patrick to clean his hearth;[188] another was midwife to Senan's mother;[189] others assisted Ciaran to grind his corn;[190] changed oats into wheat;[191] brought an epistle to Patrick;[192] dictated "the whole sacred ecclesiastical Rule" to Brenainn;[193] showed Findian where to build a church in Leinster;[194] in the form of white virgins fostered Brenainn;[195] and came for saints on their death-beds.[196]

Comminatory stories using angels as authority for practices which sprang up later were often told. Angels placed a veil over the head of a consecrated virgin;[197] taught Patrick and Secundus to sing the hymn *Sancti venite, Christi corpus*;[198] inaugurated funeral wakes;[199] and even became patron angels: "Because Michael was the angel of the race of the Hebrews, so Victor was of the Irish. Hence he cared for them by means of Patrick."[200]

Patrick accepted the possibility of man's having personal encounters with the Devil; he had had such himself:

> Now on that same night, when I was sleeping, Satan assailed me mightily, in such sort as I shall remember as long as I am in this body. And he fell upon me as it were a huge rock, and I had no power over my limbs ... I believe that I was helped by Christ my Lord, and that his Spirit was even then calling aloud on my behalf.[201]

The glossator believed that the Devil rebelled, and, with his followers, was cast out of heaven to this earth, and henceforward ranged himself in opposition to Christ and his followers: "As Christ works in the righteous, according to what St Paul says: 'God worketh in you,' so does the devil work in the children of unbelief. Sons, then, are those by works, not by nature. The children of unbelief or despair are they who despaired of their salvation through Christ's passions."[202] "Despair" was a concept of Pelagius. Notwithstanding the power of evil God always helps those who cry to him, so that "we are not deceived, that is, through despair, for he [Satan] is cunning in persuading the sin so that it is complete; after its completion, he persuades the sinner to despair".[203] The Devil tempted Juliana in the shape of an angel,[204] but the advice of the commentator was, "Let him not come into your heart instead of God".[205] This simple dualism later degenerated into fabulous tales of the work of the Devil, who passed through the air to carry off the souls of the wicked.[206] Brigit was made to see "Satan beside the table, his head down and his feet up, his smoke and his flame out of his gullet, and out of his nose";[207] Brenainn was believed to have observed the Devil, "awful, hideous, foul, hellish",[208] "Squirting the waters from him, and killing those who would drink them".[209] Pagan and superstitious views of angels were encrusted around the earlier, simpler biblical ones by later hagiographers.

DOCTRINE OF LAST THINGS

Patrick and early Celtic Christians believed in the second advent of Christ. The Apostle of Ireland declared: "We look for his coming soon as the Judge of the quick and the dead", to render just rewards to all,[210] after "his descent for the judgment of Doom".[211] Columba also looked for "Christ the Most High Lord coming down from heaven".[212] The commentator was of the opinion that Christ's second advent would not be like his first,[213] for Christ would come the second time with the sound of the trumpet which accompanied God, as on Mount Sinai.[214] And faithful Christians who recognized the first advent by the gospel would "know the second advent by revelation".[215]

The final event in history was believed to be the second advent "at the last trump". This meant the last invitation to accept the gospel, "for there will not be any sound of assembly after that".[216] Then Christ will pour out his judgements upon all sinners, for "he protects neither those who never heard Him, nor those who having heard transgress".[217] But when Christ as the true Judge[218] pronounces the sentence on all, "none will be able to absent himself", but will be compelled to give an account of even his smallest sins before the judgement seat of Christ the Lord.[219] The glossator corroborated Patrick's view, remarking that "God the Father shall execute judgement by Jesus Christ; that is, the Son shall judge in the day of judgement, according to our Lord's words (John 5.22)".[220]

Connected with the second advent was the resurrection of the dead, not "to be examined, but resurrected in order to receive the condemnation to which they have been sentenced".[221] Evidently there was some belief that judgement had preceded the advent, at which time the sentence would be meted out. Then every man would be compelled to answer for himself,[222] for no excuse would be tolerated by the divine tribunal: "If they reply, 'We did not recognize him, for his human nature concealed his divinity', the answer will be, 'You believed in the devil, though he also was incarnate.' It is right, then, that they who are not admitted to the glory of Christ share the condemnation of the devil."[223] Patrick and the early Celtic Christians believed that the second advent of Christ and the end of the world were near at hand. The glossator remarked that "time is short—that is, the end of the world".[224] Patrick was certain that he had been called by God to preach a vital message to the wicked so that they might prepare for eternity. He believed, in fact, that he was actually living "in the last days":

> I ought to receive it with an equal mind, and ever render thanks to God who showed me that I might trust him endlessly, as one that cannot be doubted; and who heard me, so that I, ignorant as I am, and in the last days, should be bold to undertake this work so holy and so wonderful; so that I might imitate in some degree those of whom the Lord long ago foretold, when forshewing that his Gospel would be for a witness unto all nations before the end of the world. And accordingly, as we see, this has been so fulfilled. Behold, we are witnesses that the Gospel has been preached to the limit beyond which no man dwells.[225]

Patrick could therefore affirm, "We look for his coming soon to be."[226] Columbanus likewise believed that "the world is already in its last days".[227]

A consideration of these Celtic doctrines reveals a significant independence of thought and exegesis. There might be here and there the echo of some phrase coined by a theologian of the West, but for the most part the Celtic teacher phrased his understanding of the meaning of the Bible in his own words, seeking always to apply it to some practical need. Celtic theology is biblical theology with no patristic emphases. A study of the Deity was made to reveal qualities of benevolence working toward the salvation of fallen man. Human redemption was procured solely by the sacrificed merits of the Son of God without any works on the part of man to earn his salvation. And yet man was believed to be required to exercise his will in obeying the Decalogue, albeit through the generously bestowed grace of God to empower his efforts. Great stress was laid upon God's law in all its bearings, especially in its function as the revealer of sin. Man's personal responsibility for his own sinning, like the stress laid on the law, is an echo of the teaching of Pelagius. Angels were held to be celestial assistants to man, while a simple dualism sets him against the Devil and evil angels. At the end of human history Christ was believed to return to re-establish man in that state for which he was originally created. The reader in the sources of Celtic Christian theology finds only a simple devotional study of the Scriptures, which, taken in their most literal sense, form the basis of Celtic beliefs.

There is no involvement in theological argumentation or in any attempt to reach definitions of obscure and theoretical terms. Aloof from the religious stresses of Mediterranean countries the teachers of the Celtic west went their own ways, seeking to understand the will of God for them as revealed in the Scriptures.

CHAPTER 3 the christian year

Particular days have been connected with acts of worship in the Christian calendar. Some of these times of devotion recurred weekly, while others fell annually.

Like other Christian bodies in both the East and West, the Celtic Church set aside special days to fulfil its sacred obligations. The Sabbath was ever carefully kept by the Hebrews, and was observed by our Lord.[1] The first converts to the Christian faith had been Jews. They continued to observe the Sabbath. But several factors combined to induce Christians to give up the observance of the Sabbath in favour of Sunday in succeeding centuries. After the fall of Jerusalem in 70, and then the crushing of the revolt led by Bar Cochbar in 135, the Jews were scattered and their name and religion execrated. One of the more obvious marks of a Jew was his observance of the Sabbath. Christians, keeping the Sabbath, not because they were Jews but in honour of creation and in obedience to the fourth commandment, were, however, stigmatized as Jews. They were accused, especially in Roman metropolitan areas, of practising an illegal religion.

Soon after the founding of the faith Gnosticism and Mithraism raised tensions in Christian thinking.[2] Gnostics "celebrated the Sunday of every week, not on account of its reference to the resurrection of Christ, for that would have been inconsistent with their Docetism, but as the day consecrated to the sun, which was in fact their Christ".[3] The influence of Mithraism tended in the same direction, for, as G. L. Laing declared rightly: "Our observance of Sunday as the Lord's day is apparently derived from Mithraism. The argument that has sometimes been used against this claim, namely, that Sunday was chosen because of the resurrection on that day, is not well supported."[4] Those Christians who were looking for a way out of their difficulty with Sabbath observance moved towards a greater regard for the first day of the week. But others on the outskirts of the Empire, where anti-Semitism did not exist, continued their veneration of the seventh day Sabbath.

For two centuries the issue was undecided, but gradually Sunday proved to be more popular. When, on 7 March 321, Constantine decreed the observance of the "venerable day of the Sun",[5] the extinction of Sabbath observance among the majority of Christians became a foregone conclusion. But there are records that both days, Saturdays and Sundays, were kept in Mediterranean lands for at least two centuries after Constantine's edict.[6]

The Council of Laodicea in 364 went so far as to rule that the Sabbath should be deliberately desecrated: "Christians shall not Judaize and be idle on Saturday,[7] but shall work on that day: but the Lord's day they shall especially honour, and, as being Christians, shall, if possible, do no work on that day. If, however, they are found Judaizing, they shall be shut out from Christ."[8] But these ecclesiastical legislators apparently spoke only for a faction of Christians. At the beginning of the fifth century Socrates (+ 445) wrote of the situation as it then existed: "Although almost all churches throughout the world celebrate the sacred mysteries on the Sabbath of every week, yet the Christians of Alexandria and at Rome, on account of some ancient tradition, have ceased to do this."[9] He makes it plain that Christians at Alexandria and Rome had once observed the Sabbath but had moved to Sunday. In north Africa Augustine noted to what purpose Saturday was devoted on his own age: "On this day, which is the Sabbath, mostly those are accustomed to meet who are desirous of the Word of God ... in some places the communion takes place daily, in some only on the Sabbath and the Lord's day, and in some only on the Lord's day."[10] Jerome (+ 420) has left this picture of how Sunday was observed in his own community: "On the Lord's day only they

A page from the Latin Commentary of A.D. 815 found at Würtzburg, with marginal and interlinear glosses in Old-Irish on Romans 11.25–35.

proceed to the church beside which they lived, each company following its own mother-superior. Returning home in the same order, they then devoted themselves to their allotted tasks and made garments either for themselves or else for others."[11] Seemingly after divine worship on the morning of Sunday the rest of the day was regarded as secular time in which work might be done. The sabbatizing of Sunday had not yet begun.

Since Celtic practice received much of its inspiration from the monachism of Egypt, it would be helpful to consider the position of the Sabbath in Egypt during monasticism's formative years. Palladius in the fifth century observed that the monks of Nitria "occupy the church only on Saturday and Sunday",[12] at which time they celebrate the Lord's Supper.[13] When Palladius called on John of Lycopolis, he

> found the vestibule of his cell closed; for the brethren built on later a very large vestibule holding about 100 men, and shutting it with a key they opened it on Saturday[14] and Sunday. So, having learned the reason why it was closed, I waited quietly till the Saturday. And having come at the second hour for an interview I found him sitting by the window, through which he seemed to be exhorting his visitors.[15]

John evidently conducted his spiritual counselling and preaching on the Sabbath as well as on Sunday. Paesius and Isaias decided to become monks on the death of their father. One bestowed his fortune on the Church, and having learned a trade, supported himself by his own labours. "But the other parted with nothing, but making himself a monastery and getting together a few brethren welcomed every stranger, every invalid, every old man, every poor man, preparing three or four tables every Sunday and Saturday.[16] In this way he spent his money."[17] Various modes of monasticism were practised in Egypt: "For having divided the property, they applied themselves each to his purpose of pleasing God, but by different tactics."[18]

Elpidius established his hermitage in a cave near Jericho. "During his twenty-five years' life there he used to take food only on Sunday and Saturday[19] and would spend the nights standing up and singing the psalms."[20] Marcarius ate only on Sunday.[21] The virgin Taor and her companions went to church for communion on

Sunday.[22] One of Nathaniel's visitors identified himself thus: "I am so-and-so's little servant and I am carrying loaves, for it is this brother's *agape*, and to-morrow when Saturday[23] dawns offerings will be wanted."[24] Dom C. Butler summed up the evidence[25] in these words:

> The celebration of the Sabbath as well as the Lord's Day, the Saturday as well as the Sunday, common throughout Egypt and the East, is well illustrated in the *Lausaic History*. These were the only days on which the monks assembled at church, took communion, received visitors, fed the needy, and relaxed their fasts.[26]

Accounts from the sources showing that both the Sabbath and Sunday were kept throughout the early centuries of the Christian era might be multiplied. Out of this background the Celts drew their understanding of the days which should be observed.

Since the Celtic Church began when Sabbath observance had not been relinquished by Christians at large, it would be surprising, were the Sabbath not revered among them.[27] The early life of Patrick by Muirchu has two stories indicating Patrick's attitude towards the seventh day. These traditions had persisted for more than two centuries after the saint's death. His biographer observed:

> The angel was wont to come to him on every seventh day of the week; and, as one man talks with another, so Patrick enjoyed the angel's conversation.
>
> Moreover in the sixteenth year of his age he was taken captive, and for six years he was a slave, and throughout thirty changes of service the angel used to come to him; and he enjoyed angelic counsel and conversation.[28]

Muirchu identified Patrick's visitor: "Victor was the angel who was wont often to visit Patrick."[29] The saint himself referred to an acquaintance of his with this name. In his account of his call to missionary service in Ireland he wrote:

> I saw in the night visions a man whose name was Victoricus,[30] come as it were from Ireland with countless letters. And he gave me one of them, and I read the beginning of the letter, which was entitled, "The voice of the Irish"; and while I was reading aloud the beginning of the letter, I thought that at that very moment I heard the voice of them who lived beside the Wood of

Foclut which is nigh unto the western sea. And thus they cried, as with one mouth, "We beseech thee, holy youth, to come and walk among us once more."[31]

Years ago Alfred Anscombe made an illuminating suggestion identifying Victoricus.[32] Victricius (+ 407), bishop of Rouen, paid a visit to Britain, possibly to help the Christians to combat Arianism, but also to minister to believers from among the Morini and Nervii who were serving in the Roman legions, encamped near the Wall in Cumberland. Anscombe suggested that Victricius probably penetrated as far as Cumbria, and that Patrick might well have heard him preach, and that Victricius was changed to Victoricus in later accounts. Traditions of Patrick's contacts with Victoricus transformed him into an angel. Victricius might well have been the inspiration for Patrick's missionary ambition. Muirchu simply recorded that Patrick and Victricius met "every seventh day of the week" for prayer and spiritual converse.[33] Worship on the seventh day is quite in keeping with the milieu and the age in which Patrick lived.

Muirchu noted the method used by Patrick in working for the conversion of pagans. This narrative also makes reference to the seventh day. A young lady of royal birth (in eulogies converts of the saints were frequently of royal birth!) named Moneisen, contrary to her parents' wishes, desired to remain unmarried. In their quandary her mother and father "having taken advice given to them by God, heard of Patrick as a man who was visited by the everlasting God every seventh day; and they sought the Scottic country with their daughter, looking for Patrick".[34] And so the legend grew. Patrick's sabbatic devotions, associated with Victricius, became in course of time converse with an angel Victor, and finally developed into Patrick's weekly visit by the everlasting God on every seventh day! Patrick himself says nothing of Sunday.

Almost five centuries later, when the movement to sabbatize Sunday was under way, in accounts of Patrick's activities several comminatory anecdotes for Sunday observance are fathered on the saint. Patrick's journeys were occasionally terminated in the records by the phrase "and he rested there on Sunday".[35] Then stories were introduced into his activities as propaganda for stricter Sunday observance. For instance, at Mag Reta, "Patrick abode there through a Sunday. And on that Sunday they were digging the foundation of Rath Baccain, the royal stronghold of the district. Patrick went to forbid this. Nothing was done for him."[36] So Patrick was recorded as cursing the building and its builders. A storm vindicated the saint by destroying what had been erected. Another anecdote was told to show how carefully the saint kept Sunday and how heaven blessed him for this:

> From vespers on Sunday night until the third [Roman] hour on Monday, Patrick used not to go out of the place wherein he was biding. [And] on a certain Sunday Patrick was afield at the hour of evening, and a great rain poured on that earth, but it poured not on the place wherein Patrick was staying, as happened in the case of Gideon's shell and fleece.[37]

Since the day was held by the Celtic Christians to begin at sundown, Patrick is said to have commenced his devotions on Saturday evening and to have continued them until dawn on Monday. "These are among the earliest Irish attempts to persuade Christians to observe Sunday as Sabbath"[38] is the correct observation of A. O. Anderson.

In the *Senchus Mor*, ancient Irish laws believed to have been framed with the help of Patrick, the relationship between the "tribe of the church" and the "tribe of the people" is carefully spelled out. These Christianized Brehon laws required that "every seventh day of the year" should be devoted to the service of God.[39] The first section of the paragraph in which this directive occurs dealt with the Christian's goods, defining the tithes and offerings which he should dedicate to God. Next, the time which the Christian should spend on sacred duties was regulated. That the later legal glossator understood the expression "every seventh day" as applying to the weekly rest day is proved by his comment, "he puts Sunday in the reckoning".[40] This, of course, would be a natural conclusion for him to draw after Sunday had superseded the Sabbath in the Celtic Church. Skene rightly observed on this point: "It is very characteristic of the spirit of these laws that the day of rest— the seventh day—should form one of the demands of the Church upon the lay tribe, which its members were bound to render for the service of God with their other dues."[41] When all regard for the seventh day had finally disappeared from the calendar of Celtic

Christians, the tradition still persisted that Patrick had believed that there was some special significance attached to the Sabbath. In a propaganda story to establish the virtue of Secundus' "Hymn in Praise of St Patrick" is a conversation between the saint and an angel:

"Is there aught else that he granted to me beside that?" saith Patrick. "There is", saith the angel. "Seven persons on every Saturday till Doom [are] to be taken out of Hell's pains." ... "Is there aught else, then, that will be given me?" said Patrick. "There is", saith the angel. "Thou shalt have out of [Hell's] pains seven every Thursday and twelve every Saturday."[42]

Thursday and Saturday were evidently days of devotion, in which special blessings might be claimed from God.*

A record of David's regard for the Sabbath was preserved in the *Second Life of St David*:

From the eve of the Sabbath, until the light shines in the first hour, after the break of day on the Sabbath, they employ themselves in watchings, prayers, and genuflections, except one hour after morning service on the Sabbath; they make known their thoughts to the father, and obtain his leave with respect to what was asked.[43]

The "eve of the Sabbath" was Friday at sunset. David evidently began his sabbatic devotions then,[44] and continued them until dawn of Sunday.

In later Roman and Western Church usage Saturday was made a fast while Sunday always was a festival. In the *Book of David* (c. 500–25) Sunday and Saturday were put on equal footing as far as the prohibition of fasting was concerned: "A bishop who wilfully commits murder, or any kind of fornication or fraud, shall do penance for thirteen years; but a presbyter seven years on bread and water, and a repast on Sunday or Saturday."[45] That fasting and abstinence from baths were not part of the ritual of Celtic Christians for Sabbath observance is illustrated by this anecdote: "A certain rich neighbour having prepared himself to bathe on the Sabbath day, as was his custom, saw them coming, weary from their journey and voyage; and seeing them, he would not bathe until the strangers, who were more worthy of bathing,

---

* See pp. 90–1 below.

had first bathed."[46] David observed Sunday as well as the Sabbath. His biographer recorded that "on Sunday, David sang mass, and preached to the people";[47] and that on one occasion "on the intervening Sunday, a great multitude heard him preach a most excellent sermon".[48]

This Welsh church leader, David, once called a synod in the absence of Cadoc, who was away on pilgrimage. The story records that on his return Cadoc was very incensed, but was admonished by a celestial messenger to be patient because "the irregularity of this business was allowed to blessed David by angelic intervention".[49] Cadoc was mollified and rewarded by the angel in these words:

> Because thou hast obeyed my voice, and at my entreaty hast forgiven what was committed against thee, the Lord my God will deliver thy castle full of the souls of men from eternal punishment, in the day of judgement; and as many shaggy hairs as are in thy cloak (a kind of garment which the Irish wear out of doors, full of prominent shaggy hairs, woven into a kind of plush), so many will be delivered by thee from eternal punishment. And also on every Sabbath, from this night for ever, one soul will be delivered from eternal torments for thy love.[50]

The Sabbath was held to be a day of blessing in Wales as well as in Ireland and other Celtic lands.

Columba was also vitally concerned with the Sabbath. In the story of the monastery of Tallaght the old point of view was preserved that there was little difference between the sacredness of the Sabbath and Sunday: "In the Rule of Columcille, Saturday's allowance of food and Sunday's allowance are equal amounts, because of the reverence that was paid to the Sabbath in the Old Testament. It differs from Sunday in work only. And in other rules there is similarity of allowances on Sabbath and on Sunday."[51] The Sabbath was revered by those who lived by the Rule of Columcille, and other monastic rules as well, and evidently, as in the case of Jerome's nunnery noted above, work might be performed by Columba's followers on Sunday after attendance at morning worship. But with the shift away from Sabbath observance after the Romanizing of the Celtic Church the regulation regarding the Sabbath was dropped, for, as A. O. Anderson points out, "The surviving 'Rule of Columcille' does not contain this item, but no authentic Rule of Columcille has survived."[52] Against the Celtic Sabbath observance the penitential of Theodore inveighs in no uncertain tone.[53]

There does not appear to be any direct evidence from his own works that Columbanus observed the Sabbath. But there does exist an epistle which has been attributed to him in which the topic is mentioned. This letter, which Walker included in his appendix to the works of Columbanus, has been variously attributed. Its title page has been lost, and so both the name of the author and that of the recipient are missing. On linguistic ground it is believed to have been composed by Columbanus, but "the authorship of the letter can only be left an open question" for the present.[54] The epistle, however, is held to be contemporaneous with Columbanus, and might well have been written by someone close to that saint. It dealt with the Hebrew festivals as well as with the Sabbath, and shows an affinity with early Celtic practice in quoting solely from the Scriptures, except for a possible allusion to an epigram by Jerome. The third section of the letter runs like this:

> We are bidden to work on six days, but on the seventh, which is the Sabbath, we are restrained from every servile labour. Now by the number six the completeness of our work is meant, since it was in six days that the Lord made heaven and earth. Yet on the Sabbath we are forbidden to labour at any servile work, that is sin, since he who commits sin is a slave to sin, so that, when in this present age we have completely fulfilled our works, not hardening our hearts, we may deserve to reach that true rest, which is denied to the unruly, as the Lord says through David, If they shall enter into my rest.[55]

This passage reveals that the writer believed that Saturday has been the Sabbath, but that in his segment of the Church it was esteemed only in a spiritual sense as a type of resting from sin. This is borne out by a previous statement in the epistle: "And also in the Gospel the Lord Jesus declared the ending of the Sabbath, when he bade the cripple, Take up thy bed, which is clearly forbidden in the law, I mean the bearing of burdens on the Sabbath."[56] The significance of this letter lies in the light it throws on the controversy which was apparently going on regarding the Sabbath and other festivals of the Hebrews. This tension is understandable in a Celtic Christian setting with its overtones of stress on the validity of the Old Testament.

Adamnan made several references to the Sabbath in his life of Columba. He told of a Sabbath service in which Columba blessed a barn.[57] Adamnan invariably employed the original biblical name, Sabbath, for the seventh day of the week, and spoke of it in a manner betokening a respect which is not detected in writers two centuries later. In discussing this matter with Diormit Columba is reported as declaring:

> This day is called in the sacred books "Sabbath", which is inter-preted "rest". And truly this day is for me a sabbath, because it is my last day of this present laborious life. In it after my toilsome labour I keep Sabbath;[58] and at midnight of this following venerated Lord's day, in the language of the Scriptures I shall go the way of the fathers. For now my Lord Jesus Christ deigns to invite me.[59]

From this and other passages it is true that Columba had some regard also for the first day of the week.[60] But a sabbatical Sunday had not yet been accepted in Iona at the time when Adamnan wrote.[61]

This respect for both days is illustrated also from the canons of various penitential books. Finnian ruled that "married people, then, must mutually abstain ... on Sunday night or Saturday night ..."[62] So from sunset on Friday until after the hours of Sunday has passed reverence for both days had to be shown. There are traces that the earliest settlers on the Faroes and Iceland probably observed the Sabbath, and so were accused of Judaizing:

> these islands were first inhabited by the Picts and *papae*, ... the *papae* had been named from their white robes, which they wore like priests; whence priests are all called *papae* in the Teutonic tongue. An island is still called, after them, Papey. But, as is observed from their habit and the writings of their books aban-doned there, they were Africans, adhering to Judaism.[63]

This is perhaps the earliest record of Celtic Christian settlers who were stigmatized as Judaizing. The statement that they were Africans is most baffling. It might indicate that their Scriptures had affinity with the African version, as had already been pointed out. But this is only a guess.

But with the acceptance of the Roman Easter and other rules the movement to sabbatize Sunday gained momentum. Pope Gregory (+ 604), as champion of Roman usages, had upheld the careful observance of Sunday, and had stigmatized any respect for the Sabbath as Judaizing. In a letter to the Roman people he wrote:

> It has come to my ears that certain men of perverse spirit have sown among you some things that are wrong and opposed to the holy faith, so as to forbid any work being done on the Sabbath day. What else can I call these but preachers of Antichrist, who, when he comes, will cause the Sabbath day as well as the Lord's day to be kept free from all work.[64]

It is not at all surprising, then, with the coming of Theodore of Tarsus (+ 690), the most successful protagonist of the Roman Church Britain had yet seen, to note a mounting emphasis on the observance of Sunday to the exclusion of all regard for Saturday. In his first book of Penitentials, Theodore drew up seven canons to deal with the keeping of Sunday, and in his second book he added a further four.[65] In fact a whole section was entitled "Those who despise the Lord's day, and neglect the appointed feasts of the church of God". Theodore prohibited all labour on the Lord's day, and forbade all fasting on it. One canon ruled: "If he fast out of contempt for the day, he shall be abhorred as a Jew by all the Catholic churches."[66]

In marked contrast with what has been noted regarding the attitude of Patrick and Columba to the observance of the Sabbath and the Lord's day is the directive in the later Old-Irish Penitential (c. 800): "Anyone who fasts on a Sunday through carelessness or austerity does a week's penance on bread and water."[67]

But the long debate continued among the Christians of Britain, and especially in Ireland, between those who advocated the observance of the Sabbath, and those who wished to keep both the Sabbath and Sunday, and those who pressed for a sabbatizing of Sunday only. A protagonist of Sunday observance went so far as to substitute "Lord's day" for "Sabbath" in the Ten Commandments as recorded in Exod. 20.8-11, in a sermon preserved in the Leabhar Breac.[68]

Columbanus allowed his monks to wash their hair or feet on Sunday.[69] This was, of course, contrary to a strict sabbatarian view of Sunday, and also went counter to Hebrew Sabbath regulations.

Columba made journeys on Sunday,[70] and Adamnan mentioned quite casually that pilgrims reached Iona who had travelled on Sunday.[71] In his description of the last night of Columba, a Sunday night, Adamnan tells of men who were fishing. Among them was a future holy monk and pilgrim for God.[72] So even at the end of the seventh century the washing of hair, travelling, or the gathering of food by fishing were not regarded as infractions of the laws of Sunday observance as they were understood by Celtic Christians.

But during the next two centuries the Romanizing of Celtic Christianity continued apace and the attitude towards Sunday altered greatly. Travelling was condemned in a comminatory story describing the arrival of Cronan's relatives with food for his monastery for the feast of Easter. When the visitors were still some distance away, they heard Cronan's vesper bell on Saturday evening. Immediately they camped by the river until Monday morning.[73]

But it would seem that the advocates for the secularization of the Sabbath and the rigidly sabbatic observance of Sunday found their progress too slow. They therefore fabricated propaganda to impress the rude masses of the people. An "Epistle of Christ" was said to have fallen from heaven in Rome[74] on the altar of St Peter. Its opening paragraph consisted of a catalogue of pseudo-biblical episodes which the author averred had occurred on Sunday, and so enhanced the sacredness of that day. But most of the stories are not to be found in the Scriptures. This would suggest that the rank and file of the Christians in Ireland during the later decades of the ninth and tenth centuries, had become ignorant of the contents of the Bible. The introduction to the "Epistle of Christ" concluded: "Therefore, it is through these commands that God has enjoined Sunday to be kept holy, for God's own hand has written that command to men, lest they should do either work or servile labour on Sunday."[75] The ancient annalist recorded for 886: "An Epistle came with the pilgrim to Ireland, with the *Cain Domnaig*, and other good instructions."[76] The following paragraphs present some of the arguments contained in the "Epistle" and give its flavour:

Here begins the Epistle of the Saviour our Lord Jesus Christ concerning the Lord's Day, which his own hand wrote in the presence of the men of Heaven, and which was placed upon the altar of Peter the Apostle in Rome of Latium, to make Sunday holy for all time. When this Epistle was brought from Heaven, the whole earth trembled from the rising unto the setting of the sun; and the earth cast its stones and trees on high, for dread of their Creator and for joy also at the attendance of the angels who had come with the Epistle; and so great was the din at that time, that the place opened where the body of Peter the Apostle lay buried in Rome. When the abbot of Rome was at Mass, he saw the Epistle on the altar.[77]

The "Epistle" having listed many fabulous calamities which had visited mankind as a result of the transgression of Sunday, then anathematizes all desecrators of this day: " 'Whoever shall not keep Sunday', said the heavenly Father, 'within its proper boundaries, his soul shall not attain Heaven, neither shall he see me in the Kingdom of Heaven, nor the Archangels, nor the Apostles.' "[78] After tabulating further dreadful misfortunes which would follow the breaking of Sunday, the writer added this strange piece of reasoning: "Now, even if this wonderful command for keeping Sunday holy had not come from Jesus Christ himself out of Heaven, the day should be sacred, venerable, perfect, and honoured, on account of all the many miracles that have happened thereon."[79] The Irish pilgrim Conall MacCoelmaine was believed to have been in Rome when the letter arrived and made a transcript of it: "Conall then wrote with his own hand the Epistle of Sunday from the Epistle which was sent from Heaven unto the altar of Peter the Apostle in Rome. When it was time to lift the shrine, the saint revealed it in a vision to the priest who was at the altar."[80] Now Conall MacCoelmaine died about 590. The fact that the bringing of the "Epistle" to Ireland had been fathered on one who had gone to his rest three centuries before its actual arrival (886) indicates the doubts which must have filled the minds of many regarding its authenticity and acceptability.

The "Epistle" presented a detailed list of what might not be done on Sunday, and then stipulated that

Whosoever shall do this on Sunday, unless he shall perform great penance for it, his soul shall not attain Heaven. "I swear," saith the abbot of Rome, "by the might of God the Father, and by Christ's Cross, that this is no invention of mine, and no fiction or fable; but it is from God the Father this Epistle was sent unto the altar of Peter in Rome of Latium to make Sunday holy."[81]

Even baptism was prohibited on Sunday. What was permitted was the "seeking a person in orders for the sake of Communion; but baptism is not sought unless it is likely that the infant shall be dead".[82] The "Epistle" ended with this recommendation to all duly constituted legal organizations to enforce Sunday legislation: "There is a further enactment of this law: whatsoever meeting and whatsoever assembly in which tribes or kings meet, that it be the law of Sunday which is first passed therein. It is enacted: The curse of every person on all who shall break this law of Sunday."[83]

That the *Cain Domnaig*, or the Law of Sunday, was actually brought with the "Epistle of Christ" from Rome is to be doubted. The *Cain Domnaig* appears to be a Christianized Brehon law tract based on the "Epistle". It has a definitely Irish flavour, and was probably devised as part of the movement to sabbatize the observance of Sunday. It was the first ecclesiastical Sunday law in Ireland. Not only did it regulate the keeping of the day, but it also pronounced the most terrible curses on any who failed to observe Sunday.[84]

Following the arrival of the "Epistle of Christ" and the formulation of the *Cain Domnaig*, the *Lives* of the Saints are filled with comminatory anecdotes showing how they enforced Sunday observance. Aed was cross with a woman for washing her hair on the Lord's day. If women persisted in doing this, he fumed, they would become bald. If later they repented, their hair would grow back.[85] Colman was averse to chopping wood on Sunday. A man who persisted found that his axe was caught in the log and he himself could not let go of its handle.[86] Cellach passed Guaire in silence, insulting him. On being invited to make things right, he retorted, "I will not go, 'tis vesper-time, and no transgression of the Lord's day do I."[87] The sons of Ua Corra, becoming lepers, went on a pilgrimage to a distant island. They there saw a man digging with a spade, the handle of which was on fire. Asked the cause, he confessed that he had worked on the Lord's day, and now this had happened to him! Another unfortunate was discovered riding on a horse of fire.[88] An Irish sage used to wander round a cemetery periodically meditating on death. One Sunday he inadvertently flicked a chip of wood from the path with the end of his staff. Because of this he was deprived of the visit which an angel used regularly to pay to him.[89] And the list of stories like these might be multiplied. They portray a very obvious and rustic desire to influence what would seem to be a primitive and quasi-pagan Christian populace towards a more pharisaical observance of Sunday.[90]

Gradually, concurrently with the Romanizing of the Celtic Church, the observance of Sunday became more and more sabbatical, and the observance of the Sabbath fell into disuse. When Queen Margaret of Scotland (+ 1093) summoned the remnants of Celtic Christian clerics to her synods to discuss doctrine with a view to their uniting with the Roman Church, she found that

> They were accustomed also to neglect reverence for the Lord's days; and thus to continue upon them as upon other days all the labours of earthly work. But she showed, both by reason and by authority, that this was not permitted. She said: "Let us hold the Lord's day in veneration because of the Lord's resurrection, which took place upon it; and let us not do servile labours upon [the day] in which we know that we were redeemed from the devil's servitude."[91]

After due pressure the ancient Celts capitulated, for "none dared on those days to carry any burdens, or to compel another to do so".[92]

There is a hint that, when the Romanizing party sought to bring the remnants of Celtic Christians into the orthodox fold in Iceland, one of the points necessary was the regularization of the observance of the Lord's day. "Thorgeir then dealt with the observance of the Lord's Day and fast days, Christmas and Easter, and all the important feast days."[93] All these records of the secularization of Saturday, coupled with earlier traces of sabbatizing strongly suggest that in Celtic lands, as was also the case in other countries, there was a gradual shift from the keeping of Saturday, the seventh day Sabbath, to the observance of both Saturday and Sunday and then to the celebration of Sunday exclusively.

The time at which the Celtic Christians commenced their Sabbath and Sunday observance is of interest. The Hebrews began their day with sunset.[94] The early Christians also started their Sabbaths at sunset on Friday and concluded worship at sundown on Sabbath. As has been stated, Celtic Christians likewise commenced their day with sunset, but might end it at dawn on the following day. When Sunday took on a religious character, it too was so observed. The *Cain Domnaig* stipulated that "the sanctity of the Lord's day is from vespers on Saturday till after matins on Monday".[95] But apparently, as in many points of Celtic belief and practice, there were no set rules which were observed by every section, and the sacred hours might end at sunset or at dawn the next morning according to choice.

As ascetic practices became widespread, fasting on specified days of the week grew more common. This custom was also a survival of Jewish custom, being endorsed by the example of John the Baptist and the precept of our Lord. Fasting was observed by the Apostles, and, as the Christian community became more thoroughly organized, Wednesdays and Fridays are mentioned as days of abstinence by the church fathers. Fasting on these two days each week is also noted by Celtic writers. In the monastery of Iona Wednesday was regularly a day of abstinence:

> On a third day of the week, the saint thus addressed the brothers: "On the fourth day of the week, tomorrow, we propose to fast; but nevertheless a disturbing guest will arrive, and the customary fast will be relaxed." ... For on the same fourth day of the week, in the morning, another stranger shouted across the strait: a very religious man, by name Aidan, Fergno's son, who (it is said) for twelve years attended upon Brenden mocu-Alti. He, when he arrived, relaxed that day's fast, as the saint had said.[96]

Evidently the rules for fasting might be waived in honour of guests. Adamnan does not mention that Friday was a fast day on Iona. But the Old-Irish glossator, Diarmait, called this the "day of the last fast".[97]

Aidan, the Celtic missionary to Northumbria, fasted "on Wednesdays and Fridays",[98] and this custom was imitated by "many devout men and women who were inspired to follow his example".[99] The penitential of Cummean (*c.* 650) required fasting "on the two appointed week days",[100] without, however, specifying which. Theodore regulated that those who had been baptized a second time should fast on Wednesdays and Fridays for seven years.[101] This suggests that fasting on those days was not obligatory upon other members of the Christian community. He imposed fasting "on Wednesdays and Fridays during the three forty-day periods",[102] for those who had been married twice or more times. While there is this dubiety in the early Anglo-Saxon Church, the Celtic Christian sources leave no doubt that these two days were devoted to fasting and prayer from the earliest times.[103]

The *Amra Coluimb Chille* recorded of Columba that "knowledge of the Godhead ... used to be sent to him, for every Thursday he used to go *ad Dominum*".[104] What this weekly act of worship was is not clear, but, as has been noted,[105] Patrick was believed to have regarded Thursday as possessing something of a religious character. Thursday might have been a primitive Celtic Christian day of minor devotion.

Besides weekly celebrations Christians also had regular annual feasts. The earliest one was the observance of Easter. This festival attracted a great amount of attention through the centuries, and during the seventh proved to be one of the major bones of contention between the Celtic and Roman Christian parties. There are also references in later Celtic literature to the observance of three forty-day periods of special fasting, the celebration of Pentecost and Christmas, and later, the observance of various saints' days.

The Easter controversy between the Celts and the missionaries led by Augustine and later advocates of the Roman party was concerned with the date on which the festival should be celebrated. Its overtones finally embraced the question of ecclesiastical authority. The Hebrew year was lunar. Each month commenced with the crescent moon. The lunar year is approximately eleven days short of the solar, so Nisan, the first Hebrew month, moved nearer to winter by eleven days each year. To keep the Hebrew calendar synchronous with the seasons an extra month was occasionally added, seven during each nineteen-year period. When this month was to be intercalated was determined by the Sanhedrin by means of a simple rule. The precipitating factor was the offering, with the Passover lambs, of "the first fruits" of the barley harvest on the sixteenth of the month.[106] According to the law, the Passover had to be sacrificed on the fourteenth or full moon, and from the fifteenth the feast of unleavened bread continued for a week. Two ripe sheaves of barley were to be presented on the sixteenth. During the closing days of the preceding month, Adar, the barley, in a secluded field near Jerusalem, was carefully observed. Should it appear impossible for it to ripen in time for the presentation on the sixteenth, an extra month, Ve-Adar, was added. The Passover was, therefore, a moveable feast which occurred during the spring on any day of the week, but it had to fall on the full moon. It came earlier when the spring was warm, later in colder weather.

Nisan, the first Jewish month, generally contained the vernal equinox. It was possible, however, for the full moon, that is, the Passover, to occur prior to the equinox. Christ was a Jew and lived according to Hebrew ceremonial regulations. He died during the Hebrew Passover. The earliest Christians, converts from Judaism, also followed Hebrew customs. They early recognized that Christ had fulfilled the Paschal types by his death.[107] His resurrection, they believed, was typified by the wave sheaf of barley.[108] These Christians looked upon the fourteenth of Nisan as the anniversary of the crucifixion and carefully kept it in remembrance of Christ's death. With the spread of Christianity among the Gentile peoples and the rise of anti-Semitism the Paschal season lost much of its flavour. Emphasis moved from an honouring of the crucifixion to a celebration of the resurrection. Those Christians who continued to observe Easter at the same time as the Passover were stigmatized as "Quartodecimans". But others in some places, with Socrates, held that:

> The aim of the apostles was not to appoint festival days, but to teach a religious life and piety. And it seems to me that just as many other customs have been established in individual localities according to usage. So also the feast of Easter came to be observed in each place according to the individual peculiarities of the people inasmuch as none of the apostles legislated on the matter. And that the observance originated not by legislation, but as a custom, the facts themselves indicate. In Asia Minor most people kept the fourteenth day of the moon, disregarding the sabbath: yet they never separated from those who did otherwise, until Victor, bishop of Rome, influenced by too ardent a zeal, fulminated a sentence of excommunication against the Quartodecimans in Asia ...[109]

In the same way as the Jewish Sabbath gave place before the pagan

Sunday, the Passover was displaced by the feast of the resurrection, Easter. Not satisfied with this partial departure from Jewish usages, a party in the Church sought to arrange that Easter should never fall on the same day as the Jewish Passover, even once in seven years. This change was attributed to Pius (+ *c.* 154), Eleuther, and Victor.[110] But this sixth-century record smacks of pious fraud. An angel was said to have informed Hermas, the brother of Pius, that Easter should be observed only on the Lord's day.[111] The story was regarded as fiction by the Eastern Church leaders, who strenuously objected to the Bishop of Rome's assumption of growing authority.[112] There followed a period of considerable disagreement and dissension, as Epiphanius (+ 403) summarized:

> For even from the earliest times various controversies and dissensions were in the church concerning this solemnity, which used yearly to bring laughter and mockery. For some, in a certain ardour of contention, began it before the week, some at the beginning, some in the middle, some at the end. To say in a word, there was a wonderful and laborious confusion.[113]

While a discussion of the details of the controversy during the first six centuries of the Christian era is beyond the scope of this chapter, a short summary of the final stages is necessary to clarify the relationship of the Celtic Church to the paschal dissensions.

With the coming of the peace of the Church the Emperor Constantine, determined to bring about unanimity, entered the controversy. The Council of Arles (314) ruled that Easter should be observed on the same day by all Christians, but there was no mention as to which day was intended. The paschal cycle then accepted was probably the nineteen-year one, and this would probably have been carried back to Britain by the British delegates. Some ten years later, by the decision of Nicaea in 325, the observance of Easter on Sunday became a legal necessity. But the Council laid down no rule for determining on which Sunday Easter should be kept.

But while the Council of Nicaea might legislate, and the Emperor, with his mastery for compromise, might decide that Alexandria should calculate the date of Easter and Rome should promulgate it, the results, as far as unity was concerned, were far from satisfactory. The original fourth-century cycle was probably closely related to the Hebrew nineteen-year period attributed to Meton (*c.* 423 B.C.). The decree of Nicaea lasted uneasily until 342. Clerical mathematicians produced several short-lived and unpopular cycles, until the mode of reckoning Easter was altered into the eighty-four-year cycle traditionally attributed to Sulpicius Severus (+ 420–5) but in use in different areas at an earlier date. In 457 Victor of Aquitaine produced a 532-year table which continued in popular use till 525, when the nineteen-year cycle of Dionysius Exiguus (+ 550) was adopted. This in turn was modified in Rome before 664.[114] But there was no unanimity about any of these cycles. Scattered sections of Christians followed quite different modes of reckoning. The point on which this controversy finally focused was a discussion of authority: Whose cycle should be followed? East was against West, and there were factions within the larger groups.

The Christianity into which Patrick was born quite possibly followed the eighty-four-year cycle of Sulpicius Severus, although this is by no means settled.[115] Bury suggested that Celtic Easter computations were based on the very earliest of the Christian cycles, that is, on the nineteen-year unit, discarded before 343.[116] Whatever may be the truth, the fact remains that when Augustine and his mission encountered the British ecclesiastics, the cycle and method of calculating Easter used by the Celts differed radically from those employed by the visitors from Italy. As had been the case in the Mediterranean lands, the bishop of Rome regarded the settlement of the Easter question according to his solution a matter of supreme importance.

The sources dealing with Celtic Easter observances are contradictory. It is possible to select some statements and form a picture which is oversimplified. But a study of the details presents a view which is true to type: there existed among Celtic Christians many factions with differing observances.

The Celtic Church reckoned Easter week from the fourteenth to the twentieth of the month.[117] When the fourteenth, or full moon, fell on Sunday some apparently celebrated Easter on it. This is what seems to have happened in the home of King Oswy.[118] Rome had moved away from this to avoid holding Easter on the same day as the Jewish Passover. The Celts reckoned their equinox on 25 March, but Rome had adopted 21 March as the more accurate date. Wilfrid alluded to the nineteen-year cycle, which he attributed to Anatolius,[119] but Bede recorded that the Britons held to the eighty-four-year cycle,[120] and that they observed Easter day on Sunday only,[121] although Eddius affirmed that they did not.[122] The Celts themselves declared that they followed John,[123] and this would make them Quartodecimans. Apparently the same confusion was also existent in Ireland. The ancient annalist for 704 recorded a most significant paragraph, noting that

> In this year the men of Erin consented to receive one jurisdiction and the rule from Adamnan, respecting the celebration of Easter, on Sunday, the fourteenth of the moon of April, and respecting the tonsuring of all the clerks in Erin after the manner of St Peter, for there had been great dissension in Erin up to that time; i.e. some of the clergy of Erin celebrated Easter on the Sunday (next after) the fourteenth of the moon of April, and had the tonsure of Peter the Apostle, after the example of Patrick, but others, following the example of Columbkille, celebrated Easter on the fourteenth of the moon of April, on whatever day of the week the fourteenth should happen to fall, and had the tonsure of Simon Magus. A third party did not agree with the followers of Patrick, or with the followers of Columkille; so that the clergy of Erin used to hold many synods, and these clergy used to come to the synods accompanied by the laity, so that battles and deaths occurred between them; and many evils resulted in Erin in consequence ... They were thus for a long time, i.e. to the time of Adamnan, who was the ninth abbot that took [the government of] Ia after Columbkille.[124]

This long quotation is given to demonstrate that even at the opening of the eighth century there still existed many different points of view on the celebration of Easter. That there were some who were genuinely Quartodecimans it would seem unreasonable to doubt.

The third order of Irish saints "had different rules and ... a different Paschal festival. For some celebrated the resurrection on the fourteenth moon, or the sixteenth ... These continued to that great mortality in the year 666."[125] Theodore inveighed against the heretic, who was obviously a Celtic Christian, who "flouts the Council of Nicaea and keeps Easter with the Jews on the fourteenth of the moon, he shall be driven out of every church unless he does penance before his death".[126] These Christians he also called

"Quartodecimans".[127] Half a century before, Columbanus, writing to Gregory the Great regarding the question of the celebration of Easter, had stated: "For you must know that Victorius has not been accepted by our teachers, by the former scholars of Ireland, by the mathematicians most skilled in reckoning chronology, but has earned ridicule or indulgence rather than authority."[128] It was not merely a blind adherence to tradition which induced the Celts to adhere to their views; they believed that their Easter calculations were more accurate and authoritative than those of Rome. The details of this conflict, violent at times and long continuing, are confused and, at this date, theoretical. What is significant is their outcome. While Rome and the Western Church had altered its reckoning from century to century, the Celtic Christians had failed to follow.

The result of the conflict has often been traced. The settlement of the dating of Easter appears to have been the major plank for the establishment of the authority of the bishop of Rome in Celtic lands. Whether the Celtic Christians were right or wrong is of little consequence now. They believed they were right. When they eventually relinquished their adherence to this point in favour of Rome, they surrendered their independence on all points and soon became fused with Roman Christianity.

Before the period of the Danish invasions there was apparently little veneration of saints, or observance of their feast days, although there are traces that the cult of the saints was commencing in the thinking of Celtic Christians at an earlier date. In the tenth and following centuries, however, the festivals of saints were a marked feature of the Christian year, and were celebrated with homilies based on the traditional lives of the saints.

In the *Life of Samson of Dol* there is a very early reference to this practice:

Therefore, my brothers, to honour the festivals of the saints is nothing else than to adjust lovingly our mind to their good qualities, of which we are fully cognisant; [so that] by imitating them we may be able to follow the same men, under God's guidance, by the straightest course to that unspeakable and heavenly kingdom to which they have happily attained, not rivalling them in great deeds, but sharing their difficult tasks, which by abstinence, prolonged and incredible, so to speak, to the untried, with whom all things are not thought possible to him that believeth, they engaged in until the happy close of this life.[129]

But there is nothing suggesting the invocation of saints in this paragraph. The example of the departed was held up as an encouragement to the living to emulate his life and deeds.

While it is impossible from the meagre sources which have survived to reconstruct a complete list of the saints who were eventually celebrated each day of the Christian year, some picture is possible. The festival of the return of the Holy Family from Egypt was celebrated on 11 January, "Out of Egypt—splendid gladness! came Mary's great Son."[130] The feast of the circumcision of Christ occurred on 2 February, "the reception of Mary's Son in the Temple, sure inestimable".[131] On 27 March fell the feat of the conception and crucifixion of our Lord, "Jesus' Conception on the same day as his crucifixion without respect".[132] Holy Thursday, 24 March, was devoted to cleansing ceremonies, the washing of the head and cutting of the hair, and the washing of the feet. The old record declares: "At the washing of the feet the *Beati* are recited as long as the washing lasts. After that comes the sermon on the washing."[133] On Holy Saturday a peculiarly Irish rite was followed, the lighting of the sacred fire. This practice might well have been a survival of a pre-Christian ceremony:

They left their vessel in the estuary and went along the land till they came to Ferta Fer Feicc [the Graves of Fiacc's Men], and Patrick's tent was pitched in that place, and he struck the paschal fire. It happened, then, that that was the time at which was celebrated the high-tide of the heathen, to wit, the Feast of Tara. The kings and the lords and the chiefs used to come to Tara, to Loegaire sone of Niall, to celebrate that festival therein. The wizards, also, and the augurs would come so that they were prophesying to them. On that night, then, the fire of every hearth in Ireland was quenched, and it was proclaimed by the King that no fire should be kindled in Ireland before the fire of Tara, and that neither gold nor silver should be taken (as compensation) from him who should kindle it, but that he should go to death for his crime.[134]

Having lighted his fire before the king lighted his, Patrick was believed to have struck a death blow against this heathen practice. From this event the Irish Easter fire ceremony probably arose. This later developed into the ritual of the blessing of the Irish Easter candle which is found in no other liturgy.[135] But it might very well be traced to the Hebrew typical service.

The *transfiguration* was celebrated on 26 July.[136] As time went by more and more festivals were added, and with the final merging of the Celtic and the Western Churches the regular Christian year came to be observed. At each solemnity it was customary to read a homily or eulogy, based on the biography of the holy man. This practice resulted in the innumerable *Lives* which later panegyrists prepared with so much imagination.

Besides these regular feasts Celtic Christians also observed three special fasts of forty days each,[137] occasionally called the three Lents. Great Lent occurred during the forty days before Easter. Another occupied the forty days prior to Christmas, and might be compared with Advent of the Eastern Churches. The third was observed during the forty days following Whitsun.[138] The Celtic clerics who worked as missionaries to Northumbria observed these fasts. Egbert, an English nobleman, having learnt from his Irish teachers, "ate only one meal a day during Lent ... He practised a similar abstinence for forty days before Christmas, and as many after the Feast of Pentecost."[139] When this third practice began is not known, "but no traces of it can be discovered in the sixth century",[140] in Celtic lands. That the Celtic method of observing the fast of Lent was different from the way in which it was celebrated by the Roman Church is suggested by Queen Margaret's reaction to the Scottish Christians:

> They did not legally keep the fast of Lent; because they were accustomed to begin it, not (with the holy church universally upon the fourth day of the week) on the beginning of the fast (Ash Wednesday, beginning on the evening of Shrove Tuesday), but on the second day of the [following] week. They said in reply: "The fast that we hold, we keep for six weeks, according to the authority of the Gosepl, which describes the fast of Christ." She replied: "You differ in this widely from the Gospel: for we read there that the Lord fasted for forty days, and it is

obvious that you do not. Since six Sundays are deducted during the six weeks, it is clear that only thirty-six days remain for the fast. Therefore it is clear that you do not keep the fast by authority of the Gospel, for forty days; but for thirty-six days. It remains for you therefore to begin to fast with us four days before the beginning of Lent, if you wish to preserve abstinence for the number of forty days, according to the Lord's example; otherwise you alone resist the authority of the Lord himself, and the tradition of the entire holy church."[141]

That it was the custom of the Celtic Church to fast for forty days excluding Sundays is also vouched for by the Lenten experience of Cedd: "During this time he fasted until evening every day except Sunday according to custom. Even then, he took no food but a morsel of bread, an egg, and a little watered milk. He explained that it was the custom of those who had trained him in the rule of regular discipline."[142] When the two lesser Lents died out the records fail to indicate. The Old-Irish Penitential mentioned periods of fasting "between the two Christmases and between the two Easters and at Pentecost, and such persons have relaxation on the high festivals of the year, and on Sundays and on the fifty nights between Easter and Pentecost".[143]

The day of our Lord's nativity was observed with the same regulations as was Sunday. The "Epistle of Christ" mentioned this fact:

On whatsoever day Great Christmas[144] falls, or Little Christmas, it counts as Sunday, and none shall travel thereon. It is on the conscience of each one to whom God has given sense and reason, though others violate the law of Sunday that his neighbours should not take as an evil example from him; for it is of himself he shall endure his pain, and it is for him who shall fulfil it that his rewards shall endure.[145]

There are traces of other festivals, derived from the Old Testament, to be found in the laws and penitentials. In discussing the length of time Patrick spent in servitude in Ireland, his biographer remarked: "He abode in his bondage six years after the manner of the Little Jubilee of the Hebrews."[146] There is a defective law regarding land tenure which reads: "It is forfeit unless it be claimed to the end of the seven years."[147] This seems to go back to the Pentateuch and applied to Irish land tenure regulated by the *Liber ex Lege Moisi*.

Closely connected with the Sabbatical Year, or the Little Jubilee, as the Irish writer pleasantly called it, was the Great Jubilee, also based on the *Liber ex Lege Moisi*, or the fifty-year release, when "the enslaved shall be freed, and plebeians shall be exalted by receiving church grades, and by performing penitential service to God".[148] The penitential canons attributed to Patrick recorded: "Truly the laws of the Jubilee are to be observed, that is, the fifty years, that a doubtful method be not established in the change of time."[149]

Light on this obscure and probably garbled penitential is thrown by a comment from the ancient laws to the effect that "there are with the Feine seven prescriptions which transfer perpetual right according to the customs of their merits; land which is offered to a church on behalf of a soul ... land which has been away fifty years ... it is upon fifty years it goes into utter bondage."[150] Whether all these rules were ever practised or not is unknown. These regulations, however, underline the interest of the early Celtic Church in following Old Testament laws, and is still further evidence of the pervasive influence of the *Liber ex Lege Moisi*.

As we conclude this chapter it would be well to summarize the facts. Celtic Christians differed from their Roman brethren, not only in their computation of Easter, but also in the observance of lesser feasts and fasts, and of course in the observance of the Sabbath. They held a religious service on Sunday to honour the resurrection and then spent the rest of the day on their chores or pleasures.

CHAPTER 4 **divine services**

From the beginning of Christianity its ministry has conducted religious services to meet the needs of its members. In the old Hebrew economy rituals were connected with birth and death, mourning and rejoicing, and at set seasons of the year. The New Testament Church carried over some of these ceremonies modified to fit in with the changed conditions.

At his initiation into the Church the catechumen died to his past and was born to a new life[1] through baptism. Connected with baptism was the act of laying on of hands.[2] When infant baptism eventually became the regular practice of the Church this rite of confirmation took on a different connotation. In some areas Christian worship also included a little baptism or foot-washing. Initially occasionally, then weekly, finally daily, "the Lord's supper" was celebrated, for the living and for the dying.

In the New Testament baptism was carried out by immersion, and was so practised by Christians for centuries. As performed by the Celtic Church baptism was also by immersion. The glossator saw in it a symbolic fulfilment of Christ's burial. 'When we [pass under] baptism," he said, "it is the likeness of his burial and death to us."[3]

There would seem to be little doubt from the sources that triple immersion was the mode practised in the section of Celtic Christianity represented by the Old-Irish glossator. On St Paul's teaching that there was "one baptism" he carefully noted, "though the immersion is triple".[4] By the Apostle's observation to the Colossians that Christians should be "buried with him", the Irish theologian understood that "three waves pass over us in baptism, because he was three days in the sepulchre".[5] This was the reason generally assigned by the Greek writers for triple immersion, while Augustine and the fathers of the West felt that this threefold act symbolized the Trinity.

The question whether there should be one or three immersions was a subject of controversy in the Western Church even as late as the seventh century, particularly in Spain. Single immersion apparently was practised in Brittany even after the seventh century. A. W. Haddan conjectured that single immersion was a Scottish or British practice. It would appear from the glosses, however, that single immersion was not in use by the Celtic Church in Ireland.

Since instruction was invariably given before baptism, it would seem that adults alone were required to comply with this rite during the early period of the Celtic Church. This would be the only way possible in a missionary movement dealing with pagans. The glossator explained that St Paul's use of the term "prophesying" indicated "preaching; the stirring up of every one to belief, that he may be ready for baptism".[6] Another comment pointing to adult baptism is found in this sentence: "As catechumens are at first taught by a priest, and are baptized, and as they are then anointed by a bishop, so then John had begun to teach men and to baptize them at first, and they have been anointed by Christ, i.e. the work which John had begun has been perfected by Christ and has been completed."[7]

The earlier penitentials corroborated this practice of careful instruction. A canon of the Synod of Patrick discussed another method of "preparation for baptism" in these terms: "If anyone of the brothers[8] wishes to receive the grace of God [i.e. baptism] he shall not be baptized until he has done [penance for] a period of forty days."[9] Even then instruction was to be continued for the baptized catechumen, since the glossator observed: "Teaching every one after baptism".[10]

Following careful indoctrination the proselyte's belief in God was deemed necessary before his acceptance for membership. This is suggested in Patrick's contact with Sescnech, who, after hearing the saint preach, believe in God and was baptized.[11] Cairthenn simply "believed in the Lord. And Patrick baptized him in Saingil."[12] Dichu, on the other hand, showed contrition. When he was about to kill Patrick, the priest prayed for him, "and grief of heart seized Dichu, and he believed, and Patrick baptized him after that".[13] Findchua was called "a perfect child" at the time of his baptism.[14] That this "belief" was considered necessary by Patrick is underlined by the anecdote of Cathboth's seven sons who "went to him [Patrick]; he preached to them, and they believed and were baptized".[15]

Instruction, belief in God, repentance, grief of heart, and penance, were prerequisites of baptism. On the Apostle's declaration, "by grace are ye saved and that through faith", the commentator noted an allusion to "the faith which they confessed in baptism".[16] This faith springs from the preaching of "baptism of repentance for remission of sins", and further brings "men into faith, the forgiveness of their sins to them through baptism".[17]

The instructor's role is that of "the bridesman, i.e. John. He had prepared the nuptials, i.e. he had wooed the Church for Christ."[18] The catechumen was united in fellowship with the believers through his baptism. The Old-Irish theologian summed up his understanding of the significance of this ceremony in the comment: "Though Christ be in you through confession of faith in baptism, and the soul is alive thereby, yet the body is dead through the old sins, and, though it has been cleansed through baptism, it is unable to do good works until the Holy Spirit awakes it."[19] The ministry of the Spirit's awakening was signified by the anointing with oil or chrism before actual baptism in water. The candidate was also required to declare his acceptance of the faith "through the creed which was recited at baptism".[20]

A legend is preserved of the encounter of Patrick with the two princesses, Ethene the Fair and Feidelem the Rosy, daughters of the high king Loaghairie. A dialogue ensued which might be arranged in the form of a catechism something like this. The girls (G) questioned the saint (P) regarding the faith, and he answered them:

G Whence hast thou come, and where is thy home?

P It were better for you to believe in the true God whom we worship than to ask questions about our race.

G Who is God? Of whom is he God?

P Our God is the God of all men.

G Where is God? Where is God's dwelling?

P He has his dwelling around heaven and earth and sea and all that in them is. He inspired all, he quickens all, he dominates all, he supports all. He lights the light of the sun. He furnishes the light of the night. He has made springs in the dry land. He has set stars to minister to the greater lights.

G Is he fair? Has he sons and daughters, thy God, and has he gold and silver?

P He has a Son coeternal with himself, and like unto himself.

G Is he immortal?

P The Son is not younger than the Father, nor the Father older than the Son.

G Has the Son been fostered by many?

P The Father, the Son, and the Spirit are not divided.

G Is he in heaven or in earth? In the sea, in the rivers, in the hill places, in the valleys?

P He is the God of heaven and earth, of sea and rivers, of sun and moon and stars, of the lofty mountain and the lowly valley, the God above heaven and in heaven and under heaven.

G Tell us how we may know him, in what wise he will appear?

P I wish to unite you with the heavenly King, as ye are daughters of an earthly king.

G How is he discovered? Is he found in youth or in old age?

P Believe!

G Tell us with all diligence how we may believe in the heavenly King that we may see him face to face.

P Believe!

G How may we be prepared to meet him?

P Do you believe that by baptism you can cast away the sin of your father and mother?

G We believe!

P Do you believe in life after death?

G We believe!

P Do you believe in the resurrection in the day of Judgement?

G We believe!

P Will you be baptized?
G We will do as thou sayest.

And Patrick baptized them and placed a white veil on their heads.

G How may we behold the face of Christ?
P You cannot see the face of Christ until you shall taste of death.
G How may we taste of death?
P You taste of death when you receive the sacrifice.
G Give us the sacrifice that we may see the Son, our bridegroom.

And they received the Eucharist, and fell asleep in death.* This credal catechism was probably based on an early formula used at services of baptism, and later incorporated into an interesting story.

The use of a white veil on the candidates after baptism is also found in the narrative of the captives of Coroticus.[21] Following the immersion, Communion was administered to the catechumens. This ritual is preserved in the baptismal service of the *Stowe Missal*. In this rite the feet of the neophites were washed after the baptism and before the Communion was received.

Through baptism the candidate was "born again in Christ".[22] Sinners were thus brought into one family, "massed into one body by baptism",[23] and thus "united in Christ".[24] Only after their baptism were they allowed to join in religious exercises[25] among Celtic Christians. Considering the Pauline teaching on "benefit or grace" the glossator asked: "What is the first grace? The answer is not difficult. The grace of forgiveness of sins through baptism. The second grace is the forgiveness of sins through repentance."[26] Applying the allegorical significance of Christ's baptism, the commentator observed that the sinner should be "baptized, i.e. after the likeness of his death in the mortal body, from which he parted in his passion. He does not return to that body, but is now in a spiritual resurrection body, without expectation of death or decay. Let us therefore not return to the mortal body of sins."[27] Another belief, voiced by Finnian, regarding the effect of this ceremony was that "the sins of all are indeed remitted in baptism".[28]

---

* This statement is often interpreted to mean that the young women were martyred. The truth probably lies nearer to an allegorical interpretation of the case. They died to sin and to the world and were baptized by Patrick in the symbol of burial. The original story is published in *Analecta Bollandiana* II. 49, and is translated by J. B. Bury, *Life of St Patrick*, 138–40.

F. E. Warren noted that the baptismal formula invoking the names of the Persons of the Trinity has been left out of the service found in the *Stowe Missal*. He pointed out the similarity between this and the *Gelasian Sacramentary*. F. C. Conybeare argued[29] that it was this omission which rendered baptism by Celtic clerics invalid in the eyes of the Western Church. Pope Gregory II replied to Boniface in 726 to the effect that

> You have informed me that certain persons have been baptized by adulterous and unworthy priests without their having been interrogated about the symbol or creed. In such cases you shall adhere to the ancient custom of the church, which is that one who has been baptized in the name of the Father, and the Son, and the Holy Ghost, must on no account be rebaptized, for the gift of grace is not received in the name of the baptizer, but in the name of the Trinity.[30]

The expression "adulterous priests" probably referred to married Celtic clergy, who were regarded as being even more unworthy because they had not been consecrated by bishops duly authorized by the Roman Church. Notwithstanding these considerations, Gregory recommended that should any Christian have been baptized in the name of the Trinity his baptism was valid. But, in spite of the arguments which Conybeare summoned, it would seem to be still true that "the precise defect intended [by Bede] is left to conjecture. Single immersion seems most probable."[31] But this can hardly be the case in view of the references to trine immersion in the glosses. The criticism might have arisen in connection with the pedilavium which followed baptism in the Celtic ritual.[32]

Later Celtic Christian writers recorded other ceremonies connected with baptism. The *Stowe Missal* noted that the breast and shoulders of the candidate should be chrismated before baptism. Here is an example from the life of Brigit: There appeared "clerics in shining garments, who poured oil on the girl's head; and they completed the order of baptism in the usual manner. Those were three angels."[33]

It seems that baptism was believed, on occasion, to have been performed in milk:

> But on the morrow, when the bondmaid went at sunrise with a vessel full of milk in her hand, and when she put one of her two

footsteps over the threshold of the house, the other foot being
inside, then she brought forth the daughter, even St Brigit.
The maidservants washed St Brigit with the milk that was still in
her mother's hand.[34]

While the earlier Celtic clerics accepted no fees from those for
whom they performed this service, in later centuries it became
quite normal for payments to be made to them. When Findchua
was baptized, his parents presented "a scruple, that is seven pennies
of gold, ... to [Ailbe of Imlech Ibair] for baptizing the child".[35]
On the occasion of the baptism of Ciaran of Clonmacnoise "a vessel
of choice honey was given to deacon Justus as his fee for baptizing
Ciaran".[36] And Bishop Eirc received "three purple wethers ... out
of the well as the fees for baptizing Brenainn".[37]

Not only were fees presented for baptism, but, when Ciaran was
receiving his last Communion, he also gave "the scruple of his
communion" to Coimgen the priest.[38] There seems to be some connection between baptizing for fees and the ruling of a canon of
the penitential of Finnian: "Monks, however, are not to baptize,
nor to receive alms; if, then, they do receive alms, why shall they
not baptize?"[39]

Since baptism was carried out by immersion, it obviously required
a substantial quantity of water. In Celtic lands the rite was often
performed in a well. It was recorded that on one of Patrick's trips
"the site of his tent is in the green of the fort, ... and to the north
of the fort is his well wherein he baptized Dunling's two sons".[40]
Findian "was baptized out of the well named Bal, as was meet for
his merits".[41] Another anecdote suggested a ceremony which Patrick was believed to have used in this service:

> Thereafter Patrick went in his chariot, so that every one might
> see him, and that they might hear from him his voice, and the
> preaching of God's word by him. And then they believed in God
> and in Patrick. So Patrick repeats the order of baptism to them on
> the river, which was anear them, and all the hosts are baptized
> therein.[42]

Here the baptismal service was conducted in a river,[43] after "the
order of baptism", whatever that might have been, had been recited.
Apparently any place with sufficient water for immersion was considered satisfactory.

Adult baptism appears to have been the practice of early Celtic Christians. It is not known when infant baptism was introduced among them. The penitential of Cummean proves that it was already in existence in the ruling that "one who instead of baptism blesses a little infant shall do penance for a year".[44] It added the warning that "if the infant dies having had such a blessing only, that homicide shall do penance according to the judgement of a council".[45] This is very interesting as it indicates that blessing a little infant was an early Celtic Christian rite which was no longer to be tolerated. It is well within the realms of possibility that the original practice of the Celts had been the simple blessing of infants in following the example of our Lord. Patrick was believed to have baptized pregnant women and their unborn infants,[46] but this is very likely a comminatory story to authorize an innovation of the author's time. But that infant baptism finally became the regular practice among Celtic Christians there is no doubt, as is witnessed by this story in the life of Columba: "At that time when Saint Columba passed some days in the province of the Picts, a certain layman with his whole household heard and believed the word of life, through an interpreter, at the preaching of the holy man; and believing, was baptized, the husband, with his wife and children, and his servants."[47] But the age of these children is not specified. The penitential of Finnian ruled that "If a cleric does not receive a child [to baptism], if it is a child of the same parish, he shall do penance for a year on bread and water."[48]

It was a custom for a white veil or white napkin to be placed on the catechumen's head during the baptismal service. Patrick put a veil upon the heads of the daughters of Leoghaire.[49] When the saint baptized the infant daughters of Maine, he draped "a veil on their heads".[50] The Old-Irish glosses mention the veil or mantle used during the service of baptism.[51] The placing of this veil followed the anointing of the candidate with oil or chrism. When Patrick upbraided Coroticus for his inhuman massacre of Irish Christians, he recalled that this oil was still seen shining upon the brows of the newly baptized persons on whom the white veils had just been placed.[52]

So, immediately following the baptism, it appears that the head of the candidate was anointed. The Old-Irish commentator remarked that after Christians have been baptized "they are then anointed by a bishop".[53] Other references to this custom have been noted above. The drawing on page 101 above illustrates this pouring of oil from a spoon on his head while the candidate remains standing in the water.

From the *Stowe Missal*[54] it is possible to reconstruct what was probably the sequence of the ritual of baptism among the Irish Christians of the ninth century. Here is a summary: the service opened with a prayer followed by a special petition that God would exorcize the devil from each organ of the body and reign within the candidate. This detailed enumeration points to the fact that the expected catechumen would be an adult and most likely a pagan. The consecration of the salt, the exorcism of the water, and a prayer then follow.

The candidate was then asked to renounce the devil and his works, and the confession of the Creed began. The administrator breathed upon him, a symbol of the infilling of the Holy Spirit, and proceeded to anoint his breast and shoulders with oil and chrism in the name of the Trinity, finally asking him a second time whether he wished to renounce the devil and his works. After a response in the affirmative, a prayer followed. Salt was then placed in the mouth of the catechumen and a benediction spoken. The neophite was once more anointed and sections of the Psalms were recited and prayers said. After the font had been blessed by means of a sign of the cross made of chrism placed on the water, those present were sprinkled with the consecrated water and a deacon interrogated them on their belief in God, after which the candidate entered the font and was baptized. While he remained standing in the water, oil was poured upon his head in the name of the Trinity and a deacon placed a white veil upon him as the priest prayed for the forgiveness of the penitent's sins and invoked the blessings of God.

The candidate was clothed in a white robe by the deacon while he was being asked whether he would accept the robe of Christ's righteousness in preparation for his final judgement before the tribunal of God. Oil was then put on the catechumen's right hand with a prayer that his activities might be dedicated unto life eternal. Next, there followed the washing of the candidate's feet while appropriate passages were read from the Psalms, such as "Thy word is a lamp to my feet, and a light unto my path", and the reading of St John's account of Christ's washing the apostles' feet. This part of

E

the ceremony ended with the directive that, as the Lord had washed the disciples' feet, "You, clad in splendid white linen, must also wash".

The concluding rite of the baptismal service, immediately following the pedilavium, was the first Communion of the newly baptized. Possibly because of this, an altar, at which the Communion was to be celebrated, was often erected close to the baptistery, as is suggested by the account of Patrick: "A church, moreover, was founded on that well in which Patrick was baptized, and there stands the well by the altar."[55] Another comment is that Patrick's "well is in front of the church".[56] Was this the position of the altar too? Both the bread and wine were received and the service ended with prayers, thanksgiving, and petitions for cleansing and dedication on behalf of the candidate.

But the *Stowe Missal* baptismal service is not pure Celtic, it contains an admixture of Western Christian usages, introduced after the process of Romanizing the Celts had begun. The sources which are available are so meagre that the reconstruction of a genuine early Celtic service is impossible. T. Thompson summed up his analysis:

> The Irish rite appears to have borne a strong resemblance to the Gallican, as for instance in the matter of the washing of the feet of the neophites. The effeta and the unction just before baptism, to judge from Bobbio and the fragments of the Stowe, had some peculiarities ... The Gallican books were superseded by Roman books. ... nor did the Irish books succeed any better in maintaining their position against the aggression of the dominant Roman influence.[57]

It seems impossible to say when the service of confirmation was introduced as a regular part of the Celtic ritual. There is a hint that it was held to be theologically necessary in the Old-Irish comment: "Though Christ be in you through confession of faith in baptism, and the soul is alive thereby, yet the body is dead through the old sins, and, though it has been cleansed through baptism, it is unable to do good works until the Holy Spirit awakes it."[58] The glossator evidently felt that the rite of baptism alone was not completely efficacious for the convert until the Holy Spirit had empowered him to live as a Christian. This dynamic was believed to be imparted to him by the ceremony of the laying on of hands.

The "Rule of Patrick",[59] a late composition, also stipulated that "the perfection of the Holy Spirit comes not, however fervently a person is baptized, unless he 'goes under the hand' of a bishop after baptism". Cuthbert likewise laid his hands on those who "had been lately baptized ... when his hands and feet had been washed in accordance with the custom ..."[60] But this kind of "confirmation" had nothing to do with endorsing infant baptism. It was a service performed immediately after the baptism of adults, at which time the impartation of the Holy Spirit was believed to occur. The later *Lives* contain several references to confirmation of a different sort. Patrick was described as confirming, consecrating, or blessing. Cormac's *Glossary* defined caplait or Maundy Thursday as "a name for the chief day of Easter, i.e. 'head washing', i.e. since every one is tonsured then, and his head is washed, in preparation for his confirmation on the Easter Sunday".[61]

After the practice of infant baptism had been established, confirmation took on added meaning. The faith of the child, which had been affirmed by his godparents, needed to be certified by the child himself, grown to the use of reason. Theodore evidently had this Celtic rite in mind when he ruled: "We believe no one is complete in baptism without the confirmation of a bishop; yet we do not despair."[62] And he further remarked: "Chrism was established in the Nicene Synod. It is not a breach of order if the chrismal napkin is laid again upon another who is baptized."[63] So this ancient British custom was a recognized part of the ritual of the Christians in these islands whom Theodore was seeking to absorb into his own organization.

The history of feet washing as a ceremony of the Christian Church is tantalizingly elusive. That pedilavium was practised by the first Christians in response to our Lord's directive, "This do as I have done unto you", is most probable. There are passing references to this rite in the first centuries. Continued for many years by the Eastern Church, feet washing eventually fell from favour in the West. But it was carried out long enough to be introduced among the earliest Celtic Christians.[64] The practice of washing the feet of those newly baptized was noted by Augustine, but he denied the pedilavium was vital to their baptism. Augustine remarked:

Now, regarding feet washing: this was commanded by the Lord

as a form of humility, which he came to teach and appropriately demonstrated himself, electing the best time to inculcate a religious truth. But many, lest it appear to be tied to the sacrament of baptism, do not admit feet washing into their ritual. Some deny its usefulness altogether. Still others celebrate it at some appointed sacred time, perhaps on the third of the octave, carefully distinguishing it from the sacrament of baptism.[65]

Sir Edwyn Hoskyns, in his excursus on "The Liturgical use of the Pedilavium" rightly explained the implications:

> There are indications in the ancient liturgies of the Church that the pedilavium once formed an integral part of the baptismal office. Saint Ambrose reminds the newly baptized of the Gospel lesson which had been read at the washing of their feet, when they had "gone up from the font." The author of the closely related treatise *De Sacramentis* adds that "the high priest was girt up (for though the presbyters also carried it out, yet the ministry is begun by the high priest) and washed thy feet." He also states that the Church in Rome did not have this custom, and suggests that this was "on account of the numbers". Presumably the ceremony took too much time.[66]

The rite seems to have persisted in certain areas in spite of the ruling of the Synod of Elvira (306), which forbade priests and clerics to wash the feet of those who had just been baptized, and is found in the Gallic and Gothic services.[67] The *Missale Gothicum*, as its seventh item, included the rite: *Dum pedes ejus lavas, dicis, "Ego tibi lavo pedes; sicut Dominus noster Jesus Christus fecit discipulis suis, tu facias hospitibus et peregrinis, ut habeas vitam aeternam."*[68] There were similar rubrics in the Gallic service book,[69] and also in the *Bobbio Missal.*[70]

That interest in pedilavium continued in the Spanish Church is borne out by the ruling of the Council of Toledo (694) that it should be performed only on Maundy Thursday.[71] While its use continued in the East, in Rome feet washing lapsed, but was for some time practised by the congregation at Milan. But in Spain, Gaul, and Germany and the various Celtic lands, feet washing long persisted, as is abundantly attested by the sources.

F. E. Warren suggested that the Italian Augustine's demand that the Celtic ecclesiastics should conform to the Roman method of administering baptism was, in fact, a demand that they abolish pedilavium.[72] But in spite of this, feet washing was carried out in several other connections in Celtic lands.

As a gesture of hospitality pedilavium was used to make guests comfortable. From his isolated retreat at Lindisfarne Cuthbert used often to go forth to meet the brethren who came to visit him for counsel, and, "when he had devoutly washed their feet in warm water, he was sometimes compelled by them to take off his shoes and to allow them to wash his feet".[72a] Even earlier in Ireland, Brigit was reputed to have been accustomed to wash the feet of her guests: "For she used to say that Christ was in the person of every faithful guest ... The wizard and his wife, ... went to the dairy ... Brigit made them welcome, and washed their feet, and gave them food".[73] The same practice was followed by the brethren on Iona. On one occasion Columba had a presentiment that pilgrims were about to land on the island. Calling one of the brothers he said, "Prepare the guesthouse quickly, and draw water for washing the feet of guests."[74]

Feet washing was held to produce miraculous results. The length to which this belief was carried by later hagiographers is shown by this anecdote:

> When Brigit's fame had sounded through Teffia, there was a certain devout virgin in Fir Tethbai, even Brig, daughter of Coimloch, who sent a message that Brigit should come and commune with her. So Brigit went, and Brig herself rose up to wash her [Brigit's] feet. At that time a devout woman lay in sickness. When they were washing Brigit's feet, she sent for the sick person who was in the girl's house, to bring her out of the tub some of the water which was put over Brigit's feet. It was brought to her accordingly, and she put it on her face, and straightway she was every whit whole, and after having been in sickness for a year she was on that night one of the attendants.[75]

On another occasion Brigit "washed the feet of the nuns of Cuil Fobair, and at that washing healed four nuns, to wit, a lame one, and a blind, and a leper, and an insane".[76] Cairan of Saigir was also a believer in feet washing. When Crichid of Cluain, Ciaran's farmer, went to Saigir to see his master, wolves killed him. Ciaran went to the place where he lay and washed his feet. As a result of this ceremony Crichid was restored to life.[77] It may well be that these comminatory stories were used to support a practice which was falling into disuse? In the following stories the miraculous is introduced to add authority to the waning practice of pedilavium.

Sometimes Cuthbert acted as guest-master in his own establishment. On one occasion this saint, "having received him [a guest] kindly in accordance with his wont, still thinking him to be a man and not an angel, he washed his hands and feet and wiped them with towels, and having in his humility rubbed his guest's feet with his own hands to warm them on account of the cold"[78] was miraculously given spiritual insight to discern that he was a visitor from heaven. Iona and its monks, too, witnessed miracles in connection with pedilavium. A well had been cursed by magicians, so Columba "first raising his holy hand in invocation of the name of Christ, washed his hands and feet; and after that, with those that accompanied him, drank of the same water, which he had blessed. And from that day, the demons withdrew from that well."[79]

Another use for pedilavium was the fostering of humility and penitence. This is illustrated by a story concerning Patrick, who

> went into the district of Mag Luirg, and his horses were forcibly taken by the tribe of the Sons of Erc, and he cursed the people of that country. But bishop Maine of the Hui-Ailella besought Patrick to forgive his brethren, and Patrick weakened the malediction. And Maine washed Patrick's feet with his hair and with his tears, and he drove the horses into a meadow and cleansed their hoofs in honour of Patrick.[80]

Even the "feet" of horses were washed as a gesture of humility and repentance! Brigit demonstrated her devotion and meekness by washing the feet even of lepers:

> Once upon a time two lepers came to Brigit to be healed of the leprosy. Brigit bade one of the two lepers to wash the other. He did so. "Do thou", said Brigit to the other leper, "tend and wash thy comrade even as he hath ministered unto thee." "Save the time that we have seen," saith he, "we will not see one another. What, O nun, dost thou deem it just that I, a healthy man, with my fresh limbs and my fresh raiment, should wash that loathsome leper there, with his livid limbs falling from him?

A custom like that is not fit for me." So Brigit washed the lowly miserable leper.[81]

Evidently the initial washing had healed the first leper, who then did not wish to recontaminate himself with his leprous companion. The saint showed her humility by washing his feet. "Great indeed was the humility of Colum Cille, for it was he himself that used to take their shoes off his monks, and that used to wash their feet for them."[82] Other stories might be added, but one more will suffice. "In the miraculous legend of St Brendon (+ 578) it is related that he sailed with his monks to the island of Sheep [Faeroe], and on sherethursdays, after souper, he wesshe theyr feet and hyssed them lyke as our Lorde dyd to his dyscuples."[83] As this story portrays, it was on Maundy Thursday[84] that this ceremony was popularly practised among Celtic Christians. It was carried out by Brigit, following the example of Christ and the disciples in the upper room:

Brigit went to a certain church in the land of Teffia to celebrate Easter. The prioress of the church said to her maidens that on Maundy Thursday one of them should minister unto the old men and to the weak and feeble persons who were biding in the church. Not one of them was found for ministering. Said Brigit: "I to-day will minister unto them." [There were] four of the sick persons who were biding in the church, even a consumptive man, and a lunatic, and a blind man, and a leper. And Brigit did service to these four, and they were healed from every disease that lay upon them.[85]

Apparently no impropriety attached to a woman's washing the saints' feet, as in New Testament times.[86] Other details of the story, the unwillingness of anyone to perform the act and the uncleanness of some who were present hark back to the initial narrative of the institution of this Christian custom by our Lord.[87] Bede noted that Cuthbert sometimes would not remove his shoes of animal skin from one Easter to the next; and, the historian added, "then only for the washing of the feet which takes place on Maundy Thursday".[88]

As may readily be concluded, Maundy Thursday was specially devoted to the caring for the needs of the body in preparation for Easter among later Celtic Christians. The hair of the monks was then shorn. The brethren also washed their heads in honour of the season. In the north of England Maundy Thursday was called Skyre Thursday, probably from Old Norse, *skira*, to purify. In the south of England it was known as Shere Thursday, and so mistakenly its etymology has been traced to the cutting of hair on that day.

On one occasion Brendan reached the island of Procurator, who prepared a bath for the voyager and his disciples, for it was the day of the Lord's Supper,[89] on another Kentigern is reported to have washed the feet of lepers on the Saturday before Palm Sunday.[90]

As has already been mentioned in connection with the ceremonies carried out in the ritual of baptism, pedilavium followed the immersion and preceded Communion in the Celtic rite. It is said of Cuthbert, that he laid "his hand on those who had been lately baptized ... when his hands and feet had been washed in accordance with the custom of hospitality ..."[91] The import of this appears to be that the catechumen, after being immersed, was blessed by the laying on of the cleric's hand. Then his own hands and feet were washed as he was accepted into full fellowship with his brethren. Feet washing following immersion is also found in the Gothic, Gallic, Bobbio, and Stowe orders of service for baptism.

Pedilavium seems to have been employed in connection with the Communion service. In the *Stowe Missal* it preceded the first Communion which the recently baptized celebrated. In the penitential of Columbanus it was ruled that "he who unwashed receives the Holy Bread, [should receive] twelve strokes".[92] It has been suggested that this "holy bread" referred to the "Eulogia," a loaf of ordinary bread, which was cut up into small pieces and distributed to the poor after the celebration of Communion. It is possible, however, that this regulation, influenced by Celtic Christians in Ireland, actually had reference to the washing of hands and feet before the Communion service, as is illustrated by the usage in the *Stowe Missal*. The Celt's adherence to a literal interpretation of the Scriptures seems to have led him to follow the procedure of the upper room exactly. For in that service Christ washed the feet of his disciples before he distributed the bread and wine to his followers.

In a narrative recorded to show the power of Columba over wind and storm an incident is embedded which throws light on one use of feet washing at Iona. By God's protection, Adamnan wrote, "we arrived at the harbour of the island of Io, after the third hour of the day; and later, after the washing of hands and feet, we entered the church with the brothers, and at the sixth hour we celebrated with them the holy ceremonies of the mass."[93] This, too, suggests that at Iona a recognized preparation for the celebration of Communion was the washing of hands and feet. L. Gougaud inquired, "Was it a ritual ablution?"[94] The travellers arrived by boat, and hence would not be so footsore and dirty. If it be granted that this was a ritual washing of feet, and like the pedilavium in the *Stowe*, preceded the Communion, an interesting feature of the Celtic service emerges. In the ninth century and later the Irish and Scottish Christian reformers, the Culdees, continued pedilavium: "At the washing of feet the *Beati* is recited as long as the washing lasts. After that comes the sermon on the Washing."[95]

In the penitential of Theodore is a ruling that "washing the feet of laymen is also within the liberty of the monastery".[96] In spite of the indifference of the fathers and the proscriptions of the councils Theodore evidently decided, when he framed his penitentials, that pedilavium was too deeply rooted in Britain to eradicate at the sweep of the pen. He therefore left each ecclesiastical community free to decide whether it should be carried out.

The most important and frequently repeated service of the Christian Church has been the celebration of the Lord's Supper. Through the centuries it has been given many names, each suggestive of some aspect of its significance. That there ever was a peculiarly Celtic liturgy has been doubted by H. Leclercq. The later Celtic Christians travelled widely, he felt, and incorporated into their celebration a variety of rites and ceremonies. The result was a conspicuous difference between Celtic and Roman usages. Gildas (+ 570) asserted that a variation existed between the British and Roman liturgies: "The Britons are at variance with the whole world, and are opposed to Roman customs, not only in the Mass, but also in their tonsure."[97] The Council of Clovesho (747), in its thirteenth canon, ordered the adoption of the Roman sacramental usages throughout England, stressing particularly "*in Baptismi officio, in Missarum celebratione*".[98] These differences were also noted by Bede.[99] The Catalogue of the Saints of Ireland likewise recorded that the Christians of that island differed in their usages. While the first order "observed one mass, one celebration", the second "celebrated different masses, and had different rules", and the third still "different rules and masses". This statement reflects the various parties among Celtic Christians. Some evidently were slower at accepting the changes the Romanizing party used.

When Queen Margaret came to Scotland, one of the first points she noted, according to her biographer, was that there were some of the remnants of the early Celtic Christians "in certain districts of the Scots, who were wont to celebrate mass contrary to the custom of the whole church; with I know not what barbarous rite. This the queen, fired with the zeal for God, so sought to destroy and uproot, that henceforth none appeared in the whole Scottish nation who dared do such a thing."[100] *Could this "barbarous rite" be pedilavium?*

The available evidence has been sifted by F. E. Warren, A. A. King,[101] H. Leclercq,[102] L. Gougaud,[103] and others. A detailed study of the liturgy is outside the scope of this chapter, and only essential differences between the Celtic usages and other forms must suffice for this sketch.

Warren called attention to "a peculiar feature of the Celtic Liturgy, at least in its Irish form". It was "a multiplicity of collects",[104] the Lord's Prayer, and Scripture lections. There was seemingly no use made of incense.[105] A unique ceremony is illustrated by a practice at the island of Iona:

> At another time, there came to the saint from the province of the men of Mumu a stranger who humbly kept himself out of sight, as much as he could, so that none knew that he was a bishop. But yet that could not remain hidden from the saint. For on the next Lord's day, when he was bidden by the saint to prepare, according to custom, the body of Christ, he called the saint to assist him, so that they should as two presbyters together break the Lord's bread. Thereupon the saint, going to the altar, suddenly looked upon his face, and thus addressed him: "Christ bless you, brother; break this bread alone, according to the episcopal rite."[106]

Evidently it was the custom for two priests or one bishop to celebrate at the same time. There have survived no Celtic consecration prayers, but that they were probably said audibly is witnessed by an incident in which Columba "heard a certain priest consecrating the sacred elements of the Eucharist".[107]

Communion consisted of both kinds. In one of his addresses

Columbanus recommended: "If you thirst, drink the Fountain of life; if hunger, eat the Bread of life. Blessed are they who hunger for this Bread and thirst for this Fountain; for ever eating and drinking they still long to eat and drink."[108] But stronger than this evidence, which might be interpreted metaphorically, is the warning Columbanus gave to any who injured the chalice with his teeth![109] In Secundus' Hymn eulogizing Patrick, that saint is described as one "who draws heavenly wine in heavenly cups, and gives drink to the people of God from a spiritual chalice".[110] The two daughters of Loeghaire asked how they might see Christ face to face. Patrick replied, "Ye cannot see Christ unless ye first taste of death, and unless ye receive Christ's Body and his Blood."[111] This was also the practice at the time the *Antiphonary of Bangor* was compiled. A hymn preserved in it, sung while the people were communicating began, "Come, ye saints, take the body of Christ, drinking his holy blood, by which you were redeemed.[112] Molling of Luachair once administered the chalice to a person who was a leper.[113] The Würtzburg glossator, in his exposition of the Christian concept of salvation through Christ, recorded that eternal life came "through the material blood which poured from his side when he was on the cross, and through the spiritual blood which is offered every day upon the altar.[114] There is no evidence in the sources that the actual Presence at Communion was believed by Celtic Christians.

The custom of the primitive Church was to mix water with the wine of the eucharistic cup. Twice Columba is reputed to have changed water into wine miraculously.[115] A later comminatory story informs us that on one occasion Patrick baptized an unborn infant, and the commentator remarked, "aqua baptismi filii, ipsa est aqua communionis mulieris."[116] Stokes suggested that this phrase indicates that the water which had been used for the baptism of the infant provided water for administering Communion to the dying mother. A rubric in the *Stowe* directed, "Wine then on water into the chalice",[117] and an old poem read:

When a shower of gore had speckled
 The breast of Diamait's steed
The water wherewith Grip [the horse's name] is washed
 Is not clear for the Sacrifice.[118]

Some form of service was performed, whenever possible, to provide Communion for the dying. For instance, "When Patrick had completed his victorious career in the present world, . . . he received from bishop Tassach communion and sacrifice."[119] Stories to the same effect are preserved of Brendan. For example, he resurrected a mermaid, and "after the girl had received the Body of Christ and his Blood she died without anxiety"; and another: "The old man pointed out to them the land of which they were in search, i.e. the Land of Promise, and having received the Body of Christ and his Blood he went to heaven."[120] Cuthbert sent a priest to the dying queen of King Egfrid of Northumberland to administer "the sacrament of the body and blood of the Lord".[121] On his own deathbed Cuthbert received the Blessed Sacrament in both kinds from the hands of Herefrith, abbot of Lindisfarne.[122] The *Annals* record that Maelseachlainn More, the "pillar of the dignity and nobility of the west of the world died . . . after intense penance for his sins and transgressions, after receiving the body of Christ and his blood, after being anointed by the hands of Amhalghaidh, successor of Patrick".[123]

That a service of healing, similar to the injuction of St James,[124] was carried out among Celtic Christians is suggested by this narrative in the life of Samson:

> And it came to pass when he had entered within the palace, God as we may suppose, exercising power on his behalf, he found a certain great chief harassed by suffering at the hands of a demon; and, when he was aware of this, St Samson came to him and, having taken oil, blessed it and fully anointed him on the head, face and breast while many watched him; and, with God's help, he who had been sick was made perfectly whole.[125]

An office of visiting the sick of later date has survived,[126] but no service books of the time of Patrick or Columba are to be found in their original form. But J. F. Kenney has well noted:

> Of the importance of the *Antiphonary of Bangor* there is no question. It may be the oldest extant Irish manuscript: it is the oldest to which precise dates can—with probability—be assigned. Apart from some fragments it is the only record surviving of the old Irish church services unaffected by the Romanizing movement of the seventh and eighth centuries, and is one of the very few

western liturgical books of the seventh century which we possess ... Through its pages the general student can receive the voice of the daily worship of God carried across twelve centuries from those famous, but shadowy, monasteries of ancient Ireland.[127]

With the help of this book, the Bible, and a book of whatever hymns might have been composed by the day of the *Antiphonary*, "the abbot would be in a position to direct all the offices and devotions, habitual or special, of the monastery"[128] Included in it were suggestions for conducting the Divine Office during Easter and on Easter day; on Sabbaths and Sunday in Easter-tide; on Sabbaths and Sundays through the year; and on the Feasts of the Martyrs.

The general picture emerges, from a study of the sources available, which portrays Celtic Christian services tending to resemble earliest Christian practice, and as having an individuality of their own, and characteristics which marked them out as singular. Each differed from other Celtic rites. This complete lack of uniformity, this apparent improvisation of order and content, of prayers and blessings, probably contributed to the weakening of the position of the Celtic Church and eased its absorption into the flood tide of general Western Christianity.

CHAPTER 5 ministry

Organization developed in the Church out of necessity. It was Christ who appointed the apostles to promulgate the principles of his kingdom, and they immediately set about winning converts.[1] After Pentecost the numbers of Christians multiplied. They met for devotion in the porticoes of Herod's temple and held seasons of fellowship in the larger homes of the more wealthy.[2] The poor were helped with material necessities, but only in a haphazard sort of way. When murmuring arose because of supposed inequalities, the Christian community authorized a special group of persons to serve the business needs of the Church, while the apostles were free to minister in prayer and preaching.[3] This picture of the primitive church is filled in by St Paul. Writing both to Timothy and Titus he advised them to appoint leaders in every church they established, with other subordinate helpers called deacons and deaconesses. As the number of groups of believers increased in a locality a leader was probably chosen to superintend the affairs of several churches, as St Paul himself had done. In the early Church this overseer was elected from among the elders of the Christian communities, and, because of the lack of available evidence, it must be concluded, apparently received no special consecration. He was seemingly first among equals.

The title bishop meant overseer, or one who supervised the affairs of the Church; it stressed authority. The term presbyter, with its shortened form, priest, indicated a man who was older in experience; its emphasis was seniority, maturity, and a sense of responsibility. The terms bishop and presbyter were used interchangeably in the New Testament, and for centuries later. With modifications in ecclesiastical organization gradually coming about, the functions of bishop and priest grew to be different;* but for a long time this difference was not clearly defined. The two categories of church official, the bishop–priest–elder on the one hand, and the deacon and deaconess on the other, were the only functionaries in Pauline and later church life.

The evolution of the simple presbyter into a monarchical bishop was a gradual one. In some areas of the Church the bishop ruled over presbyters at an early date, possibly from the middle of the second century, while in other localities the movement progressed more slowly. When Celtic Christianity was carried to Ireland by Patrick, this clearly marked differentiation between bishop and priest appears not to have existed in the section of Christianity in which he had been brought up. In the writings of Patrick references are found to his ordaining only bishops. Later records present a picture of the earliest Celtic church organization simply swarming with bishops! There are fewer problems in understanding why this is so if it be granted that bishop and priest were still apparently different names for the same office, and that these Patrician bishops were the ministers of the various groups of believers, without any of the authority or functions which are associated with the accepted meaning of the title bishop. The catalogue of the saints of Ireland according to their different periods is perfectly intelligible in this light: "The first order of Catholic saints was in the time of Patrick, and then they were all bishops, famous and holy and full of the Holy Ghost; 350 in number, founders of churches. They had one head, Christ, and one chief Patrick."⁴ This order continued to the year 534. Taken at its face value this record presents a view of the organization of the primitive Celtic Church in Ireland which would be quite natural in the circumstances. Neither episcopacy nor monasticism had de-

---

* A full discussion of the rise of episcopacy from the primitive New Testament church organization is outside the scope of this chapter. The study has been done before, see DCA I, 208–40, and J. Bingham, Works II, 1-22.

veloped beyond the experimental stages, even in Gaul, by 400. In Ireland, at the remote extremity of the west, and in a semi-pagan land, many of the later refinements of both systems were lacking in the opening decades of the fifth century.

In this catalogue Patrick was the "chief" of the Church. There is no hint of dependence on any organization or authority outside of the Celtic Christian community. While the believers looked to Patrick as their leader, Christ was regarded as the "head" of his people. Each bishop was apparently the pastor of his congregation,[5] appointed so by Patrick when the believers were first grouped together. The Pauline practice of placing a bishop or presbyter in charge of each community seems to have been carried out by Patrick in Ireland.

The Celtic glossator presented a remarkable picture of what he regarded as the ideal bishop, It was based on his understanding of St Paul's teaching. The bishop was to be a man of probity, acknowledged as such by those who were not even members of his community. He should show that he was able to control his family before his ordination, and most certainly after it.[6] His fellow-Christians should be unanimous in their estimate of his fitness for office.[7] He must never become intoxicated,[8] nor must he be even fond of drink.[9] He should be free from avarice,[10] and have no quarrel with any person.[11] He, of course, must be a baptized Christian,[12] and his life should be characterized by good works.[13] He should be inclined to hospitality and ready at all times to receive every sort of person in need.[14]

Ecclesiastical authorities should not confer orders on him unless they have weighed his reputation and character,[15] checking his fitness for his responsibilities most carefully, to see that his personal life was above reproach,[16] for if he had failed to correct his family when not a bishop, he was hardly likely to be an effective leader of a multitude.[17] His ability as a preacher should be reviewed to see whether he was a suitable person to teach the flock of God,[18] since he should be studious, skilled in knowledge, and wise in his exhortation,[19] exemplifying in his own life the principles he sought to propound.[20]

In the fifth century clerical celibacy had not yet been enforced in all parts of the Christian Church, nor had it reached Celtic lands. Patrick's great-grandfather was a deacon, his grandfather was a priest, and his father was a deacon. Patrick wrote these facts without embarrassment. He evidently had no notion that his readers would regard them as anomalous. That bishop-priests and deacons were married in the Patrician period of the Celtic Church is also attested by other sources. The *Book of Armagh*, written about 807, preserved a record of the type of bishop Patrick was believed to have sought. The saint once asked Domnach Mac Criathar of Leinster to recommend a suitable candidate, one who must be "a man free, of good kin, without defect, without blemish, whose wealth would not be over little nor over great; 'I desire a man of one wife, unto whom hath been born only one child.'"²¹ When Fiacc the Fair had been found to possess all these characteristics, he was ordained as a bishop by Patrick, the first man so consecrated in Leinster. It was evidently not necessary to have to pass through any lower grades in church office as a prerequisite to installation as a bishop. Patrick was only seeking to carry out the New Testament regulation, and was so followed by the later leaders of the Celtic Church. This is vouched for by the remark of the Old-Irish glossator on the Pauline stipulation that the bishop should be married to one wife only, "before ordination and after baptism: needless to say 'afterward' then".²² His children should be examples of a well-disciplined family.²³

It will be noted* that inside the monastic *familia* marriage was permitted to the bishop, priest, or any other Christian who might so desire. The same is apparently true of bishops who were not within monastic jurisdiction, for the law tracts recognized the son of a bishop without any opprobrium.²⁴ The later homilists also regarded marriage in a bishop as not censurable: "Patrick himself went and founded Ath Truimm, twenty-five years before the founding of Armagh; . . . Now [these are] the progeny that belongs to Patrick by consanguinity and by faith and by baptism and by doctrine; and all that they obtained by land and of churches they offered to Patrick for ever."²⁵ Does this statement mean that Patrick had "progeny by consanguinity", or does it indicate that his successors did? It might possibly point to the episcopal succession which remained in the family. Whatever its significance, an intriguing story has been preserved of the marriage of Patrick: "Now when Milluic considered how he should retain Patrick, he bought a handmaid

---

* See pp. 155, 179–82 below.

for him, and when the feast was prepared on their wedding-night they were put together in a house apart."[26] Another account, which sought to establish the point that Patrick and his bride never actually consummated their marriage, noted that "Patrick preached to the bondmaid, and they spent the whole night in prayer". Patrick was then supposed to have recognized his bride as his sister whom he had not seen for six years. "Then they gave thanks to God, and go into the wilderness. Now, when Patrick was biding in the wilderness, he heard the voice of the angel, saying to him, 'Ready is the ship.' ..."[27] The knowledge of Patrick's marriage and family must have persisted for centuries for these later comminatory stories to be thought necessary. Their point seems to have been, not that Patrick was not married, but that his wife lived with him "in the wilderness" as a spiritual spouse or sister. Stories like this are frequently met in Irish sources. Here is one which fathered on Patrick the rule that men and women should not continue to live in this "spiritual" relationship, but should separate one from the other:

> At a certain time Patrick was told, through the error of the rabble, that bishop Mel had sinned with his kinswoman, for they used to be in one habitation a-praying to the Lord. When bishop Mel saw Patrick coming to him, to Archachad, in order to reproach him, bishop Mel went to angle in the furrows whereon rain had poured ... Then bishop Mel's kinswoman came having fire with her in her chasuble. And her raiment was not injured. Then Patrick knew that there was no sin between them, saying, "Let men and woman be apart, so that we may not be found to give opportunity to the weak, and so that by us the Lord's name be not blasphemed."[28]

These tenth and eleventh-century narratives were used to establish clerical celibacy and reinforce the penitential canons. But even a canon attributed to Patrick acknowledges a married clergy:

> If any clergy, from sexton to priest, is seen without a tunic, and does not cover the shame and nakedness of his body; and if his hair is not shaven according to the Roman* custom, and if his

---

* This canon has caused a great deal of discussion. Parts of it must be of a later date. A married clergy and "the Roman custom" seem mutually exclusive. The ministry of sextons would also appear to require a later dating of that

wife goes with her head unveiled, he shall be alike despised by laymen and separated from the church.[29]

At the beginning of the seventh century Gregory had recognized that there were clerics in Britain who did "not wish to remain single", and recommended to Augustine that he permit them to marry and draw their stipends separately.[30] And at the time the penitential of Finnian was written the pressure towards establishing a celibate clergy was mounting:

> If anyone, who formerly was a layman, has become a cleric, a deacon, or one of any rank, and if he lives with his sons and daughters and with his own concubine, and if he returns to carnal desire and begets a son with his concubine, or says he has, let him know that he has fallen to the depths of ruin, his sin is not less than it would be if he had been a cleric from his youth and sinned with a strange girl.[31]

Yet even Finnian dedicated his penitential book "to the sons of his bowels".[32] But the implication of the Old-Irish Penitential is that celibacy was optional with priests or deacons, but mandatory for bishops:

> Anyone holding the rank of bishop, who transgresses in respect of a woman, is degraded and does penance twelve years on water diet, or seven years on bread and water.
>
> If he be a priest, or a deacon who has taken a vow of perpetual celibacy, he spends three and a half years on bread and water.[33]

There were, as has been noted, priests and deacons who had not taken vows of perpetual celibacy. The Burgundian and so-called Roman penitentials also prescribe penances in case "any cleric or his wife overlays a baby, he (or she) shall do penance for three years, one of these on bread and water".[34] The baby was obviously their own.

The attitude against a married priesthood hardened through the years as the result of the idea that he was a holy receptacle of sacramental grace. In later centuries it was declared that "a priest, practising coition, small is his profit in baptizing; [i.e. he cannot baptize] baptism comes not from him, after visiting his nun".[35]

---

portion. Todd and Bury have both tried to deal with the problem at length. It would seem that later writers have corrupted the original canon for propaganda purposes.

That this most probably referred to married priests is suggested by the word "coition" and not adultery or fornication which would be the case were he celibate. This Irish sentiment is also met with in penitentials other than Celtic.[36] As noted above, married clergy were also accepted in England and Wales. Commenting on the Pauline qualifications of a bishop, Gildas observed:

> Well governing his house, saith the apostle, having his children subjected with all chastity ... Imperfect therefore is the chastity of the parents, [i.e. the bishop and his wife] if the children be not also endued with the same. But how shall it be, where neither the father [i.e. the bishop] nor the son, depraved by the example of his evil parent, is found to be chaste?[37]

Gildas was not censuring bishops who were married; what he was deploring was episcopal promiscuity and lasciviousness in the sons of bishops. Nennius dedicated his *History* "to Samuel, the son of Benlanus, the priest",[38] his master, regarding it as an honour, rather than any kind of disparagement to him, to be esteemed the son of a learned presbyter.

That married bishops continued in Ireland until the tenth century is established by the story of Cormac Mac Cuilennain, king of Munster, who is called "bishop and martyr". The story went:

> He was always a virgin, and he used to sleep in a very thin tunic, which he wore at matins also, and he used to sing his psalms frequently immersed in water. Now Gormlaith, daughter to Flann, son of Maelsechlainn, son of Domhnall, was his wife, and he never sinned with her except by one kiss after matins; and he sang thrice fifty psalms as penance for it in the fountain of Loch Tarbh. He was seven years king.[39]

This pious king-bishop was also a bandit and marauder, for the annals record "the plundering of Osraighe by Cormac, King of the Deisi, and many [secular] churches and monastic churches were destroyed by him".[40] He was eventually slain in the battle of Ballymoon near Carlow, in 903 (?). His widow Gormlaith married Cormac's conqueror in 909, and on his death, Neill, king of Ireland.[41]

When Malachi became archbishop of Armagh he set about correcting the practice which had been going on for about two centuries, that the bishops of Armagh were married men who passed on their bishoprics to their sons. His biographer, Bernard, recorded in horror that

> A very wicked custom grew up through the diabolical ambition of some powerful persons to obtain the holy see [Armagh] by hereditary succession. Neither would they suffer any persons to perform episcopal duties unless they were of their own tribe and family ... Finally eight married men held the office before Celsus.[42]

The Old-Irish glossator reflected the tensions in his community regarding the values of celibacy as against matrimony among the clergy in his comment on the Apostle's expression "a sister": "These are the women who attend on us, and are not for any other purpose."[43] But he added: "It is not enough for thee to be without a wife, unless thou do good works (or live a right-acting life); whatever the condition in which one is, whether it be celibacy or matrimony, it is necessary to fulfil God's commandments therein."[44] So evidently when he wrote, celibacy of the clergy, discussed by all and accepted by some had not yet become mandatory.

The organization of the Celtic Church, as will be noted,* was originally tribal. Communities of Christians lived in settlements with a presbyter-bishop to conduct their religious services. With the spread of Christianity and the moulding influence of the teachings of the gospel the dangers from pagans probably grew less. As the popularity of monasticism increased in the West, the divisions between the ordinary Christians and those who entered the religious life grew wider. The picture which the Celtic sources present is most confused, and a clear understanding of the relationships involved seems impossible to gain. But, at the risk of oversimplification, a tentative solution may be suggested, and is here submitted.

There were evidently monastic bishops and bishops who were free from community restraints. Some of the original Celtic presbyter-bishops founded monasteries, in the later definition of the term, that is, celibate men and woman banded together to live a life of devotion apart from the world. But even all these monks did not renounce possessions nor were they averse to labour. Their communities were presided over by abbots who might be bishops or

* For a discussion of this topic see ch. 7 below.

priests. Gradually rules were formulated to govern their lives. But all this took centuries to develop.

But the presbyter-bishops who did not live in monasteries evidently acted as spiritual helpers to Christians whom they served as counsellors and whom they led in worship. These bishops seem to have been tied neither to locality nor to congregation, and were free to perform the functions of the office wherever Christian people might desire it. Under the jurisdiction of no authority, they were found wandering throughout all Celtic lands, much to the disgust of later metropolitans who wished for the discipline and organization of diocesan authority.

Because of the power vested in him by his clan the abbot of a tribal monastery was also its chief. Under him the bishop functioned in spiritual matters only. But with the Romanizing of the Celtic Church the authority of the bishop increased while that of the abbot decreased. The prestige of the bishop-priests was always high. The laws and penitentials ascribe special honour to them, comparing them with chiefs or kings. In case of injury compensation was to be paid to them, while any misdemeanour on their part was punished by heavier penalties than those imposed on the people. They possessed power to grant clerical letters of introduction to any Christians who might be journeying to other parts of the country or to foreign lands. They were exempted from taxes and were freed from military service. Like Celtic chiefs, the clergy evidently wore special clothes, which appeared "austere, and should be unusual".[45] Another gloss called these garments "his badge of office".[46]

The penitentials contain abundant data indicating the failings and foibles of clergymen, and the way in which they were disciplined and rehabilitated. The penalties meted to them varied with their rank and dignity, and the sort of crime or misconduct which they had committed. As with the monastic clerics, penances consisted of corporal punishment, such as fasting and other austerities, prayers and vigils, peregrinations and exile, and fines of various kinds.

The authority of the clergy came to Celtic lands with Christianity. Patrick had apparently been ordained in the first place by clerics who had set his father apart as a deacon. Patrick consecrated the first bishops in Ireland of whom we have some kind of certain record, and these clerics passed on their authority through a simple service of ordination. When a layman or a deacon who showed potential abilities was considered to be a suitable candidate for the position of presbyter or bishop, he was consecrated immediately.

No order of service has been preserved to show the way an ordination was conducted in early Celtic Christian times. Gildas has left a record of the lections of Scripture[47] used in the ordinal of his day. These lessons, different from those in use in other Western services, were read as the candidate stood by the altar, possibly awaiting a Communion service. Gildas also noted the custom of anointing the hands of deacons and priests at the time orders were conferred. F. E. Warren pointed out that this "anointing of the hands at the ordination of deacons is not found in any form of the Roman Ordinal, ancient or modern, nor in any Gallican Ordinal".[48] A single bishop was permitted to consecrate another bishop.[49] Warren has tried a reconstruction of the ceremony, but all that may be said regarding the service is guesswork. He also conjectures that it is likely that the giving of the stole to deacons at their ordination, the delivering of the book of the Gospel to them, and also the investing of priests with a stole were all probably of Celtic origin.[50] In later times two or more bishops co-operated in carrying out the Ordinal. The candidate might feel his need for episcopal authority and request ordination. He might be chosen by his fellows and have the dignity conferred on him. This seems to have been the way of Aidan's consecration, when the brethren of Iona in conference (*conventu seniorum*) decided to set him apart to preach.[51] The seniors might have called for a bishop to carry this out, or there might even have been one present. But there is no record by Adamnan that there was a bishop at Iona before 654.[52] It certainly appears that the joint resolution by the elders of Iona to honour Aidan for the gospel ministry was similar to the decision of the brethren at Antioch at the consecration of Barnabas and Saul for their sacred functions.[53]

But with the final absorption of the Celtic Christian organization into that of Rome monarchical episcopacy became the practice. In 1609 a jury of inquisition was set up in Ireland to investigate the state of the Church. Here is part of their report:

The said jurors doe, upon their oathes, finde and say, that Donnel

Mc. Hugh O'Neale, kinge of Ireland, did, longe before any bushopps were made in the said kingdome of Ireland, give upon certaine holy men, whom they call *sancti patres*, severall portions of land ... and that the said portion of land, and third parte of the tiethes soe contynued free unto the corbe or herenagh, for many yeres, untill the church of Rome established bushopps in this kingdome, and decreed that everie corbe or herenagh should give unto the bushoppe (within whose dioces he lived) a yerely pension, more or less, accordinge to his proportion out of his entire erenachie.[54]

In the Celtic Church there was no territorial jurisdiction or predial endowment which later bishoprics possessed. The introduction of bishops by the Church of Rome, spoken of above, refers most probably to the Synod of Rathbreasil (1118) when, for the first time, a papal legate presided in an Irish council. The initial item on the agenda was to decide upon the regular bounds of the dioceses and settle the endowments for the bishops.[55] It would seem, then, that episcopal government, as it is understood in the Western Church, did not exist in Celtic Ireland until after the Norse invasions, and came about as part of the process of Romanization.

But the early Celtic bishop-priest had many varied duties to perform. Preaching and presiding at the altar were his regular tasks. Teaching the Scriptures to the young, and baptizing catechumens he carried out as opportunity occurred.[56] He acted for the believers in conferring church orders, ordaining deacons and priests, and, later, other bishops, when the episcopal dignity grew in stature. He also possessed the authority of "binding and loosing".[57] He provided for the circulation of the law books, the Gospels, and the Psalms, by writing out the Scriptures, and he officiated at the consecration of houses of worship. Occasionally a bishop might even become the chief of his tribe and lead his people to battle. A bishop might also act as a champion, farmer, or blacksmith, and might even be a physician to the sick and dying.

Through the centuries, and with the increasing influence of Roman Christianity upon Celtic polity, the position of the bishop grew in power. The process was very gradual and may be noted by little hints. Columba recognized a visitor at Iona and deferred to him the privilege of celebrating the Communion.[58] But is this a comminatory story to underline a state desired by the Romanizer Adamnan?

The student of the Celtic sources notices mention of deacons, here and there. The glossator has also left a picture of the qualifications for the diaconate, basing his views on the writings of St Paul. Deacons, like bishops, should be married to "one wife before ordination",[59] and should "have corrected their households".[60] The commentator advised, "Let testimony concerning them be given before they are ordained",[61] for they, too, "are teachers of the faith",[62] and therefore they must not be "double tongued", i.e. "let not what they say and what they think be different";[63] neither must they "sell the divine gifts for worldy gain".[64] For on a faithful deacon of this kind "it is proper to confer a bishop's rank".[65]

In the post-Viking period the number of functionaries in the Celtic Church grew. There are records of readers, singers, door-keepers, bell-ringers, stewards, catechists, treasurers, scribes, teachers, or doctors. A man might fill one or more of these functions. Probably in deference to the use of the number in the Apocalypse, the organization was occasionally termed "the seven-graded church" to suggest perfection. Deacons are mentioned, but not much is indicated about their actual duties. The glossator, in his comments on St Paul's statements regarding the offices of bishop and deacon in his letters to Timothy and Titus, indicates that these offices were similar in the Celtic Church to what they were in New Testament times.

CHAPTER 6 discipline

Discipline in the early Church was concerned with the conduct of its members so as to maintain purity of life. As the Church grew in popularity its adherents were sometimes such in name only. Persecution shook out those who were fearful or weak. Eventually, when peace returned, some desired to be reunited with their brethren.

The problem of how to treat lapsed or fallen Christians was always a grave one. While privileges were withheld from those who had sinned grievously, the Church was always reluctant to cast off any who might be reclaimed. Some clerical leaders were lax while others were rigid. To cope with this uncertainty a system of penance gradually evolved.

Great differences in the practice of discipline may be noted among early Christians compared with later developments; for example, primitive confession was public. Numbers were few, and the sinner was reinstated as he would be within a family. This procedure continued for centuries in the Western Church. It was recommended: "In church thou shalt confess thy transgressions and shalt not betake thyself to prayer with an evil conscience."[1] Another directive was: "Every Lord's day gather yourselves together and give thanks, first confessing your transgressions, that your sacrifice may be pure."[2] The apostolic advice, "Confess your faults one to another",[3] was evidently carried out literally. Little consideration was shown to the sensitivity of the penitent's feelings, for his humiliating experience was regarded as a salutary base on which his later stability might be built. At the close of the fourth century, in Rome at least, both secret and open sins required public penance.[4] Ambrose could well report: "I have seen penitents whose tears had hollowed a furrow on their faces, and who prostrated themselves on the ground to be trampled upon by the feet of every one; their pale faces, worn by fasts, exhibited the image of death in a living body."[5] But he recommended that after the sinner had confessed "to a man" he ought also to make a public acknowledgment.[6] It seems that by this time some leaders were advocating private and others public confession. Sometime towards the end of the fourth century, presbyter-penitentiaries were appointed to rehabilitate those who had lapsed. Through scandals which arose, however, this office was eventually abolished.[7] But the idea that a kindly pastor should counsel penitents was not a new one, nor did it perish. In 470 Pope Simplicius appointed a special week in which confession, penance, and baptism would be administered by priests in three churches in Rome. This developed into the annual reconciliation on Maundy Thursday.

When penance came to be regarded as a sacrament is not known. The gesture of absolution seems to have been the laying on of hands, but even its "use was by no means universal".[8] Nor have formularies of penance and absolution been preserved. For centuries the reinstatement of the penitent to Communion "probably took the form of a deprecatory prayer"[9] only. "No verbal absolution in any form but that of prayer is known to have been preserved",[10] nor is there any early statement on sacramental penance.

The question soon arose whether penance might be repeated for the same sin. "As one baptism," Ambrose ruled, "so one penance."[11] The rigour of this order often caused penance to be postponed until the hour of death. In the West the administration of this discipline eventually attained a formal methodology. The priest heard confession privately and assigned penance. For serious sins the penitent was not allowed to partake of Communion. On Maundy Thursday the bishop brought the sinner back into the fold in a public service of reconciliation. Exceptions were made for persons involved in accidents or sicknesses in which there was the possibility of immediate death.

With the break-up of Roman society, morals rapidly deteriorated. This had its effect upon the Church. "How changed is the Christian people now from its former character!" sighed Salvian of Marseilles about the middle of the fifth century.[12] This ancient historian drew so graphic a picture of the depravity of his age that it has hardly been paralleled. All seemed bent on committing the basest crimes even into old age. "Some of them, I suppose," Salvian said, "are relying on a foolish assurance of a long life or the intention of eventual penitence."[13] Because it could not be repeated, "in the fifth century penance in time of health was nearly lost in the West as in the East".[14] This is one aspect of the background of the Christianity introduced by Patrick.

The penitential discipline of the Celtic Church was of Irish origin. When and by whom it was started cannot at present be determined. The rules seem to be a synthesis of Christianized Brehon laws and prescriptions being developed by Cassian and others for dealing with sin-sick souls. While the church fathers discussed capital crimes, no logical, formalized catalogue of human frailties is to be found before John Cassian's list. As physicians studied the diseases of the body, their causes and cure, so progressive monastic leaders sought to classify sins, and to find their motives and their remedies. Under each of eight heads families of sins were eventually arranged. From these origins Celtic penitential books seem to have sprung.[15]

While the Celtic Christians were in the flood of their missionary zeal virtue was probably at is peak. With the passing years and increasing complexity in organization coupled with independence in views among the different Celtic communities, it soon became apparent that some help was needed for both priest and layman, to enable each to decide what should be done with the various classes of sinners. It is probable that in some such way the Celtic penitential books came to be. At first these slim volumes contained simple rules. They gradually took on a systematized form which finally covered every exigency which a priest might meet in the confessional.

It appears from the ancient Celtic laws that a "soul-friend" functioned even before the arrival of Christianity. The Irish word *anmchara* has been rendered "spiritual guide",[16] or "spiritual director". The glossator felt that "pastors and teachers", expressions used by the apostle Paul, referred to "soul-friends",[17] remarking, "good is my soul-friend", that is, Jesus Christ.[18] Every Celtic chief had a counsellor or druid at his court. While little is actually known about them, Caesar has left a description of their position and authority in Gaul:

> They judge in almost all controversies, public and private, and if any crime has been committed, or slaying done, or if there is a controversy over inheritance or boundaries, they determine rewards and adjudge penalties. Whoever, whether a private person or a tribe of people, does not recognize the award, they interdict from the sacrifices. This penalty is with them, most grave. Those who come under this interdict are looked upon as in the number of the impious and the criminal; these all persons shun, avoiding their touch or speech, lest they should be hurt by the contagion. Nor to these is justice given if they seek it, nor is any honour shared with them.[19]

Druids were married, and frequently passed their offices to their sons.[20] Incantations, fortune-telling, and magical spells were part of their stock-in-trade. They were the genealogists and annalists of their tribes, and also acted as leeches.[21]

Druids were powerful not only in Ireland, but also in Scotland and Wales. When Columba arrived in Iona, he was believed to have ousted two druids, who, in the guise of bishops, disputed his presence.[22] In fact, Iona is still known to some highlanders by its old name *Inis Druineach* or *Nan Druihean*, i.e. Druid's Isle.[23] The ancient Welsh laws included the procedure which was to be followed in druidical excommunications or banishments. The outcast was known as a "kinwrecked" man.[24] After the murderer had been sentenced, the old law required "every one of every sex and age within hearing of the horn to follow that exile and to keep up the barking of dogs to the time of his putting to sea, until he shall have passed three score hours out of sight".[25] Caesar noted that these banished criminals were so numerous in Gaul that they were recruited into companies to oppose him.[26] Druids were understood to have practised sorcery. Commenting on the coming of Antichrist the glossator remarked, "He will perform false marvels and false signs, as wizards have done through him."[27] The druids or wizards fulfilled the prophetic picture for the commentator.

In their social position and political influence the powerful saints were, on occasion, seemingly the successors of the druids. Druidism and Christianity were superficially similar. Both had seasons in which fires were ceremonially extinguished, and were then relighted from a symbolic flame. Both baptized infants, at which time the child's name was bestowed upon it. Both claimed to work magical cures to predict events, and to transfer diseases from human beings to plants or other objects. Both were teachers of youth and counsellors of kings. Like the druid, the Christian soul-friend might banish a sinner. Both cursed their enemies, and, as Senan once exclaimed, "Stronger is the spell that I have brought with me, and better is my lore."[28]

Christian religious leaders apparently took over some lands which had been sacred to the druids.[29] They, too, organized ordeals by fire and water; they circumambulated sacred places, and taught the pagans to regard their deities as devils. Patrick was believed to have been *anmchara* to King Loeghaire after he became a Christian,[30] as Columba was to Aidan, king of Dalriada,[31] and Adamnan to Finnsnechta Fledach, king of Ireland.[32] In short, the evidence seems to point to the fact that "the cleric supplants the druid as the king's chief adviser, under the title *anmchara*, soul-friend".[33]

On one occasion Columba declined the request to become the soul-friend to Donnan of Eig.[34] It was evidently optional for a cleric to accept this office, and it was the privilege of the one so refused to select another. This would suggest that confession was by no means obligatory, neither in making nor in hearing it. The position of the soul-friend was an important one; the saying, attributed both to Brigit and Comgall, Columba's teacher at Bangor, "anyone without a soul-friend is a body without a head", became a proverb.[35]

In early Celtic Christianity, women occasionally filled the position of soul-friend.* Women brought up foster children, and these, grown to maturity, might return to their "spiritual mothers" for help and counsel. Ita of Cluain Credill was confessor to Brendan.[36] Brigit acted in this capacity.[37] Columbanus confessed to a woman, but later in life he seems to have felt that this was not the wisest practice, and appointed priests only for this function.[38]

* See below, ch. 8.

J. T. McNeill maintained that the Celtic Christian always confessed in private in contradistinction to the Roman practice of public confession. But among Celtic Christians exceptions abound. There is evidence that both public and private confession were used. The penitential of Finnian (c. 525–50) suggested that anyone who sinned in secret should "seek pardon from God and make satisfaction, that he may be whole".[39] He further recommended that, "if one of the clerics or ministers of God makes strife, he shall do penance for a week with bread and water and seek pardon from God and his neighbour, with full confession and humility; and thus can he be reconciled to God and his neighbour".[40] In the canons attributed to Patrick, of uncertain date but with parts which very probably go back before Finnian, there was provision for public confession and retribution: "At the completion of a year of penance he shall come with witnesses and afterwards he shall be absolved by the priest."[41] A slanderer was also treated like the murderer or adulterer covered in the above ruling:

A Christian who believes that there is a vampire in the world, that is to say, a witch, is to be anathematized; whoever lays that reputation upon a living being, shall not be received into the Church until he revokes with his own voice the crime that he has committed and accordingly does penance with all diligence.[42]

Even in the Anglo-Saxon Church, when Cuthbert's preaching turned men and women to Christ, the record observes that "they all made open confession of what they had done, because they thought that these things could certainly never be hidden from him; and they cleansed themselves from the sins they had confessed by 'fruits worthy of repentance', as he commanded".[43] But, on the other hand, the Old-Irish Penitential (c. 800) laid down a definite directive for private confession: "Anyone who is himself conscious of any falsehood or unlawful gains let him confess privately ...";[44] while the Irish Canons (c. 675) ruled that certain works were to be performed "after confession of sins in the presence of priest and people",[45] and others "after confession of sins to the priest".[46] An episode in the life of Samson preserves the belief that public confession was permissible on occasion. When Samson visited his dying father, the old man was conscience-stricken.

And forthwith, having turned them all out of doors, his mother only remained with those there. There were Samson himself and his deacon and his father and mother. Without more ado Amon himself, craving their indulgence, in the presence of the three already mentioned, confessed in their midst a principal mortal sin, which he had kept hidden within himself, and vowed that, from that very day until his death, he would serve God with all his heart, his wife especially supporting him in his resolve. He found strength to shave his head that same hour, his wife, as I have said, very strongly urging him.[47]

It would appear that J. T. McNeill's statement that "according to the penitentials penance is to be administered privately at every stage; confession is to be made in secret to a qualified person, who is regularly, of course, a priest",[48] did not apply to all sections of the Celtic Church. The evidence of the penitential books suggests that confession could be made in public before witnesses or before the church, to an abbot, or even to a woman.

While all this is so, the practice of confessing to a priest was by no means infrequent among Celtic Christians. The *Old-Irish Penitential* recommended both private confession to God, and also confession to a suitable cleric: "Anyone who is himself conscious of any falsehood or unlawful gains let him confess privately to a confessor, or to an elder who may be set over him. If there be none such, let him make his own confession to God, in whose presence the evil was done, so that He shall be his confessor."[49] So that even at the beginning of the ninth century auricular confession was not yet mandatory. Advantages were recognized in both methods. But the work of the confessor was still only to admonish, advise, and pray for his charge. The discussion as to whether it was necessary to confess to God only, or to a priest, went on for many years,[50] and was not settled in the Celtic Church until the ordinances of the Roman party ultimately prevailed.

There is no mention in the penitential books of any sacramental quality to confession and absolution. The priest or soul-friend served as a counsellor only. The glossator recommended that the penitent should "purify himself through repentance, so that there is nothing in him which his conscience may "reprehend",[51] for "the Lord will be with him provided he cleanse himself by repentance".[52] The Irish commentator Malgairmrid noted; "My confession will not be

F

in vain to me, for whatever I shall pray for, God will give it".[53] Confession to God and cleansing from sin by repentance through his grace are stressed in these comments. That there was therefore no ritual absolution in the Celtic Church is suggested by the Old-Irish comment on the story of Nathan's dealings with David's sin in connection with Bathsheba: "It was said to David that his sins were forgiven him; it is not, however, said to us, when our sins are forgiven us."[54] In his note on the psalmist's assurance that God will answer their prayer for pardon is this advice: "Pray for forgiveness and make repentance, even as Hezekiah did. That is, when any man sins, that he seek the forgiveness of God at that time."[55] And explaining the psalmist's petition, "Deliver me in thy righteousness", he noted that it was a request to "God, to forgive him his sins".[56]

J. T. McNeill also believed that "public reconciliation was not in use".[57] But the fourteenth canon attributed to Patrick, of later date, as noted above, prescribed that "at the completion of a year of penance he shall come with witnesses and afterwards be absolved by the priest".[58] This must have been some sort of public cere-mony, but it might also be a local exception. Finnian, on the other hand, ruled that "sins are to be absolved in secret by penance and by every diligent devotion of heart and body".[59] It thus seems clear that there were no fixed rules.

In the Western Church, as already noticed, penance was mainly non-recurring, and hence was often postponed till the hour of death. But there is no hint in any of the Celtic penitential books that penance could not be received frequently for the same sin. It might be prescribed as often as it was needed.

Several interesting points, which later had far-reaching effects on discipline in the whole Western Church, had their roots in the penitential books of Irish Christians. Penance was described as medi-cine for sin. This concept originated long before the origin of the Celtic Church. It grew out of an old philosophy that "contraries are cured by contraries".[60] The sinner was regarded as a sick soul needing to be cured. The earliest reference to the application of this philosophy in the Irish Church is found in the penitential of Finnian:

If a cleric is wrathful or envious or backbiting, gloomy or greedy, great and capital sins are these, ... But by contraries, as we said, let us make haste to cure contraries and to cleanse away the faults from our hearts and introduce virtues in their places. Patience must arise for wrathfulness; kindness, or the love of God and of one's neighbour, for envy; for detraction, restraint of heart and tongue; for dejection, spiritual joy; for greed, liberality.[61]

Columbanus also accepted this principle. The talkative person, he maintained, "is to be sentenced to silence; the disturber to gentleness; the gluttonous to fasting; the sleepy fellow to watchfulness".[62] Cummean added, "The idler shall be taxed with an extraordinary work, and the slothful with a lengthened vigil."[63]

Those whose positions were high and whose knowledge was great were judged to have deeper guilt.[64] This was very different from the legal views of the time, which often permitted a king to go free while his slave would be slain for the same crime. Equality of sexes was another feature of penitential discipline,[65] at any rate following the law promulgated by Adamnan.

Another characteristic was composition. This indicated the kind of satisfaction which should be made to the injured party or his family by the offender or his relatives. In the old laws of Ireland and Wales composition had particular reference to homicide: "At this day ... no one is put to death for his intentional crimes so long as *êrec* is obtained."[66] If the culprit fled, his relatives were obliged to pay,[67] or, if the murderer had not absconded, he was to be handed over, together with his cattle and land. The *êrec* fine consisted of two parts. The first was the body-fine for the murdered person, which amounted to seven female slaves, the usual unit of value. The second was the honour-price for the insult. This was graded according to the rank of the injured person, the higher his position, the greater was the honour-price.

On these points some provisions of the early Celtic penitentials were based. According to the *Irish Canons* penalties were to be calculated with the rank of the injured and that of the criminal carefully taken into consideration: "The blood of a bishop, a superior prince, or a scribe which is poured out upon the ground, if the wound requires a dressing, wise men judge that he who shed the blood be crucified or pay [the value of] seven female slaves."[68] This kind of payment had its parallel in the Anglo-Saxon laws.

Examples of composition might be multiplied, suggesting their debt to ancient Celtic usage. But the citation from the influential penitential of Finnian will suffice:

> If any cleric commits murder and kills his neighbour and he is dead, he must become an exile for ten years and do penance seven years in another region. He shall do penance for three years of this time on an allowance of bread and water, and he shall fast three forty-day periods on an allowance of bread and water and for four years abstain from wine and meats; and having thus completed the ten years, if he has done well and is approved by testimonial of the abbot or priest to whom he was committed, he shall be received into his own country and make satisfaction to the friends of him whom he slew, and he shall render to his father or mother, if they are still in the flesh, compensation for the filial piety and obedience [of the murdered man] and say: 'Lo, I will do for you whatever you ask, in the place of your son.' But if he has not done enough he shall not be received back forever.[69]

The penitential of Columbanus also ordered the murderer to accept a penance almost exactly like the above.[70]

Another characteristic of the penitentials was called "commutation".[71] This meant the substitution of one form of penalty for another. Penitents who possessed property or who could obtain help from their relatives were allowed to pay fines in place of exile or long penances. This idea went wild in the *Irish Table of Commutations* some time in the eighth century.[72] The principle is well illustrated from the *Irish Collection of Canons*:

> He who has stolen treasure either from a holy church or within the city where martyrs and the bodies of the saints sleep—the lot shall be cast on three things: either his hand or his foot be cut off; or he shall be committed to prison, to fast for such time as the seniors shall determine and restore entire what he carried off; or he shall be sent forth on pilgrimage and restore double, and shall swear that he will not return until he has completed the penance and [that] after the penance he will be a monk.[73]

There seems to have been little logic in the substitution of one penalty for another. The *Irish Canons* suggested:

The equivalent of a special fast, one hundred psalms and one hundred genuflections, or the three fifties and seven canticles.[74] The equivalent of a year, three days with a dead saint in a tomb without food or drink and without sleep, but with a garment about him and with the chanting of psalms and with the prayer of the hours, after confession of sins to the priest and after the monastic vow.[75]

Crucifixion was the equivalent of a fine of seven female slaves.[76] There is no record that the fine could not be raised!

Since the penitentials varied so much, it is impossible to say that any penance was imposed in all the books or in all places or at all times. The general tendency of the handbooks may, however, be noted. The earlier the book, the more severe the penance; commutations there were none, but they came into use in later books to a degree not originally envisaged. The penalties prescribed varied greatly. In the early penitentials it was insisted that sorrow for sin be exhibited,

> with weeping and lamentations and garment of grief, under control, a short penance [is more desirable] than a long one, and a penance relaxed with moderation.[77]

> There is required of them also remorse and lamentation for their sins, and that they should desire their brethren to pray God for them that their sins may be remitted by means of penance and penitence.[78]

In other penances the cries of the repentant sinner were put to better use, he sang psalms and sacred songs. The number of songs he was obliged to render varied all the way from three or six[79] or eight[80] or twelve[81] or fifteen[82] or thirty[83] or fifty[84] to one hundred and fifty.[85] In the *Lives* of the saints, the record of the singing of the entire Psalter is not uncommon. Since most of the monks would be performing penances, this singing might have given rise to the idea of "perpetual praise" for which some monasteries grew famous.[86] On occasion the penitent was ordered to sing the Psalms in uncomfortable positions, such as "kneeling at the end of each",[87] or in "cross-vigil",[88] with his arms outstretched, and "without lowering of arms".[89] At other times saints might spend entire nights standing in water, or in a tomb with a corpse,[90] or in a cold church, or even lying on nutshells.[91] An anchorite of Clonard made 700 genuflections a day and became a cripple "by reason of the excessive number he had formerly made".[92] Findchu sat suspended by a sickle in each armpit.[93] Ite kept a stag-beetle under her clothes to nip her flesh.[94] The list of such bizarre penances might be enlarged greatly.

Blows with a rod or lash are frequently mentioned.[95] A sinner might be sentenced to "one hundred lively blows";[96] another to "365 blows with a scourge on every day to the end of a year";[97] or to "one hundred blows with a thong on the hand";[98] or even to "seven hundred palm thumpings",[99] or beating the palms on the hard ground. Columbanus fervently believed in the use of the rod or lash. Flagellation might have been self-inflicted, but the Irish penitentials give no evidence on this point.

Banishment was part of the ancient legal code of the Celts. For the more serious offences, particularly homicide, the culprit was exiled from his country. In the *Lives* and the penitentials this was called a "pilgrimage". Banishment might be for "seven years",[100] or "ten years".[101] The exile might roam as did Cain, "a vagabond and a fugitive upon the earth",[102] or he might be required to spend his time in "a monastery of another country";[103] or even "in the yoke of exile under another abbot".[104] Judging by the number of Irish pilgrims who wandered about England and on the Continent this must have been a popular form of penance.

It might happen that the pilgrim, sent on a trip for the good of his soul, was loth to leave. The homilete in the introduction to the life of Colum Cille declared:

> For when one leaves his fatherland in body only, and his mind doth not sever from sins and vices, and yearneth not to practise virtues or good deeds of the pilgrimage, then, that is made in that wise there groweth neither fruit nor profit to the soul, but labour and motion of the body idly. For it little profiteth any one to leave his fatherland unless he do good away from it.[105]

By far the commonest of punishments were fasts of various durations and degrees of intensity. Sometimes the diet was merely restricted, and certain luxuries excluded. At other times the sinner went "without supper" only for refusing to bow to his superior.[106] For another sin he might be required to spend as long as a year on bread and water,[107] while on occasion a fast for two days or forty days or any duration might be administered. The amount and kind of food which might be eaten during a fast also varied. A modifying recommendation was laid down:

> It is established that after the coming of Christ the Bridegroom, he shall set forth no fixed laws of fasting. But the difference between the Novationists and the Christians is that whereas a Novationist abstains continually, a Christian does so for a time only, that place, time, and person should in all things be regarded.[108]

In the preface to the writings of Gildas on penance a very detailed list of dietary items was given. It is interesting also as an index of the Celtic bill of fare:

> He shall seek pardon every hour and keep a special fast once every week except during the fifty days following the Passion. He shall have bread without limitation and a refection with some butter spread over it on Sunday. On the other days his allowance of bread shall be a loaf of dry bread and a dish enriched with a little fat, garden vegetables, a few eggs, British cheese, a Roman half-pint of milk in consideration of the weakness of the body in this age, also a Roman pint of whey or buttermilk for his thirst, and enough water if he is a worker. Let him have his bed meagrely supplied with hay. For the three forty-day periods let him add something as far as his strength permits.[109]

He might be required to "abstain from wine and meats for a whole year";[110] or for "two days in each week on bread and water, and two days at the end of each month";[111] or just for "seven days".[112] For murder the penance might be "twelve years on bread and water".[113] David stipulated "another penance is for three years, but with a half pint of beer or milk with bread and salt every second night with the ration of dinner".[114]

On the other hand so severe might fasts become that death would result. "A great gathering of the saints of Ireland" convened because "they were grieved that penitents died on bread and water in the days of the elders who lived before them. Then they fasted against God for this."[115] The advice given by the *Rule of Tallaght* was that fasting should not be continued to the endangering of life. An angel was said to have come with a special message to this effect:

Wonder not if the bread and the water cannot sustain the penitents today. The fruits and plants of the earth have been devastated so that there is neither strength nor force in them today to support anyone. The falsehood and sin and injustice of men have robbed the earth with its fruits of their strength and force. When men were obedient to God's will the plants of the earth retained their proper strength. At that time water was no worse for sustaining anyone than milk is today. Then the angel told them to mix some meal with their butter to make gruel, so that the penitents should not perish upon their hands [?], because the water and the bread did not suffice to support them.[116]

Monstrous penances were sometimes imposed. "Crucifixion",[117] amputation of hand or foot or both,[118] perpetual slavery,[119] going without sleep,[120] repaying twofold or fourfold of what had been stolen,[121] and periods of silence. This list is illuminated by an amusing anecdote. Two clerics went into the wilderness together under a vow of silence. After a year one observed, " 'Tis a good life we lead." After the lapse of another year in silence his companion exclaimed, "If I cannot have peace and quiet here, I'll go back to the world!"

With the collapse of law and order which followed the invasions of Europe by the barbarians during the fifth and following centuries, the Irish penitential books played an increasingly important role on the Continent. Their influence tended in the direction of order and discipline, exercising a not inconsiderable influence towards civilizing the rude pagans with whom the Celtic missionaries laboured.[122] These little books, however, marked a departure from previous practice. They formed convenient handbooks to help confessors in their tasks. They might also have been permitted to laymen, to teach them the degrees of guilt and the kinds of redress which ought to be made to the injured.

The penitentials were moulded by many of the social and legal practices of the pagans. J. T. McNeill concluded that "we may feel confident that the rise and success of the penitentials as a basis of discipline was aided by the accommodations they made to pre-Christian elements in the life of the Goidels, or Irish Scots, and of their close relatives, the Britons of Wales".[123] And so the little books grew popular among the Anglo-Saxon Christians as well as those on the Continent, and were extensively used. But they rendered the priest to some extent independent of the bishop, and hence were regarded as suspect by well-organized metropolitans. Celtic penitentials were not written by any ecclesiastical body. They were the product of individual clerics, and differed among themselves, even the names of their authors being sometimes lacking. Several of them were fathered on early saints to add some measure of authority. After years of miscopying and adaptation they became confused and inaccurate. Commutations tended to neutralize any sense of guilt which sins might engender in the conscience.

At the beginning of the ninth century the Synod of Châlons-sur-Saône (813) angrily decreed that the "*libelli* called penitentials, of which the errors were certain, the authors uncertain" should be abolished.[124] The Synod of Paris (813) ordered the bishops to look for these "booklets written in opposition to canonical authority" and to burn all they could find, "that through them unskilled priests may no longer deceive men".[125] But although sentence to extinction might be passed by synodical decree and carried out by episcopal authority, the penitentials were too useful to be destroyed so easily. A compromise seems to have been unconsciously reached. The materials and methods of the penitentials were rearranged with sufficient modifications and corrections, and brought into harmony with canon law. H. S. Lea thus succinctly observed:

> Crude and contradictory as were the penitentials in many things, taken as a whole their influence cannot have been but salutary. They inculcated in the still barbarian populations lessons of charity and loving kindness, of forgiveness of injuries and of helpfulness to the poor and to the stranger as part of the discipline whereby the sinner could redeem his sins. Besides this, the very vagueness of the boundary between secular and spiritual matters enabled them to instil ideas of order and decency and cleanliness and hygiene among the rude inhabitants of northern Europe. They were not confined to the repression of violence and sexual immorality and the grosser offences, but treated as subjects for penance excess in eating and drinking, the consumption of animals dying a natural death or of liquids contaminated

by animals falling into them; the promiscuous bathing of men and women was prohibited, and in many ways the physical nature of man was sought to be subordinated to the moral and spiritual. It was no small matter that the uncultured barbarians should be taught that evil thoughts and desires were punishable as well as evil acts. Such were their tendencies, and though at the present day it is impossible to trace directly what civilizing influence they may have exercised on the peoples subject to them, ... they exercised [such] influence.[126]

The penitential books were designed specifically for Christians. The presence in them of warnings against heathen practices shows to what extent these customs were still followed by the believers. In some areas, Christianity in Celtic lands was grafted on to heathenism. When the chiefs accepted the message of salvation from the first missionaries to Ireland the people followed their example. Such mass influxes were bound to include pagan people only nominally subscribing to the principles of Christ.[127] It would seem logical to think that, the earlier the penitential book, the more references there would be to the sins which the new Christians had been used to committing as pagans. But this is not so. It is the later books which contain more references to heathen practices. This probably reflects a lapse into heathen ways of some who were descended from the early converts. The very hagiographers are the writers who have clothed their heroes in many of the trappings of paganism, as they try to outmagic their heathen opponents!

The First Synod of Patrick warned against any cleric who "becomes surety for a pagan",[128] and any "Christian who believes that there is a vampire in the world, that is to say, a witch".[129] The *Old-Irish Penitential* made rules regarding "anyone who gives drugs or makes a bogey".[130] There are several warnings against making lamentations or dirges for the dead.[131] Generally chanted by women, these songs of grief evidently were so hard to eradicate that they were eventually carried over into the modern Christian wake.

The penitential of Theodore contained an entire section on the worship of idols and other heathen practices such as sacrificing to devils, exposing children on roofs or placing them in ovens to cure fevers, burning grains of wheat where a person had died, incantations, divinations, and other magical practices.[132] The eating of horse flesh, drinking of blood or semen, and other items which are all part of the customs of the pagans, are expressly forbidden in the penitentials.[133] The clue which indicates the depth to which these heathen customs had penetrated among Christians is the expression, "if they belong to the clergy",[134] found in the penitentials.

But while these little books acted their part in combating paganism and helping to establish discipline among Christians who were converts from heathenism, they were also contributory to grave evils. C. Plummer long ago gave his sober verdict of what the penitential books eventually became:

> The penitential literature is in truth a deplorable feature of the medieval Church. Evil deeds, the imagination of which may perhaps have dimly floated through our minds in our darkest moments, are here tabulated and reduced to system. It is hard to see how any one could busy himself with such literature and not be the worse for it.[135]

Another evil of the penitentials was the corrupting effect of commutations in money,[136] which seem incredible to a present-day moralist.[137] Vicarious penance, by means of which the wealthy and powerful were able to go free, was a further ill effect. It is possible that this was a feature of medieval theology which led to the invocation of saints and angels, and the substitution of their merit for the sinner's guilt. Devised by earnest religionists eager to uphold high standards of conduct, the penitential books eventually caused more problems than they solved, and were ultimately given up entirely.

CHAPTER 7 **monasticism**

Monasticism did not originate in the Celtic west, nor was it devised fully developed. It evolved through centuries of experimentation and adaptation. Anthony founded Christian monachism in the opening decade of the fourth century. He stressed the semi-eremitical life. The cenobitic community was launched into the Church by Pachomius (*c.* 315), who also made southern Egypt the centre of his work. A house for women was first established by the sister of Pachomius.[1] Palladius, the chronicler of monachism, left a vivid picture of Egyptian monasticism in 390. Some toiled in garden and field, sowing and tending the vineyards; others worked at building, cutting logs and shaping stones; still others went quietly about the tasks of weaving, cooking, and maintaining the machinery of the settlement. Then at three o'clock each afternoon, Palladius reported, one might "stand and hear how the strains of psalmody arise from each habitation, so that one believes that one is high above the world in Paradise. They occupy the church only on Saturday and Sunday."[2]

Several factors encouraged the practice of monachism. The attempt to escape the Decian persecution drove some Christians into the desert.[3] A desire to live in piety far from a pagan society led others to seek solitude. While Gnostics regarded the flesh as intrinsically evil, orthodox Christians considered its weaknesses to be incitements to sin. Some ardent souls resolved that its passions should be subjected to the will, and the distracting images of the mind destroyed.[4]

Many expedients were used. Some practices had their inspiration in Brahminism, while others were devised by quasi-Jewish sects. Across the centuries Christians borrowed these techniques for self-mastery and modified them. Celibacy was increasingly regarded as an important attainment. At first embraced by few, asceticism gradually came to be a way of life for more and more men and women. When asked why he acted as he did, Macarius, the desert brother replied, "Tell them, 'For Christ's sake, I am guarding the walls.' "[5] Severe fasts were endured by some desert monks.[6] Dorotheus, for instance, ate only a few ounces of bread and a handful of herbs each day.[7] The motto of the masochist in subduing his body was epitomized, "It kills me, I kill it."[8]

The abandonment of all possessions was adopted to break the hold of the world upon the soul. Some lived as recluses. The hermit Serapion the Sidonite had only a cloth to cover himself; others went naked;[9] and a few attempted to rest without bedding. Occasionally the ascentic went without sleep for days, while he spent his time in prayer.[10] By curious ways the saints sought to slay the flesh. Macarius, in penance for having killed a mosquito, sat nude in the marshes for six months to be stung.[11] Pachon slept naked in a hyena's lair.[12] Unable to endure their self-inflicted ordeals a few even went insane.[13]

John Cassian was the propagandist of the ideas and ideals of monachism. He wrote his *Institutes* for those who would war against the passions of the flesh, and his *Conferences* to encourage a life of contemplation. His writings had a wide and profound influence. But in spite of all this even by the fifth century there were no orders of monks; standards of cenobitism and asceticism were not fixed, as witness Sulpicius Severus' remark, "Overeating in Greece is gluttony; in Gaul it is a matter of course."[14] Each monastery was autonomous. The abbot regulated the affairs of his colony as he and the brethren agreed. Even the monk within the settlement might act as he wished regarding his personal property and the form of austerity he practised. As late as 420 Palladius remarked that he considered it was indeed better to live freely as a monk than to have to submit to the constraint of a vow.

About 350 Martin is believed to have founded the first monastery in the west, near Tours. Caesarius established his community at Arles. Fifty years later Honorius and his friends chose to live at Lérins. It was here that Eucherius built a hut for himself and his wife.[15] No rules have survived to depict life in these settlements. Each community in Gaul was independent. Martin lived in a wooden hut by himself,[16] while some eighty of his followers chose caves in the hill near by. Each pursued his own road to holiness.

Athanasius (+ 373), writing to a monk named Draconitius to persuade him to accept a bishopric, left a description of the stage to which the philosophy of monasticism had developed in his part of Christendom:

> You may still, after you are made a bishop, hunger and thirst with Paul, and abstain from wine with Timothy, and fast frequently, as St Paul was wont to do. Let not therefore your counsellors throw such objections in your way. For we know bishops that drink no wine, and monks that do; we know bishops that work miracles, and monks that work none. Many bishops are not married; and on the other hand many monks are fathers of children, and monks that are not so; clergy that eat and drink, and monks that fast. For these things are at liberty, and no prohibition laid upon them. Every one exercises himself as he pleases; for it is not men's stations, but their actions, for which they shall be crowned.[17]

This picture of the family life of "monks" and "bishops" suggests that celibacy for either was optional in the East before 373.

Augustine (+ 430), disturbed by the attitude of a group calling themselves "Apostolics," charged that "they arrogantly assumed to themselves that name, because they rejected all from their communion, who had either wives or estates, of which sort the Catholic Church had many, both monks and clergy".[18] In the West also, during the fifth century, there were "monks" who still exercised their liberty to enjoy family life with their wives and children, and who continued to hold possessions and property. These married monks and clerics were members of the universal Church, but were seeking to live in greater discipline in their own homes. Augustine vindicated their orthodoxy.

Now this sort of monk lived side by side with those who had renounced everything. Some ascetics remained with their families while others fled into solitude. Still others banded together in colonies for mutual comfort. In Gaul there are no records that monks endured the hardships practised in Egypt. Martin was probably the inspiration for Celtic monasticism. The bee-hive huts of Ireland have their counterpart in southern Gaul. Out of this background the monachism of the British Isles probably developed.

The earliest reference to "monks and nuns" in Ireland is found in the writings of Patrick. Vindicating his mission he noted: "Wherefore then in Ireland they who never had the knowledge of God, but until now only worshipped idols and abominations—how has there been lately prepared a people of the Lord, and they are called children of God? Sons and daughters of Scottic chieftains are seen to become monks and virgins of Christ."[19] Patrick wrote this some time during the middle of the fifth century. If he held ideas of monastic practice then prevalent in the West, he probably meant that many young persons had accepted the Christian challenge of virtuous living. He left no word of monasteries in which renunciation or asceticism was followed.

When the first actual monastic foundation was laid in Celtic Britain is not known. Ardmore started by Declan and Arran settled by Enda might have preceded the traditional establishment of Armagh by Patrick in 445, but the sources are vague.[20] The first community for which any definite evidence is available was that which Finnian began at Clonard about 530. During the next fifty years his disciples, the "Twelve Apostles of Ireland", set up centres, but the dates are approximate. In 541 Ciaran founded Clonmacnoise; in 546 Columba established Derry; in 552 Brendan settled Clonfert in Longford; in 554 or 558 Comgell started Bangor in Ulster; in 560 Columba began Durrow, and in 563 sailed away to Iona.[21]

Finnian was believed by the hagiographers to have been the first to have devised some sort of monastic rule, but this has not survived. Before his time monasteries apparently resembled Christian missionary village compounds, walled off from the hostile populace, in which a cross-section of Christian society lived.

Western Christian ecclesiastical government, moulded by Roman civil organization, gradually grew to be metropolitan and imperial —a central leader with authority over the affairs of the Churches in his area. Its logical end was the papacy. Celtic monasticism, on the other hand, was uninfluenced by Roman civil organization. The Celts lived in a society in which there were no cities. The Christians were part of innumerable splintered agrarian tribes. Some consisted of a few dozen persons, while others were large. Each tribe was ruled by a chief, whose status depended upon the wealth and size of his clan. In Ireland there were generally seven grades of chiefs.[22] Occasionally a tribal leader became a high chief and dominated several septs.

Into this tribal social structure Christianity penetrated, and its organization developed along tribal patterns. Eastern desert monasticism was modified in Gaul, from where it was probably adapted to the temperament and environment of the far western Celts, and blended with their tribal form of life.

The dependence of the Celtic Christians upon Old Testament legislation has already been noted. From the background of Mosaic laws they drew their philosophy of community arrangement, regarding themselves as a tribal theocracy similar to Israel. The glossator remarked: "Confirm us to thyself, O Lord; we shall say that we are thy folk, the nation[23] of God and the people of God."[24]

Most of the founders of Celtic monasteries chose the sites for their settlements purposefully.[25] Some were placed in wide and fertile plains, as was the monastery of Brigit at Kildare, by the river Liffey. Here flocks and herds grazed and agriculture was practised. So, too, were situated the settlements of Clonard and Bangor. The story is told of the concern of Cronan for the position of his house. On one occasion a royal visitor had been unable to find him in Sean Ross. Cronan, therefore, moved his whole establishment to Roscerea, saying, "I shall not remain in a desert place where strangers and poor folk are unable to find me readily. But here, by the public highway, I shall live, where they are able to reach me easily."[26]

This urge to dispense hospitality to the wayfarer and the indigent led to the founding of Christian settlements along the main roads of Ireland. Derry, Kells, Fore in Westmeath, Clonmacnoise, and Durrow, for instance, were all easily accessible. This facilitated travelling from one monastic house to another, and provided shelter and food for pilgrims. Celtic monastic communities were placed along the main roads of south Wales also, and in later centuries, all over the Continent.

Sometimes the monastery was built within the walls of an old fort. Aedh, the chief of a section of Donegal, gave his cousin Columba such a location for his church in Derry, and Columbanus was granted the site of Annergray. But some Celtic religious had a predilection for islands. Arran early had a Christian community, probably started in the early sixth century by Enda. Inisboffin, Inismurray, and Lindisfarne, and many other islands were so occupied. Illtyd, some time at the close of the fifth century, was believed to have been the first to settle on Caldy Island, off the Welsh Pembroke coast. This house enjoyed a wide reputation because David had been a scholar there.

Skellig Michael was at once "the most westerly of Christ's fortresses in the western world", and perhaps the most dangerously situated. Twelve miles off the south-western tip of the Kerry coast,[27] perched almost at the top of perpendicular cliffs some eight hundred feet high, the settlement was located on a forty-five degree slope about one hundred and eighty feet long by a hundred wide. The path led up about one hundred feet, and then six hundred and twenty hand-cut steps, "the way of the cross", led to the top. The community consisted of the church of St Michael, oratories, and dwelling huts. There were two wells and burial grounds in five different places. Margaret Stokes long ago wrote this moving description of the place:

> The scene is one so solemn and so sad that none should enter here but the pilgrim and the penitent. The sense of solitude, the vast heaven above and the sublime monotonous motions of the sea beneath, would but oppress the spirit, were not that spirit brought into harmony with all that is most sacred and most grand in nature, by experience.[28]

The six dwellings of stone, bee-hive shaped, are still water-proof. The two smaller oratories of corbelled stone are rectangular inside, but with the outsides rounded. They each have an east window, and the entry necessitated that the worshipper stooped to enter. The wall which protected the settlement on the cliff-side stands on the edge of a sheer precipice. The courage and skill of its builders fill the beholder with amazement.[29] Some nine thousand pairs of gannets have nested on the island from antiquity, so the monks very probably used the eggs and meat they had to hand. These island locations reveal the Celtic Christian's love of isolation and his great hardihood and courage.

The picture of the Celtic monk fleeing from the world to some secluded place where he might join battle with the devil has given rise to the idea that monastic settlements were always placed in desolate and uninhabited places. But, while there were such locations, this kind of site was in the minority. Dangerous and inaccessible regions like Ardillaun or the Skelligs, or country districts like Glendalough, were chosen, but most of the settlements were in friendlier, rural places, with trees and fields and birds' songs for company, as the Celtic Christians loved the things of nature, and through them gained a sense of the nearness of God.[30]

Sometimes, as at Glendalough, the huts were built along the side of a valley. Here Kevan lived in a cave[31] overhanging the upper lake of Glendalough. His hut could be approached only by a boat. At other times the huts were ranged around a central green, while in forested areas the trees were cleared and farm land cultivated. The Norsemen found these settlements, but no cities, and attacked and burned them continually. A ninth-century poem catches the joyous desire of the Celtic Christians for peace and seclusion:

I wish, O Son of the living God, O ancient, eternal King,
For a hidden hut in the wilderness that it may be my dwelling.
An all-grey lithe little lark to be by its side,
A clear pool to wash away sins through the grace of the Holy
    Spirit.
Quite near, a beautiful wood around it on every side, ...
To nurse many-voiced birds, hiding it with its shelter.
A southern aspect for warmth, a little brook across its floor,
A choice land with many gracious gifts such as be good for every
    plant.
A few men of sense—we will tell their number—
Humble and obedient, to pray to the King:—
Four times three, three times four, fit for every need,
Twice six in the church, both north and south:—

Six pairs besides myself,
Praying for ever the King who makes the sunshine.
A pleasant church and with the linen altar cloth a dwelling for
    God from heaven;
Then, shining candles above the pure white Scriptures.
A house for all to go to care for the body,
Without ribaldry, without boasting, without thought of evil.
This is the husbandry I would take, I would choose, and will
    not hide it:
Fragrant leek, hens, salmon, trout, bees.
Raiment and food enough for me from the King of fair fame,
And I to be sitting for a while praying God in every place.[32]

Just as in biblical times the cities were allocated to the priests
and Levites scattered throughout the territories of the twelve tribes
of Israel, so Celtic monastic founders followed the teaching of the
Liber ex Lege Moisi.[33] Wherever they chose to settle, the Celtic
missionaries obtained grants of lands from the people. This was
true not only in Ireland but also in Celtic communities in Wales,
Scotland, north England, and on the Continent. Many stories fur-
nish evidence for this. Soon after Patrick came to Ireland, his
disciple Lomman converted Feidlimid, the grandson of Niall. How
Lomman obtained a grant of land for his community was thus
chronicled:

> In the morning Fortchern son of Feidlimid went and found
> Lomman with his gospel before him. A marvel to him [Fort-
> chern] was the doctrine which he heard. He believed, and was
> baptized by Lomman, ... Feidlimid himself came to have speech
> of Lomman, and he believed, and offered Ath Triumm to God,
> and to Patrick, and to Lomman, and to Fortchern.[34]

The founding of Armagh was on a site donated by Dare.[35] These
lands remained in the hands of the successors of the original
patrons for centuries. The English inquisitors reported at Lym-
mavadon in 1609, upon oath, that these lands were handed down
from generation to generation to the successors of these original
recipients.*
    This plan was also used by Columba in Scotland, for Brude
"granted Iona to Columba".[36] Iona, in turn, later responded to the

*See p. 130 above. Bede, *HE* III, 4.

invitation of King Oswald of Northumbria to send a missioner to evangelize his subjects. On Aidan's arrival, "the king appointed the island of Lindisfarne to be his see as he asked".[37] Columbanus sought and found locations in this way on the Continent. Following the Norse invasions and the later re-establishment of the monastic domains, the new generation of clerics apparently was hard put to to gain its rights. Tales were invented to provide angelic authorization for these ancient claims.[38]

Donations of animals and furnishings were also presented to Celtic settlements. The law tract *Heptads* mentions "a cow which is given to God".[39] A kitchen utensil or cauldron was donated by Dare to Patrick, who also bestowed "on him the stead wherein Armagh stands today".[40] The same tract further notes "land which is given to a church for one's soul",[41] because of services which the clerics might render to the people. Should the Church prove remiss the gift was forfeit.[42] And so by these various means the wealth of a Celtic religious house increased from generation to generation.

Tithing was carried out in early times by the Hebrews.[43] The practice passed to the Celtic Christians from the *Liber ex Lege Moisi*. Giraldus Cambrensis noted a current tradition of the twelfth century that tithing had been introduced into Britain by Germanus and Lupus about 445, as well as first-fruits and other Hebrew offerings: "They give the first piece broken off from every loaf of bread to the poor ... They give a tenth of all their property, animals, cattle, and sheep, either when they marry, or go on a pilgrimage, or, by the counsel of the Church, are persuaded to amend their lives. This partition of their effects they call tithe."[44] Cadoc, abbot of Llancarvan, directed how the tithes should be distributed: "Whoever shall decimate, ought to divide the property into three parts, and give the first to the confessor, the second to the altar, and the third to those who pray for him."[45] Eadbert, the successor of Cuthbert on Lindisfarne, was "a man who was well known for his knowledge of the Scriptures, [and] his obedience to God's Commandments ... Each year, in accordance with the Law, he used to give a tenth of all beasts, grain, fruit, and clothing to the poor."[46] The Brehon regulations appear to be an application of Malachi's message[47] of a blessing on those who were faithful in tithing. Celtic legislators noted the antidote to "the three periods at which the world is worthless: the time of a plague; the time of a general war; the dissolution of express contracts"; and then pointed out that "there are three things which remedy them: tithes, and first-fruits, and alms; they prevent the occurrence of plague; ... war; and they confirm all in their good contracts".[48] These tithes and first-fruits and alms were carefully defined in the laws: "Tithes, i.e. with limitations [the amount is limited or specified]. First-fruits, i.e. the first of the gathering of each new fruit, i.e. every first calf, and every first lamb, and everything that is first born to a man. Alms, i.e. without limitation, or charity."[49] These regulations of the law tracts, which applied the teaching of the *Liber ex Lege Moisi*, were reinforced by the penitential books. The *Irish Canons* present a picture of the Celtic methods of payment: the tithes should be presented annually from the fruits of the ground, "since they spring up each year".[50] This applied also to "animals and humans, since we have the benefits of the same every year".[51] Nothing was exempt from tithing: the produce of flock and herd and garden and field. Even the children in the family were tithed. When a father had ten sons, he was required to present one to the Church. The method used to determine which son should be given as tithe was a curious Celtic one. After the presentation of his first-born as the first-fruits,

> nothing [is] due from him [the father] afterwards until he has ten sons; and when he has, lots are to be cast between the seven best sons of them, and the three worst are to be set aside [exempted] from the lot-casting; and the reason they are set aside is in order that the worst may not fall to the church. And the son who is selected has become the tenth, or as the first-born to the church; he obtains as much of the legacy of his father after the death of his father as every lawful son which the mother has, and he is to be on his own land outside, and he renders the service of a *saer* stock [free user of the land] tenant to the church, and let the church teach him learning, for he shall obtain more of a divine legacy than of a legacy not divine.[52]

Should the family grow very large the father was also required to pay "every tenth birth afterwards, with a lot between every two sevens".[53] This rule greatly increased the wealth of the monastic settlements.

The dependence of the Celtic Church on the *Liber ex Lege Moisi* is further illustrated by the way in which the first-fruits were paid. "First-fruits are whatever is born of the flocks before others are born" in a given year.[54] All "these things ought to be presented at the beginning of harvest, and they were offered once in the year to the priests at Jerusalem", the penitential, the *Irish Canons*, continued. "Nowadays, however, each person [pays] to the monastery of which he is a monk."[55] It should be noted that it was to the custom of the Hebrews, and not to the church traditions, that this appeal to authority was made.

The laws required that a man's property be divided carefully, and "one-third of every legacy" be presented to the Church at his death.[56] Besides these regular contributions to those who ministered, later practices enlarged the offering made by the "tribe of the people" to the "tribe of the church":

> Any church in which there is no service to *manach* tenants for baptism and communion and the singing of the intercession; it is not entitled to tithes or to the heriot cow or to a third of each bequest.[57]

But even more than all this was required of the people for the support of those who ministered to them in the Church:

> Any church in which there is an ordained man of the small churches of the tribe apart from the great churches, he is entitled to the wage of his order, that is, house, and enclosure and bed and clothing, and his ration that is sufficient for him, without exemption, without neglect of all that is in the power of the church, that is, a sack with its "kitchen", and a milch cow each quarter, and the food for festivals.[58]

While the tribe was responsible for these items, each member was required to make his personal contribution: "These are his[59] reciprocal duties to the ordained man: a proper day's ploughing each year, and with its seed and its arable land, and half of clothes for mantle or for shirt or for tunic. Dinner for four at Christmas and Easter and Pentecost."[60] This comparatively late "rule" fathered on Patrick some practices which evidently had grown up following the Norse raids.

Celtic laws, especially Irish laws, were half secular, half ecclesiastical. Occasionally a monastic leader would formulate a code which would prove beneficial to the people. Irish writers frequently allude to what they designate "the four laws of Ireland": "These are the four *čana* of Ireland: Patrick's law not to kill the clergy; and Adamnan's law, not to kill women; Daire's law not to kill or steal cattle; and the law of Sunday, not to transgress thereon."[61] Besides these there are records of several other laws. Evidently the populace showed their appreciation for the results of these enactments by giving offerings to those who framed them. The monastic settlement which inherited the rights of the founder and legislator soon discovered that its revenues might be augmented by reminding the people of these benefits. There are many references in the *Annals* of tours made by the heirs of saints to promulgate these "laws" again and again.[62] Occasionally the "relics"[63] of the saints would then be taken along if he had not framed a law, and these would be used for raising revenue. The great fairs were special occasions on which the people were persuaded to pay their dues.[64] In fact the Irish word *cain* made the double meaning of "law" as well as "tax" or "tribute". By this means the wealth of the monastery was still further augmented. The cemetery of a saint was considered a privileged spot, and one who was buried in such a place would not go to hell.[65] The greater the reputation of the saint, the greater wealth would thus accrue to his settlement through burial dues.[66] But these customs grew up after the times of the Norse incursions.

The Celtic ecclesiastics had rigid views regarding those from whom they might accept alms. These "shall not be accepted from any Christian who has been excommunicated".[67] It was further stipulated that "it is not permitted to the Church to accept alms from pagans".[68] But these strict regulations were later modified: "Be content with thy clothing and food; reject other things that are the gifts of the wicked since the lamp takes nothing but that by which it is fed."[69] Later legislators went farther. The gifts which Nebuchadnezzar presented to Daniel were cited as precedent for taking whatever a pagan might offer. J. Kenney observed that this was the decision of the Roman party in the Celtic Church, and paralleled Theodore's attempts to reverse the rulings of the strictly Celtic penitential requirements.

The Old-Irish glossator left comments suggesting opposition to mendicancy. On St Paul's words, "Do your own business", he remarked "that ye be not a-begging",[70] adding: "These are other things now which he blames here, namely, unsteadiness and indolence and mendicancy; he beseeches them, then, that these sins may not be with them",[71] continuing, "we have not been restless in begging from you".[72] Commenting on the Apostle's phrase "slow bellies", the Irishman deprecated clerics who were sluggish at service, and who were constantly begging for dinners.[73] The penitential of Finnian went as far as to stipulate that monks who baptized should not receive alms for their services.[74]

It is not difficult to see that from all these sources of income some settlements might grow enormously wealthy. Here is a picture of the status of one saint which gives an idea of the position of a church leader in his locality:

> In the days of Lent, Saint Cadoc was accustomed to reside in two islands, Barreu and Echni.[75] On Palm Sunday, he came to Nant-carvan, and there remained, performing Paschal service, feeding daily one hundred clergymen, and one hundred soldiers, and one hundred workmen, and one hundred poor persons, with the same number of widows. This was the number of his family, besides serving attendants and esquires and well-dressed guests, the number of which was uncertain, a multitude of whom frequently came to him. Nor is it to be wondered at, for being rich he was able to feed so many, being an Abbot and a Prince over the territory of his progenitor; from Fynnon Hen, that is, from the Old Fountain, as far as the river Rhymny; and he possessed all the territory from the river Gulich to the river Nadauan, from Pentyrch direct to the valley of Nantcarvan; and from that valley to the Gurimi, that is the Lesser Rhymny, toward the sea.[76]

He certainly was wealthy and generous, a prince of people and Church. The impression left by the records is that during the early centuries Celtic clerics kept aloof from pagans, not even accepting their alms. Only after pagans became believers would they receive gifts of land or produce from them. In later centuries, however, they not only solicited alms, but often even "cursed" any who refused. The pious, hard working missionary finally gave way to the wandering mendicant, who, repudiating the earlier philosophy of his Church, begged in place of toiling for food and lodging.

No monastic settlement had all the buildings which are here to be described. The larger colonies probably had most, while in the smaller ones the buildings were greatly limited. Celtic monasteries had no communal dormitories. Each person, or perhaps each family on occasion, had an individual cell, which was made of wattles and plastered. The shape of the cell was round, and of the simplest form. The monk lived, worked, wrote, and studied in his hut. Sometimes caves were chosen in place of buildings. The Christian hung up his bag containing his books. His bed was the most rudimentary, the more ascetic preferring to sleep on the ground with a stone pillow, in imitation of Jacob. Skins helped to keep him warm on a floor carpeted with straw.

In larger monasteries there was a separate refectory in which the family of religious ate communal meals. These were also built of wattles and poles or planks. Stone was used when the more easily worked materials were not at hand. Hospitality was shared generously, Ciaran's case being typical of the larger places:

> Full fifty and a hundred
> Ciaran's Dun used to feed,
> Both guests, and weaklings,
> And folk of the refectory and upper room.[77]

W. Stokes suggested[78] that the word translated "upper room" is derived from the Irish term for sun, and might indicate a solarium. He could not find this word used elsewhere, and felt that it probably indicated a flat roof on which meals might be taken during good weather. The older brethren dined below, and hence two categories were mentioned in the poem. During mealtimes, at least on more solemn occasions, some member of the society might read a sermon or a portion of the Scriptures to those who "eat when preached unto".[79]

Near the refectory was a kitchen,[80] where a fire was kept burning constantly. This had been blessed and was held to be sacred, and was never to be extinguished. One of Ciaran's disciples failed in his duty and allowed the fire to go out. The Devil was believed to have instigated this lapse. "Ciaran of Saigir said that he would not partake of food until guests should come and bring him fire."[81] Presently fire was brought down from heaven, and all was well! Close to the kitchen was generally a supply of water, a spring or stream, or even a well.[82] On occasion there might also be a pool in which the monks might refresh themselves by washing their hands and feet after toiling in the fields. Once King Lugaid demanded taxes from Senan, who had refused. The king, wishing to get even with the recalcitrant holy man, ordered his horse to be maintained by the saint in lieu of the levy: " 'Take ye my racehorse to the cleric, and let it be fed on corn with him.' Thereafter the horse was brought to Senan and he was put into the pool of the refectory to be washed, and the horse was immediately drowned in the pool."[83] Cattle evidently were permitted to refresh themselves at such pools.

As the size of the monastic community increased, the need for a guest-house became imperative. The Rule of Ailbe recommended "a clean house for the guests and big fire, washing and bathing for them, and a couch without sorrow".[84] What a charming picture of simple hospitality! At the end of a long journey, foot-sore, cold, and dirty, what more would the simple pilgrim need? Hospitality was an inflexible rule of all Celtic settlements. Dire penalties were to be inflicted on those who failed to supply the wants of the needy.

The Celtic house of worship was a very small structure. The dying Ciaran was carried to his "little church".[85] Its shape was generally round, although some oratories were rectangular. There was at least one church to each Christian settlement, but there might be two or even seven. Like the huts of the people, churches were constructed of stakes driven into the ground. Between these were fixed woven wattle screens.[86] The interstices were plastered, and with Celtic artistry were probably decorated. No traces of these buildings survive. Where large trees were available, churches were made of planks. Finian sent his monks "into the wood to cut trees for the church".[87] At Iona "oak timbers"[88] were hauled in for this purpose. The oratory which the brethren from Iona built on Lindisfarne was of "hewn oak thatched with reeds after the Scots' manner".[89] Straw might also be used for roofs, or where unavailable, sods were substituted. Very rarely is a "church built of stone"[90] mentioned in the sources. One such was on an island reached by Brendan. The wattle rods were "peeled"[91] to prevent termites lodging under the bark. Windows and doors must have been of the most rudimentary sort.

Architects and craftsmen were employed whenever they were at hand. When Cadoc was erecting a church, those who were felling the trees for timber were joined by "a certain Irishman, named Linguri, a stranger, but a skilful architect, being forced by poverty, [he] came to him with his children, that by the practice of his skill, he might procure food for himself and family, and he was gladly received by the man of God, and engaging in the work . . ."[92] His assistance was appreciated by all.

Penitential cells also appear to have been provided in certain monasteries. Those under conviction of sin might retire to these either voluntarily or under the advice of a soul-friend. The *Old-Irish Penitential* declared that the habitually ill-tempered reviler should be "expelled from the church to a place of penance".[93] While this does not specify a special cell, this is probable. The penitential cell would in all likelihood be situated in a secluded spot.[94] The mention of "dark houses"[95] might also refer to them. *De Arreis* connects "hard penance" with a "dark house or in some other place where no hindrance comes".[96] This retreat might also be called a "stone prison" for prayer.[97]

The floors of churches appear to have been covered with straw, hence great care was to be exercised not to drop any holy thing, such as Communion bread, or any valuable thing into it.[98] The larger communities would also contain cells for anchorites, infirmaries for the sick, and homes for the foster children who were cared for by the monastery. There would also be a separate school house in which pupils were taught in bad weather. At Tallaght there was a "lecture room".[99] Before the church or settlement was occupied, it was always piously and ceremoniously dedicated to the service of God. The story illustrating one such ceremony of consecration has been preserved: "Now after that Senan and the angels went right-handwise[100] round the island till they came again to the Height of the Angels, after they had consecrated the island."[101] Innis Cathaigh was the monastic settlement of Senan. The survival of this pagan practice in Celtic Christian ritual is evidence of the pervasive and persistent influence of heathenism. This, however, was not the usual method. A fast of forty days, with earnest prayer for divine blessings, was the more common way. Bede described how Lastingham was dedicated to God by just such a ceremony.[102] Another way was for a high ecclesiastical official to come and carry out the solemnity. An early penitential, that attributed to Patrick, ruled that "if anyone of the presbyters builds a church, he shall not offer [the sacrifice in it] before he brings his bishop that he may consecrate it; for this is proper".[103] At the time of its dedication the place of worship was probably given a name. This, in the early Celtic period, was the name of its founder, and not that of some honoured personage. J. Haly pointed out that, with a great deal of probability,

> it is at present easy to tell by the name whether a church has been founded before or after the Anglo-Norman invasion. If it be a church of Patrick, Columba, Kevin, or any Irish saint, it is almost certainly pre-Norman, and it is so called because the saint named founded, or is supposed to have founded, a church on that spot. But if it bear the name of St Mary, or St Peter, or any saint not associated with Ireland itself, there need be no hesitation in deciding that its origin is to be overlooked for in that period when the combined influence of Rome and England was changing the old institutions.[104]

Of course there would be exceptions to this distinction in modern times, but it seems to have been true for the Celtic period.

These Christian walled settlements were called "cities". Brigit's Kildare was called "the city of Brigit", and Clonmacnoise was known as "the city of Ciaran". This procedure recalls an Old Testament custom: Jerusalem was known as the "city of David". These settlements had no cloistered court and no common refectory or sleeping room. Each monk, as has been noted, had his separate cell or cottage, where he might live with his family if he chose. The whole group of separate buildings was surrounded by a wall or cashel. It was this which imparted a kind of coenobitic touch to the encampment. The absence of one large church is another notable feature. The foundation was in the nature of a *laura* or separate huts in which each provided for himself, rather than a *coenobium* in which the *familia* had all things in common, sleeping, eating accommodations, and with joint ownership of property.

The limits of these "cities" or estates which had been given for ecclesiastical purposes were carefully and clearly marked. This Celtic practice, with its ramifications, may be traced to the *Liber ex*

Lege Moisi. The Old Testament legislation which had to do with the cities of the priests and Levites, contained this directive:

> Command the children of Israel, that they give unto the Levites of the inheritance of their possession cities to dwell in; and ye shall give also unto the Levites suburbs for the cities round about them ... from the wall of the city and outward a thousand cubits round about ... (Num. 35.2–5).

The old law tract *Precincts* reads almost like a paraphrase of this Old Testament statement, the cubit giving place to the pace: "One thousand paces is the extent of the precinct of a saint, or a bishop, or a hermit, or a pilgrim, if it be in the plain, and two thousand paces from the precinct of every noble cathedral."[105] While the general principle holds good in the cases for which records exist, the exact extent of land which belonged to a church varied from place to place. For instance: "Then did Conall measure out a church for God and for Patrick with sixty feet of his feet. And Patrick said: 'Whosoever of thy offspring shall take from this church, his reign will not be long and will not be firm.' Then he measured Rath Airthir with (?) his crozier."[106] Instead of the cubit the Celtic ecclesiastic here used his pace. Patrick was also believed to have measured Ferta with his feet:

> The way in which Patrick measured the rath was this—the angel before him and Patrick behind the angel; with his household and with Ireland's elders, and Jesu's staff in Patrick's hand; and he said that great would be the crime of him who should sin therein, even as great would be the guerdon of him who should do God's will therein.
>
> In this wise, then, Patrick measured the Ferta, namely seven score feet in the enclosure, and seven and twenty feet in the greathouse, and seventeen feet in the kitchen, seven feet in the oratory; and in that wise it was that he used to found the cloisters always.[107]

But these comminatory stories probably sought to establish a custom which had grown up later and needed Patrician authorization. Only one dimension is given for each edifice, probably because the buildings and their enclosure were circular.[108] While Patrick was said to have measured his settlements in this way, neither archaeological nor written records corroborate this fact. However, at Ardoilean, an island off the Galway coast, the area within the walls was roughly rectangular, approximately 115 feet by 70 feet.[109] Other monastic ruins have been found enclosed within irregularly shaped walls.

The nature of these walls varied with the purpose for the barriers. The simplest was a hedge or fence to keep the cattle belonging to the tribe of the church from straying, and to prevent the animals of the tribe of the people trespassing. There were many variants. At Lindisfarne the rampart was of stones held together by sods.[110] Becan also built a stone wall around his settlement.[111] At Neendrum the palisades are very considerable, consisting of three concentric walls, roughly circular. They apparently date from pre-Christian times, and were used by later Christian occupants of the site. The walls of Tara present a similar view. The bounds of a Christian steading at Dundesert, County Antrim, consisted of a trench around the walls that used to be about

> the breadth of a moderate road; and the earth which had been cleared out of it was banked up inside as a ditch, carrying up the slope to about the height of sixteen or twenty feet from the bottom. The whole face of the slope was covered with large stones, embedded in the earth. Concentric with this enclosure, and at about the interval of seven yards, was another fosse, having a rampart on the inner side, similarly constructed, and on the area enclosed by this stood the church, east and west, 90 feet long and 30 wide. The ruined walls were about six feet high and five thick. The burial ground was principally at the east end of the building, and the whole space outside the walls was covered with loose stones. The two entrances were of about the same breadth as the fosse, and were paved with large flat stones, but they had no remains of a gateway.[112]

This structure was obviously built for defence. Ditches, walls, and palisades, all speak of purposes other than worship. When need arose, the enclosure was used as a place of sanctuary for the fugitive and for the safety of its regular inhabitants. The walls were sometimes built by the saints themselves. On one occasion when visitors "arrived, thus they found Becan, building a stone wall, with a wet sheet around him, and praying at the same time".[113]

Within the walls the property was sacrosanct. Originally granted as the home of the patron saint the law stipulated that the refuge was to extend "on every side, that is their inviolable precinct",[114] that is, there was not to be unauthorized "entry into a church over its mound".[115] The number of gateways varied. Into the monastery court of Ardoilean there were no fewer than four entries. Frequently crosses were placed directly at the entrances as reminders that the area was sacred.[116] At the west gate of Monasterboice stood a magnificent cross;[117] in fact three Celtic crosses survive there to this day. Often, however, only a stone pillar, marked with a rude carving of a cross, indicated the way into the holy place, as on Skellig Michael. It was an Old Testament custom to set up a pillar to mark a boundary between two parties, and to indicate a holy place.[118] The monastic "cities" were evidently regarded as fulfilments of the Hebrew "cities of refuge" through which God's will might be carried out for all peoples.

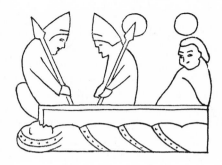

CHAPTER 8 **monasteries**

High priority must be given to the role played by the monastery during the Celtic period. It was more vital than that of an average community a thousand years later. Its functions and responsibilities were pervasive in the life of the people. The laws of Ireland carefully defined the relationships which the "tribe of the people" were to sustain to the "tribe of the church". The sanctuary which the monastery provided for offenders in need was jealously guarded. The laws and customs which supported the idea of protection were richly flavoured by regulations taken from the *Liber ex Lege Moisi*. The Old Testament contained these provisions regarding asylum:

> Ye shall appoint unto you cities to be cities of refuge for you: that the slayer may flee thither, ... and the congregation shall deliver the slayer out of the hand of the revenger (Num. 35. 10–12, 25).

The law tract *Precincts* laid down the Irish monastic concept of the asylum which the Christian Church provided: "The church protects sinners, so that they come out of it free or bond, as they entered it, ... it shelters the trespassers ... so that fines are accepted from them where death was deserved ... And she is exempt for entertaining and advising at all times."[1] This privilege of refuge was granted not only to the fugitive who entered the sacred enclo-

G

sure of the monastic settlement, but it was also given by the patron saint himself to any who might place himself under his protection. An illustration of this is the story of Curan and Columba,[2] whose sanctuary was violated and the young man Curan slain by Diarmid. In terrible indignation Columba was represented as cursing the murderer. As a result a battle ensued in which the northern prince Hugh O'Neill defeated and slew Diarmid at Culdremhe.

Adamnan has preserved a story of a young girl who fled to Columba, when he was studying with German in Leinster, while still a young man. Her pursuer, ignoring the holy man and the young disciple Columba, slew the girl before them. "Then the old man in great affliction, turning to Columba, said, 'For how long, holy boy Columba, will God, the just judge, suffer this crime, and our dishonour to go unavenged?' "[3] He then pronounced a terrible curse on the murderer, who immediately fell dead before them!

A declaratory story was told of Diarmait's son Bresal,[4] who grabbed a cow from the nun Luchair of Kells "in the sanctuary". His own father sentenced him to death for his crime. Bresal was later restored to life by Becan, and all ended well after the principle of asylum had been firmly underlined. This concept not only afforded protection to persecuted and afflicted Christians living among heathen peoples, it also worked to enhance the prestige, power, and influence of the monastic settlements themselves.

Children were often entrusted to the members of the various Christian communities to be brought up in the faith, in imitation of the way Samuel was "lent to the Lord",[5] and to be educated as useful members of society. The laws and penitentials contain several regulations covering the relationship of the child to the monastic school and the school to the child. The *Old-Irish Penitential* gives rules governing "boys of ten years old".[6] The penitential of Cummean also deals with the sins of little boys.[7] Even infants and very young children were thrust upon the monasteries. This is strong circumstantial evidence of the presence of women in some monasteries, because it would seem to be highly improbable that men would tend the smallest babies.[8] Explaining St Paul's illustration of a "nurse cherishing her children", the glossator remarked that "she makes every sound to instruct her fosterling ... of us instructing fosterlings".[9] Brigit, Ita, and Bee, Hilda and the daughters of King Cualann, were all educators of the smallest children.[10]

Cadoc received Elli as his foster-son when he was only a little boy of three, and "loved him above the love of father and mother".[11] Colman, chief of Leinster, sent his baby son to be reared by Coemgen. Rich and poor mingled freely.[12] They all lived in huts or in the outlying community.[13] After their training had been completed, the young people either continued in the settlement or went out into the "tribe of the people" to fend for themselves. The parents of the foster children were required by law to provide clothes and payments to those who looked after them. But there was also "fostering for affection",[14] in which relationship the foster parent supplied all the child's needs. If the father failed to offer his son to the Church, he was obliged to pay all the expenses of his education. If the son who had been pledged to the Church by a pious father later decided to leave its service, the parent was under obligation to pay only two-thirds of the cost and the Christian settlement made up the rest.[15] Parents were encouraged to present their boys for education, and were provided with lists of the fees, just as in the Brehon schools.[16]

In commenting on the principle which the apostle Paul laid down for Timothy: "For the Scripture saith, 'Thou shalt not muzzle the ox that treadeth out the corn', and, 'The labourer is worthy of his reward' ", the Old-Irish glossator remarked: "This is an example from the Old Law to confirm the principle that it is right to supply food and clothing to the clergy and students."[17] The implication seems to be that the students made contributions of labour to the running of the ecclesiastical seminaries, and, in consequence, should be supported.

The care of the wayfarer and pauper, the widow and orphan, was regarded as a most important part of the practice of the Celtic Christian. The *Liber ex Lege Moisi* provided for the stranger, the foreigner, and the homeless, and the Celt obeyed. No call for help was ever denied. Even to those from abroad who desired an education, the Irish monasteries provided free board, lodgings, books, and tuition.[18] The ancient laws condemned inhospitality as a crime,[19] while the penitentials inveighed against it as a sin.[20] Lasair gave food away even during a famine so that he might escape from the insults and reproaches of the poet-band.[21] But the Celt was hospitable because he loved people. His feelings may well be crystalized in these lines:

> O king of Stars!
> Whether my house be dark or bright,
> Never shall it be closed against any one,
> Lest Christ close his house against me.
>
> If there be a guest in your house
> And you conceal aught from him,
> 'Tis not the guest that will be without it,
> But Jesus, Mary's Son.[22]

Brigit is represented as making a feast for Jesus in her heart.[23] Finnian of Clonard had 3000 whom he supported in his settlement. Cadoc's generous hospitality has already been noted.

The founder or holy man to whom the original grant of land had been made was called the patron saint of the monastery or Christian community. The importance of his position can hardly be exaggerated. A gloss of the law tract *Succession* thus eulogized his person and office. He is one[24]

> who is the noblest; who is the highest; who is the wealthiest; the shrewdest; the wisest; who is popular as to compurgation; who is most powerful to sue; the most firm to sue for profits and losses. And: every body defends its members, if a goodly body, well-deeded, well-moralled, affluent, capable. The body of each is his tribe. There is no body without a head.

That this description applies with equal force to the leader of "the tribe of the church" is corroborated by the *Cain Aigillne*.[25]

The leader of the Christian settlement originally possessed the land, buildings, and the right of succession, which depended upon him and the tribe to which he belonged. Not only in Ireland but also in Wales abbatal tenancy was hereditary.[26] This tribal and hereditary occupancy was not solely of Celtic origin among Celtic Christians, it also had its authorization in the *Liber ex Lege Moisi*. Priests were chosen only from the tribe of Levi, and especially from the family of Aaron, and succeeded their fathers to holy office, and also to the possession of the sacred cities with their suburbs. This certainly looks like the authority for the Celtic Christians to continue the hereditary succession of druid and Brehon in their own

Christian communities. But while hereditary laws applied, this did not preclude the aspiring Brehon's fitting himself for his task through study. The Christianized laws provided for almost every eventuality to ensure that a suitable successor be selected for the leadership of each community.

The simplest application of this regulation of hereditary succession was to a suitable son of the original founder-abbot, as is evidenced by this couplet from the law tracts. The successor should be

> The son of the abbot in the pleasant church
> A fact established by sense.[27]

This successor was called a "coarb". Later hagiographers went to great lengths to establish him as the "heir" of the founders. This enabled all the wealth and prestige of the monastery to remain in the property of the heir. After the Viking period he was called the *erenach* or *airchinnech*. Giraldus Cambrensis noted that "the sons, after the deaths of their fathers, succeeded to the ecclesiastical benefice, not by election, but by hereditary right".[28]

Should the abbot have no son, or be a "virgin abbot", a suitable person was to be chosen from "the tribe of the patron saint who shall succeed to the church as long as there shall be a person fit to be an abbot of the said tribe of the patron saint; even though there should be but a psalm-singer of them, it is he that will obtain the abbacy".[29] Coemgen "ordained that the *erenagh* in his church should be habitually of the children and posterity of Dimma".[30] But should neither the son of the abbot nor a suitable person from the tribe of the saint be forthcoming, the law provided for a third source:

> Whenever there is not one of that tribe fit to be an abbot, it [the abbacy] is to be given to the tribe to whom the land belongs, until a person fit to be an abbot of the tribe of the patron saint, shall be qualified; and when he is, it [the abbacy] is to be given to him, if he be better than the abbot of the tribe to whom the land belongs, and who has taken it. If he [the former] is not better, it is only in his turn he shall succeed.[31]

It occasionally happened that junior members of "the tribe of the church" obtained grants of land on their own behalf in the neighbourhood, and set up subsidiary communities of Christian

believers. These were regarded as extensions of the original church
or monastery. On some occasions a foster-son of the Church settled
with a few companions at a little distance, or perhaps even across
the sea. All these ancillary houses were regarded as being legally
bound to the original settlement of the patron saint and were
under the jurisdiction of his "heirs". The law provided that

> If a person fit to be an abbot has not come of the tribe of the
> patron saint, or of the tribe to whom the land belongs, the
> abbacy is to be given to one of the *fine-manach* class until a person
> fit to be an abbot, of the tribe of the patron saint, or of the tribe
> to whom the land belongs, should be qualified; and when there is
> such a person, the abbacy is to be given to him in case he is
> better.[32]

The term *fine-manach* grade described an inferior member of the
"tribe of the church" who was a tenant on the ecclesiastical lands; or
it might also indicate members of the Church who had established
places for themselves, or it might even include the "people who give
the church valuable goods".[33] The law took care of all eventualities
thus:

> If a person fit to be an abbot has not come of the tribe of the
> patron saint, or of the tribe of the grantor of the land, or of the
> *manach* class, the "anoint" church shall receive it, in the
> fourth place; a *dalta* church shall receive it in the fifth place;
> a *compairche* church shall obtain it in the sixth place; a neigh-
> bouring *cill* church shall obtain it in the seventh place.[34]

The "anoint" church was the one in which the patron saint had
been educated, or in which he had been buried. The *dalta* church
was one established by a foster-son or pupil in the monastic settlement. A *compairche* church was one under the jurisdiction of the
patron saint, but situated at some distance. A neighbouring church
was one which, though not under the authority of the patron saint,
was simply located at a not too great distance from it.

Should all these sources prove unavailing, the monks were to
select a suitable person from among the "pilgrims"[35] who had
sought sanctuary or hospitality among them, or even a responsible
layman might temporarily rule until he found some one more
suitable.[36] This practice gave rise to many anomalies through the
centuries. The coarbs were not always bishops nor even priests.

In Kildare they were always females. There is also a record of a female coarb of St Patrick at Armagh. The one who inherited the rights of the patron saint was a chieftain of considerable power in the ecclesiastical community. The *Annals* contain a nearly complete list of the abbots or coarbs, but do not indicate successive bishops, who were more often than not in subjection to the coarb-abbot, and who did not succeed one another. The names in the *Annals* of the successors of Patrick are often called abbots, while some are called bishops as well as abbots, and others are styled simply bishops, and still others merely coarbs of St Patrick. Nothing in this last title shows whether he was a bishop or not. It is therefore well-nigh impossible to trace episcopal succession in Armagh. The co-arbs of Patrick might be bishop, priest, layman, or even a woman.[37] In the eleventh century this anomalous situation still existed in Ireland. Bernard wrote that

> There had been introduced by the diabolical ambition of certain people of rank a scandalous usage whereby the Holy See [Armagh] came to be obtained by heritary succession. For they would allow no person to be promoted to the bishoprick except such as were of their own tribe and family. Nor was it for any short period that this succession had continued, nearly fifteen generations having been already exhausted in this course of iniquity.[38]

Before the time of Celsus eight of these coarbs had been married men. After Malachy had been elected to office by the Roman party, he strove to bring Armagh and its succession into line with canonical practice.

The composition of the early Celtic monastic household may be discovered from the sources. The *Catalogue of the Saints of Ireland* recorded that the original Christians, who were drawn to the faith by Patrick and his successors, were "all bishops, ... founders of churches ... They rejected not the services and society of women, because, founded on the rock Christ, they feared not the blast of temptation. This order of saints continued for four reigns",[39] that is, to 534. T. Olden long ago strove to establish that this introduction of women into monastic households was as consorts or spiritual wives.[40] It would seem less far-fetched to suggest that at the initial stage celibacy was not enforced. Communities of men and women living together as families were more likely in vogue. S. H. Sayce pointed this out when he wrote: "As in Egypt so in the Celtic Church the *monasterium* or *collegium* was an assemblage of huts in which the monks, both cleric and lay, lived with their wives and families."[41]

In the Irish laws provisions covering the various members of the monastic family are found. They recognized "virgin" and married clerics of all grades, even lay recluses:

> There is a virgin bishop ... the virgin priest ... a bishop of one wife ...[42]

> ... a virgin clerical student ... a clerical student of one wife.[43]

> ... a lay recluse ... of virginity ... lay recluses who are without virginity, if they be beloved of God, and their works great, if their miracles are as numerous, or if they are more numerous, in the same way that Peter and Paul were to John, and in the same way Anthony and Martin were.[44]

So there were evidently in Irish ecclesiastical organizations "virgin bishops", "virgin priests", "virgin abbots", and "virgin clerical students", besides "virgin lay recluses". There were also apparently married bishops, priests, abbots, clerical students, and lay recluses. A comparison of the status enjoyed by the "virgin" and married persons shows that virginity was held to be superior. But being the "husband of one wife" did not debar a man from any clerical office, not even that of recluse. In fact the law goes out of its way to protect from censure or contempt "lay recluses who are without virginity if they be beloved of God". And so the writers of the *Lives* noted that the steward of Cadoc had a daughter,[45] while Cadoc himself had a "son-in-law",[46] and his father a "monastery".[47] The laws deplored "the son of a religious without an hour for his order".[48]

The old and infirm often found shelter in the Christian settlements. Even kings and queens entered these communities to gain peace in their declining years. The old woman of Beare, on the other hand, finding herself left behind by the march of life, sadly lamented her change of fortune:

> I had my day with kings!
> We drank the brimming mead, the ruddy wine,

Where now I drink whey-water; for company more fine
Than shrivelled hags, hag though I am, I pine.[49]

The biographers of the saints had recorded the traditional make-up
of Patrick's monastic "family":

The family of Patrick of the prayers, who had good Latin, I
remember; no feeble court [were they], their order, and their
names.

Sechnall, his bishop without fault; Mochta after him his priest;
Bishop Erc his sweet-spoken Judge; his champion, Bishop Mac-
caerthinn;
Benen, his psalmist; and Coemhan, his chamberlain;
Sinell his bell-ringer, and Aitchen his true cook;
The priest Mescan, without evil, his friend and his brewer;
The priest Bescna, sweet his verses, the chaplain of the son of
Alprann.
His three smiths,[50] expert at shaping, Macecht, Laebhan, and
Fortchern.
His three artificers, of great endowment, Aesbuite, Tairill, and
Tasach.
His three embroiderers, not despicable, Lupaid, Erca, and Cruim-
thiris.
Odhran, his charioteer, without blemish, Rodan, son of Braga,
his shepherd.
Ippis, Tigris, and Erca, and Liamhain, with Eibeachta:
For them Patrick excelled in wonders, for them he was truly
miraculous.
Carniuch was the priest that baptized him; German his tutor,
without blemish.
The priest Manach, of great endowment, was his man for supply-
ing wood.
His sister's son was Banban, of fame; Martin his mother's brother.
Most sapient was the youth Mochonnoc, his hospitaller;
Cribri and Larsa, of mantles, beautiful daughters of Gleaghrann.
Macraith the wise, and Erc,—he prophesied in his three wills.
Brogan, the scribe of his school; the priest Logha, his helmsman,—
It is not a thing unsung,—and Machui his true foster-son.
Good the man whose great family they were, to whom God gave
a crozier without sorrow;

Chiefs with whom the bells are heard, a good family was the
family of Patrick.

May the Trinity, which is powerful over all, distribute to us the
boon of great love;

The King who, moved by soft Latin, redeemed by Patrick's
prayer.[51]

If this list is taken as even partially historical as to the various
categories of helpers in a Celtic monastery of the time of its
writer, possibly the eighth century, the picture emerges of a well-
organized Christian "city" consisting of many workers, and sharing
the products of their skill with each other.

The chief was the abbot, who had under him a vice-abbot. The
religious duties, conducting services and ordaining clergy, were
carried out by the bishop or bishops. Then there were seniors, the
aged members of the society, who were consulted in matters of importance. The rank and file of the city consisted of farmers who
tended the fields and orchards, the flocks and herds; carpenters who
kept the houses in repair or built new ones; smiths who made bells
and other objects of iron; jewellers who fashioned brooches, buckles,
and decorative cases for books or the furnishings for the Communion
service, and croziers; masons who fabricated stone altars or constructed any stone building that might be made. The baker prepared
bread and other delicacies with flour provided by the miller. The
tanner took care of the skins of animals killed for food, and turned
them into leather for sandals, cloaks, or writing materials, satchels
and bags for books and other uses. The embroideresses prepared the
more decorative clothes for the abbot and other clerics, and the
cloths for the altars, out of materials prepared by carders, spinners,
and weavers. At the gate the porter functioned, with the help of the
guard or the strong man, called the champion, while the gardener
provided fruit and vegetables and herbs for the cooks in the kitchen;
and the cellarer or steward was responsible for the meal services.
On the islands fishermen procured food from the sea. The guest-
master dispensed hospitality, while nurses took care of the foster-
children and the sick and infirm. Teachers instructed in the schools,
and scribes prepared books in the *scriptoria*, which the librarians
carefully tended. Everyone had his work to do. Even when a British
king left his realm and came to Ireland on a pilgrimage in order to

gain heaven, "he gave himself to manual labour like any monk a-serving God".[52] But, on the other hand, and typical of Celtic self-contradiction, Finan protested to Mochuda: "It is a wretched thing to make your monks into brute beasts; for it were better to have oxen for ploughing and draught, than to put such torture on the disciples of God."[53] To which Mochuda replied with a chuckle, "Well, O Cleric, 'tis the sweat of his own tonsure that heals every one."[54]

The size of the monastic "city" varied considerably. Finnian of Clonard is said to have ruled over no fewer than three thousand saints,[55] while at the other end of the scale there are records of communities of only a dozen men.* Bearing in mind the comparatively small population of the British Isles, and the recurrent charge that Celtic Christians were few in number, the average settlement could hardly have been very large, consisting possibly of a few score persons.

The individuality, which is characteristic of Celtic philosophy of life, made the formulation of rules which were universally accept-able in all communities impossible. The first authenticated list of regulations which has survived was framed by Columbanus. He left Ireland and established various communities on the Continent. Here his *regulae* proved so severe that none but the hardiest and most determined were able to live by them. When Columbanus was banished from Gaul, he was very loth to return home. Could a reason for this be that his way of living was not the usual Celtic way of *laissez-faire?* It has been taken for granted,[56] without enough evidence, that the rules of Columbanus were typical of the programme of the usual Irish monastic house. There were possibly communities which lived in a manner suggested by the rules of Columbanus, but they would represent one phase only of many different kinds of Celtic monachism.

Columba's "rules", like other Celtic monastic *regulae*, were of a much later date than Columba. They were fathered on earlier saints to give them some measure of antiquity and authority. Even at the late date when these rules were devised there were still great dif-ferences between them. Each monastery went its own way. This divergence in practice is humorously underlined by the discussion between two monastic heads on the relative merits of abstinence and wine drinking. One said, in effect, My disciples are better than

* See pp. 159–60 above.

yours. They do not drink! To which the other retorted, Mine will get to heaven anyway![57]

Celtic Christians permitted "double monasteries", settlements in which both men and women lived in the same or in adjacent buildings, and generally were presided over by a woman. Palladius, in the opening years of the fifth century, described how the virgin Asella ruled over many religious persons, including husbands and wives, in a building in Rome, and taught them to live as monks and ascetics while still in their own homes.[58] Martin admitted a husband and wife to his community at Marmoutier, and, as has been noted, a couple lived in the monastery at Lérins. Double monasteries were founded in Gaul and also in Britain, and continued in existence for centuries.

The Council of Agade (506) on the Mediterranean, at which Caesar of Arles was probably present, prohibited the building of nunneries near abbeys. Justinian (529) forbade all who dwelt in monasteries with nuns even to converse with them. Double monasteries in England were permitted but deprecated by Theodore, who none the less ruled that "it is not permissible for men to have monastic women, nor women, men; nevertheless, we shall not overthrow that which is the custom in this region".[59] He evidently felt that double monasteries were too strongly entrenched to be overthrown immediately. Hilda ruled over what was perhaps the most famous double monastery of her day at Whitby. Cogitosus' *Life of Brigit* professed to describe a sixth-century monastery at Kildare:

> The number of the faithful of both sexes increasing, the church was enlarged, having within, three oratories, large, and separated by partitions of planks, under one roof of the greater house, wherein one partition extended along the breadth in the eastern part of the church, from the one party wall to the other, which partition has at its extremities two doors; through the one in the right side the chief prelate enters the santuary, accompanied by his regular school and the ministrants of the altar; through the other, the abbess and nuns, when they communicate. Another partition divides the pavement of the house into two equal parts. There are two main doors—one for men, one for the women.[60]

Brigit invited a holy man from his solitary life to join her in

governing her settlement in episcopal dignity.[61] She did not
hesitate to call her men-servants to dine with her.[62] Ita (+ 569)
and Kieran (+ 520) also associated men with their settlements,
while Mochuda (+ 637) was beloved of thirty girls who became
nuns. Evidently the hagiographers had no doubt that men and
women lived together in the same establishments, and their
readers appear to have taken this state of affairs for granted.

The same story may be repeated for double monasteries in England. Aebbe was abbess of Coldingham. On one occasion "one of
the brethren of the same monastery" spied on Cuthbert's vigils
as the holy man was standing all night in the sea and singing
psalms, and noted that otters dried and warmed the saint's feet.[63]
Verca was abbess of a monastery at the mouth of the Tyne. She
had a "priest of the same monastery" living with the sisters,[64]
as did Aelfflaed in her mixed monastery.[65] And so the evidence
might be increased to point to the stage of monastic practice
wherein men and women lived in the same establishment. This was
transitional, between communities of families and the final separation between the sexes. An insight into the actual practice of this
kind of monachism is given by this Old-Irish story of Laisran the
anchorite of Clonmacnoise. Clerical students used to take turns at
inviting him to their homes for entertainment:

> One night a certain clerical student took him to his house. He
> put a mantle under him. Laisran slept on his mantle. He sees a
> carnal vision, and he had not seen it from his birth till that
> night. He rises then. He began to weep and lament (?). "Woe to
> me ... ," saith he. Then he began to pray, and recited the three
> fifties in prayer. Then a numbness came upon his lips. Then
> came an angel to him and said, "Be not sorrowful, what you have
> seen this night you have never seen before, and what caused even
> this is because the mantle on which thou hast slept (?) is a
> mantle which has not been washed since the married couple had
> it." A demon has ... it then because it has not been washed,
> for every garment that is taken from ... folk, a demon ac-
> companies it as long as it is not washed.[66]

This anecdote reveals curious facts, evidently accepted by its writer
and its intended audience. The cloak which the clerical student
lent the anchorite had been slept in by "the married couple,"

obviously the student and his wife. While the hagiographer was intent on showing the ascetic prowess of Laisran he unconsciously recorded the fact that married couples lived in the same monastic settlement side by side with the most rigid celibate.

Because of the presence of such records in the sources the role of women in Celtic monastic practice is difficult to define. Confusion and prejudice often fog the discussion of the evidence which exists. The task of the historian is complicated because stories have been devised as propaganda for celibacy. In the Old Testament women occupied positions of honour. They could even become prophetesses. Children were regarded as guarantees of God's blessing. When the Christian Church began, the role of women was simple and obvious. But with the rise of the ascetic movement attitudes towards marriage gradually changed. What were those who were already married to do about the religio-social pressures towards celibacy? Some decided to maintain their family existence for the sake of the children, but to live as brother and sister. Single men determined to maintain a woman merely as a housekeeper. But it soon became apparent that "spiritual wifehood" of whatever kind was impracticable. In the end separate establishments for the unmarried, both men and women, were founded. Like the Western Church in general Celtic Christians seem to have passed through the stages of development between 450 and 1150.

For Celtic hagiographers of the tenth and later centuries, who probably knew little of the history and evolution of clerical celibacy, the thought that saints of previous ages had been married men with families appeared extremely anomalous. They invented stories of these early Christians as explanations. Two such fictitious anecdotes follow, quoted though long to illustrate this tendency. The point of the first narrative, written probably early in the ninth century,[67] was that Scothin lived with the ladies concerned merely as a "brother":

> Now two maidens with pointed breasts used to lie with him every night that the battle with the Devil might be the greater for him. And it was proposed to accuse him on that account. So Brenainn came to test him, and Scothin said: "Let the cleric lie in my bed tonight", saith he. So when he reached the hour of resting the girls came into the house wherein was Brenainn, with their lap-

fuls of glowing embers in their chasubles; and the fire burnt them not, and they spill [the embers] in front of Brenainn, and go into the bed with him. "What is this?" asks Brenainn. "Thus is it is that we do every night", say the girls. They lie down with Brenainn, and nowise could he sleep for longing. "That is imperfect, O cleric," say the girls, "he who is here every night feels nothing at all. Why goest thou not, O cleric, into the tub [of cold water] if it be easier for thee? 'Tis often that the cleric, even Scothin, visits it." "Well," says Brenainn, "it is wrong for us to make this test, for he is better than we are.' Thereafter they make their union and their covenant, and they part *feliciter*.[68]

A similar story is told of Ciaran. He was once on his way to the mill to seek for oats:

Then comes the daughter of the master of the mill, and she was seeking Ciaran, and he found favour in her eyes, for his form was more beautiful than that of anyone of his own age. "That is most hard for thee", said Ciaran. "Is it not this whereof thou shouldst take heed—the perishableness of the world, and Dooms-day, and the pains of hell, in order to obtain them?" When the girl had gone home, she tells those tidings to her father and to her mother. These came and offered the girl to Ciaran. "If she offers her maidenhood to God," said Ciaran, "and if she serves him, I will be at union with her." So the girl offered her maidenhood to God and to Ciaran, and all her household their continual service, and the permanent ownership of them to Ciaran, from that time forward.[69]

Dare's daughter loved Benen. She was punished and died, but after the performance of a miracle she was restored and "she loved him spiritually. She is Ercnat."[70] Of another liaison between Benen and Cruimtheris the record goes: "Benen used to carry her ration to her every night from Patrick."[71] Cruimtheris was one of the seamstresses in Patrick's *familia*.[72] The very fact that a cleric might visit a woman every night suggests a state of affairs which would certainly be highly suspect in later ages of monastic development. In the traditional story of later date concerning Columba's prowess light is shed on the presence of men and women in a community over which he presided:

so long as the Devil heard Columba's voice at celebration he durst not stir till Columba completed celebration, and till the news were asked of him afterwards by Columba. And it was a halter for the Devil who dwelt with a student at Armagh, who used to go there to another cleric's wife, i.e. when celebration and offering were made he used to visit her, until Columba once upon a time perceived the Devil beckoning to the student, and Columba forbade the student to go forth. So Columba's celebration was a halter to the Devil.[73]

This narrative was not directed against the clerical student and his wife, but was told as a warning against the irregularity of still another clerical student who visited a married woman. There evidently arose no question about regular marriage among clerics, but there was a feeling against affairs with married women.

The later hagiographers appear to have taken it for granted that women at one time lived on Iona, for "Erenat a virginal nun, ... was cook and robe-maker to Columcille".[74] In another connection the story goes that Columba "went round the graveyard in Iona and he saw an old woman cutting nettles to make broth thereof".[75] He then decided that his cook should make him "nettle broth without butter or milk" daily.[76] Stories like these might be multiplied.[77] They were evidently devised to suggest that the old Celtic saints, who according to persistent records were married, were in fact living celibate lives in spite of their relationship with women. A tenth-century poem puts the cruder narratives into poetic form:

Crinog, melodious is your song.
Though young no more you are still bashful.
We two grew up together in Niall's northern land,
When we used to sleep together in tranquil slumber.

That was my age when you slept with me,
A peerless lady of pleasant wisdom:
A pure-hearted youth, lovely without a flaw,
A gentle boy of seven sweet years.

We lived in the great world of Banva,[78]
Without sullying soul or body,
My flashing eye full of love for you,
Like a poor innocent untempted by evil....

Since then you have slept with four men after me,
Without folly or falling away:
I know, I hear it on all sides,
You are pure, without sin from man.

At last, after weary wanderings,
You have come to me again,
Darkness of age has settled on your face:
Sinless your life draws near its end.

You are still dear to me, faultless one,
You shall have welcome from me without stint:
You will not let us be drowned in torment:
We will earnestly practise devotion with you. . . .

Then may God grant us peace and happiness!
May the countenance of the King
Shine brightly upon us
When we leave behind us our withered bodies.[79]

After Mel had been accused of misdemeanours and had finally been exonerated by Patrick, the Apostle of Ireland was reputed to have ruled: "A monk and a virgin, the one from one place, the other from another, shall not dwell together in the same inn, nor travel in the same carriage from village to village, nor continually hold conversation with each other."[80] T. Olden thought that these stories represented the actual practice of having women in their lodgings as consorts.* This practice had been condemned by the Council of Nicaea (325), in its third canon. While it is possible that this state of things went on in some Celtic settlements, it would appear much more likely that these later stories were told as propaganda for celibacy, and to try to explain the condition of married monks and priests and bishops in earlier times. The evidence that marriage was openly practised by these Christians appears to be overwhelming.

The question whether or not women fulfilled any clerical functions in the Celtic Church is an interesting one. When Theodore set about regularizing the practices of the Christians, the question of the status of women in England was one with which he dealt:

* See n. 40 on p. 232 below.

It is permissible for women, that is, the handmaidens of Christ, to read the lections and to perform the ministries which appertain to the confession of the sacred altar, except those which are the special functions of priests and deacons. Women shall not cover the altar with the corporal nor place on the altar the offerings, nor the cup, nor stand among ordained men in the Church, nor sit at a feast among priests.

According to the canons it is the function of the bishops and priests to prescribe penance. No woman may adjudge penance for anyone, since in the canons no one may do this except the priests alone.

Women may receive the host under a black veil, as Basil decided. According to the Greeks a woman can make offerings [*facere oblationes*], but not according to the Romans.[81]

It would seem that these canons were designed to meet what Theodore considered abuses among the Celtic Christians whom he encountered.

There is a reference to the consecration of Brigit as a bishop. On one occasion a discussion took place:

"Why have the nuns come?" asked Bishop Mel. "To have the orders of penitence conferred on Brigit", says Mac Caille. Thereafter the orders were read out over Brigit, and bishop Mel bestowed episcopal order upon her, it is then that Mac Caille set a veil on [her] head. Hence Brigit's successor is entitled to have episcopal orders conferred upon her.[82]

There is another reference to this. Nadfraech, of the men of Tuibhi, was Brigit's lector and her preacher, "for, she said, after she had received orders from Bishop Mel, that she would not take food without being previously preached unto".[83] These comminatory stories were probably told to establish the prestige of the successors of Brigit's monastic holdings at a later date. They point to the fact that their readers were very credulous, or that in some few communities women were ordained to clerical, or even to episcopal, functions in the Irish segment of the Celtic Church.

Samuel Johnson wrote to Charles O'Connor to the effect that "the ages which deserve an exact inquiry are those times (for such they were) when Ireland was the school of the West, the quiet habitation of sanctity and literature".[84] From the days of Bede, and for two centuries after, the Irish educational system was the attraction which drew multitudes to study in that island.

The purpose of Celtic education was twofold. It sought to train clerics and to educate the lay people. Attendance at school was not compulsory, but the people were urged to send their children. Visitors from abroad were welcome. Irish schools influenced England, Scotland, and the Continent, and Irish teachers were among the most highly respected educators in the court of Charlemagne.[85] The curriculum, while including some secular studies, was mainly religious. "Comgal took Mochua with him to Bangor, where he read the canon of the Old Law and the New Testament, and the ecclesiastical order."[86] The *Lives* speak exclusively of religious texts, the Scriptures, particularly the Psalms, and monastic rules. L. Gougaud listed works which had been noted in monastic libraries founded by Celts on the Continent: Gospel books, psalters, hymn books, liturgical works, poems, rules, penitentials, martyrologies, some patristic writings, commentaries on the Gospels and Epistles and Psalms, annals, and church histories.[87] M. Esposito noted that "as far as our evidence goes, the Latin literature current in Ireland at the end of the sixth century was biblical and ecclesiastical, not classical".[88] Perhaps this is going a little too far, for Jonas recorded that Columbanus spent "much labour on grammar, rhetoric, geometry and the Holy Scriptures",[89] and became "distinguished among his countrymen for his unusual piety and knowledge of the Holy Scriptures".[90]

A legend is told of Cummine, who was once asked what he would like most in his church. "I should like it full of books", he said, "for them to go to students, and to sow God's word in the ears of every one, [so as] to bring him to heaven out of the track of the Devil."[91] In the *Lives* books are often associated with the saints. On the day of his death Columba was depicted as transscribing a book.[92]

Besides religious studies it would seem most likely, because of the excellent products which have survived, that grammar, poetry, art, and illumination, art metal work, mathematics, geometry and astronomy were also considered. There must have been some five divisions: vernacular studies, Irish legends, grammar, poetry, and history; in Christian studies, theology placed paramount emphasis upon the Bible; perhaps a slight consideration of classical studies or what ever ancient authors might be obtainable; aesthetic studies of art, poetry, and music; and scientific studies, geography and astronomy and mathematics,[93] all received attention.

Because of the smallness of the buildings instruction would most likely be given in the open air, as far as possible.[94] Small groups of students would learn from one teacher, and then move on to another.[95] The age at which children commenced their education was seven.[96] A pleasant atmosphere probably reigned to give rise to the Old-Irish comment: "It is the custom of good teachers to praise the understanding of their pupils that they may love what they hear."[96a] That oral teaching methods were used is also suggested by the sources.[97] The earliest textbooks for teaching the alphabet were seemingly made up of simple passages from the Scriptures, for we read of saints reading the alphabet when they were actually studying the Bible.[98] Columba, so the legend goes, ate the cake on which the alphabet had been written, the Bible being the bread of life, and so learned it all at once![99]

There must have been an extensive vernacular study. The glosses to the Epistles of St Paul, the Psalms, and parts of the Gospels, were in Old-Irish. The scribe would hardly have written in Old-Irish if he planned to preach in Latin. Adamnan told of the singing of Irish hymns in honour of Columba as though this were a regular practice.[100] The *Amra Choluimb Chille* is probably a ninth-century edition of a seventh-century text written in Old-Irish. The *Vita Tripartita* is the earliest hagiographical work in the Irish Church. E. MacNeill felt that it was written in Irish with a mixture of Latin at the latest early in the eighth century.[101] The *Life of Cuana* contains a statement to the effect that a blessing is invoked on the head of the scribe who translated this biography from Irish into Latin.[102] It would appear, therefore, that there must have been a study of the vernacular as well as of Latin in the Irish monastic schools.

One of the most important and far-reaching of the activities of the Celtic monastery was the work carried out in the scriptorium. This was attached to the school in which the pupils were taught.[103] Before the invention of vellum the ancient Celtic scribes evidently used wooden slats covered with wax.[104] These were carried in leather cases for protection, and a sharp stylus was used for writing on them.[105] A picture of conditions in which this work was sometimes carried on is pleasantly revealed in the story of Ciaran of Clonmacnoise and the tame fox which carried his psalter. While Ciaran taught, the fox would sit "humbly attending the lesson till the writing on wax came to an end. And he then would take it with him to Ciaran. But once the natural malice broke through the fox, and he began to eat his book, for he was greedy about the leather bands that were about it on the outside."[106] Skins were prepared and later made into vellum.[107] Now the scribe could gloat over his "white book", as he used quill pens while he supported the manuscript on his knees or on a desk of some kind.[108] Books were often borrowed to be transcribed,[109] and the story of Columba's battle as a result of copying without permission illustrates how jealously these manuscripts were guarded. The ink was made of carbon, lamp-black, or fish bone black, or the "green skinned holly" juice.[110] The quills were from geese, swans, crows, and other large birds.[111]

The work of the scribe was an honoured one. The deaths of sixty-one scribes before 900 are noted, and forty of them lie between 700 and 800.[112] They were highly skilled artists and held a respected position. Abbots and bishops also often filled the role of scribe. But these scribes could also be very human and down to earth. E. Hull has collected some personal expressions of the feelings of Irish scribes recorded in the *Lebhar Breac*:

I am weary today from head to foot!

Twenty days from today to Easter Monday, and I am cold and tired without fire or shelter.

I shall remember, O Christ, that I am writing to thee, because I am fatigued today. It is now Sunday evening.[113]

An unnamed scribe wrote a note to his companion: "Ochone, dost thou still serve for ink? I am Cormac, son of Cosnamach, trying it at Dun Daigre, the place of the writing, and I am afraid we have got too much of the mischief in this ink."[114] And yet another scribe recorded his sentiments thus: "A prayer for the students; and it is a hard little story, and do not reproach me concerning the letters, and the ink is bad, and the parchment scanty, and the day is dark."[115] It was evidently just one of those days when nothing would come out right! In still another context a young scribe boasted: "Had I wished, I could have written the whole commentary like this!"[116] But the happiness of the scribe is also reflected in the poems which were written from time to time. Here is a typical one:

> Over my head the woodland wall
> Rises; the ousel sings to me.
> Above my booklet lined for words
> The woodland birds shake out their glee.
> There's the blithe cuckoo chanting clear
> In mantle grey from bough to bough!
> God keep me still! For here I write
> A scripture bright in great woods now.[117]

Each scriptorium had its own library. The books were kept in satchels, and hung from the rafters in the scribe's hut. The satchels were of leather, and tooled and decorated.[118] The more valuable the book the more elaborate was the case in which it was stored. Sometimes the container was made of metal, and embellished with precious stones. The library of Bobbio, at the end of the tenth century, contained no fewer than seven hundred volumes.[119]

A great amount of study has been devoted to a consideration of the Celtic tonsure. The clearest description has been left by Bede:

As for the tonsure that Simon the magician is said to have worn, I ask what faithful Christian will not instantly detest it and reject it together with all his magic. On the forehead it has indeed a superficial resemblance to a crown, but when you look at the back, you will find the apparent crown cut short, so that you may fairly regard this custom as characteristic of simoniacs, and not of Christians.[120]

"Monks and clerics", Bede noted, differed not at all in their tonsures. J. Dowden appears to have hit upon the most feasible solution of the problem.[121] Noting that the Celtic tonsure had a superficial resemblance to a crown on the forehead, he concluded that there was probably a tuft or fringe of hair left in the front. The side view would suggest that the hair had been shaved "from ear to ear". Whatever the mode of cutting the hair the issue of the tonsure raised two questions. Firstly, the Celtic hair-cut was slurringly called the tonsure of Simon Magus, probably because the druids (*magi*) had cut their hair in that fashion.[122] It seems likely that, when the Christian cleric took the place of the druid in Celtic life, he not

"Axehead"

only adopted the right of hereditary succession, laws, and education from the druids and adapted them to his own Christian usages, but he apparently also dressed and cut his hair in a similar manner. In Celtic lands a tonsure was a badge of office or status. There were different kinds of tonsure. W. Stokes long ago pointed out that there were two sorts of tonsure at least, and possibly three, which were mentioned in the *Lives*. There were the clerical or monachal tonsure,[123] the tonsure of the slave,[124] and the druidical tonsure, if different.[125]

Columbanus required his monks to "wash their heads ... on every fifteenth day, or certainly on account of the growth of the flowing hair".[126] From the monuments, de Paor noted that ecclesiastics often appear clean shaven, while laymen and soldiers have drooping moustaches, and sometimes have forked and pointed beards.[127] Salvian described the tonsure of monks in his age and locale as being simply a "close crop".[128] Perhaps the short haircut was originally selected as a badge to distinguish the Christian from the "barbarian", and later became encrusted with fictitious associations of sanctity. It would seem that at different times and in different sections of the Celtic Church tonsures varied.

But, like the Easter controversy, the tonsure controversy took on overtones of authority. The Romanizing party required all the clerics to submit to the rulings of the Western Church. At this distance the question arises, Why did such a simple thing as a hair-cut rouse the feelings it did over a thousand years ago? A parallel might be found in the case of the veil and the fez in modern Turkey. Such inconsequential things distinguished the older order of tradition and religion from the new order. The veil and fez were symbols of the authority of the past. The power that imposed its way and forced its symbols on the populace was dictatorial. So was the Roman tonsure eventually imposed upon the Celtic Christians.

It apparently took some time after the Easter controversy had been settled for the tonsure controversy to be resolved. As late as 887 there still existed differences, for in that year "Anealoen the pilgrim came to Ireland, and the wearing of the hair long was abolished by him, and tonsure was accepted".[129] Although general acceptance of Roman practices came about in 695 in northern Ireland, there evidently were pockets of resistance in certain parts of the independent Celtic Church. But there was a ruling in an early Welsh law against the practice of allowing the hair to grow long, which the new mode of hair-cut ignored: "If any Catholic lets his hair grow in the fashion of the barbarians, he shall be held an alien from the Church of God and from the table of every Christian until he mends his fault."[130]

Another Celtic practice had to do with food. Besides the restriction of diet which strict asceticism imposed, other factors affected the Celtic Christian's choice of food. The Old Testament regulations on the use of "unclean" flesh has been noted already. There is evidence that some saints were vegetarians and teetotalers for health reasons, which had nothing to do with ascetic practice. Samson of Dol was very particular about his own diet: "To be sure he was one who never, throughout his whole life, tasted such a thing as the flesh of any beast or winged creature; no one ever saw him drunk; never through change of mind, or halting indecision, nor even in the least degree did any kind of drink injure him in any way."[131] The reason for this careful consideration of what he ate was health:

> Moreover, it was a custom in the consitutions of this monastery to bruise herbs from the garden, such as were beneficial for the health, in a vessel and to serve it out in small quantities to the several brothers in their porringers by means of a small siphon

for their health's sake, so that when they came in from saying
Terce they found the mixing vessel already prepared with garden
herbs.[132]

Evidently the brethren had stumbled on the benefits of vitamins
and minerals from raw vegetables and herbs !

The *Amhra Chulimb Chille* preserved an ancient tradition of the
dietary habits of Columba. He "used not to drink ale".[133] He was
just as strict on diet as Samson, for "he used to avoid flesh or the
beef or condiment".[134] He went so far as to resolve that "he would
not eat fish lest disease should take him".[135] The *Old-Irish Life of
Columba* contained a similar account of his way of life.

> And he used not to drink ale, and used not to eat meat, and used
> not to eat savoury things, as Dallan Forguill said in the *Amra*:
>
>> He drank not ale; he loved not satiety;
>> He avoided flesh.[136]

The glossator remarked on the Apostle's warning "that he may
regulate foods, that is, to forbid lust, for if gluttony were not, lust
would not be".[137] This connection between diet and lust is most
interesting. He also noted on St Paul's remark regarding "meat and
drink" that it "is not this that will bring you to heaven, though it
may be proper food".[138] The impression left by the few sources
which touch on this point is that some of the leading early Celtic
Christians had a high regard for the place of healthful living in
maintaining Christian character.

The regulations of Adamnan were based, in part, on the *Liber ex
Lege Moisi*. The law stipulated that swine should not be eaten
because they were unclean.[139] Adamnan modified this directive:
"Swine's flesh that has become thick or fat on carrion is to be
rejected like the carrion by which it grows fat. When, however, the
swine has grown smaller and returned to its original thinness, it is
to be taken."[140] Should any animal with horns push and kill a
man, it should be slain, and its flesh cast out as carrion, so stipulated
the Hebrew law.[141] Adamnan, on the other hand, ruled thus:
"Swine that taste the flesh or blood of men are always forbidden.
For in the Law any animal that pushes with the horn, if it kills a
man, is forbidden; how much more those that eat a man."[142] The
Mosaic law stipulated that only those creatures which had been

slaughtered so that the blood flowed freely from the body might be taken as food:

> Moreover ye shall eat no manner of blood, whether it be of fowl or of beast, in any of your dwellings. Whatsoever soul it be that eateth any manner of blood, even that soul shall be cut off from his people (Lev. 7.26–7).

Adamnan clearly declared that he followed this regulation. The flesh must be treated as carrion if not slaughtered correctly:

> For the fact that the higher blood had not flowed, which is the guardian and seat of life, but was clotted within the flesh . . . he who eats this flesh shall know that he has eaten the flesh with the blood; since the Lord has forbidden this, it is not the cooking of the flesh but the shedding of the blood that is lacking . . . Nevertheless, the fat and the hides we shall have for divers uses.[143]

Another Mosaic regulation had to do with the use of money, and prohibited the receiving of usury: "If thou lend money to any of my people that is poor by thee, thou shalt not be to him as an usurer, neither shalt thou lay upon him usury."[144] The "Excerpts from the *Book of David*" incorporated this Mosaic legislation into the Celtic penitential canons: "He who receives usury shall give up those things that he had received."[145] The Old Testament certainly was pervasive in Celtic thinking.

Still another Old Testament regulation dealt with feminine hygiene. Couples were to abstain from intercourse "during the entire menstrual period".[146] This was in compliance with the rule of the *Liber ex Lege Moisi* which stipulated that a woman in this condition was "unclean".[147] Another penitential regulated a mother's uncleanness after childbirth: "After the birth he shall abstain, if it is a son, for thirty-three days; if a daughter, for sixty-six days."[148] This is an application of the Mosaic law also.[149] The position of a secondary wife or *adaltrach* was carefully defined by the *Senchus Mor*, with stipulations which appear to have grown out of the relationship of Abraham with Hagar and Sarah.[150]

Among the charges which have been brought up against the Celtic Christians on more than one occasion is that a man sinned in marrying his deceased brother's widow. Giraldus Cambrensis said: "Nay, what is most detestable, and not only contrary to the Gospel, but to everything that is right, in many parts of Ireland, brothers (I will not say marry) seduce and debauch the wives of their brothers deceased, and have incestuous intercourse with them."[151] One of the points which Queen Margaret considered wrong in the conduct of the Celtic Christian remnants in Scotland of her day was "a surviving brother's marriage with the wife of a brother who had died".[152] This custom was a literal application of the statute[153] in the Old Testament known as the Levirate marriage common among ancient Semitic peoples. Its purpose was that the name of the deceased brother should not become extinct. It was only carried out when the widow was childless, and only until a male heir had been born. It was a misunderstanding of this Celtic conscientious adherence to the letter of the Old Testament which roused the censure of critics of its practices.

CHAPTER 9 Conclusions

And so the end of this investigation of the beliefs and practices of the Celtic Church in Britain has been reached. A group of Christian people has been considered, who emerge into history without a pedigree and disappear without posterity. As a desert stream, gushing from a secret spring, for a while irrigates the wilderness, bringing life and fragrance into being, and then disappears, so Celtic Christians for more than two centuries nourished Europe with the evangel of God. Carried forward with enthusiasm and devotion, seasoned with individuality and good will, the salutary message of grace crossed England and Scotland into Europe. And when the ravages of war, and the almost equally devastating arguments of angry factions, threatened the ruin of the Church on the European mainland, Celtic Christians in the far west preserved and brought again into the current of European life the vital principles of the gospel of the Lord Jesus Christ.

The seventh and eighth centuries were a time of transition and conformity for Celtic Christians. During these years their ancient usages gave place to those of Rome. Had there actually been regular intercourse between believers in the Celtic west and their fellows on the Continent before 600, it would hardly have been possible for each to be ignorant of the beliefs and practices of the other. But when, following the gospel commission, Irish Christians set out on their missionary enterprises and encountered their continental brethren, problems appear to have arisen. Co-operation finally resulted only when the Celts surrendered their peculiar traditions. These are now to be summarized.

The first had to do with authority. The Scriptures were supreme. Literally interpreted, rigidly obeyed, biblical regulations lay at the foundation of Celtic Christian belief and life. No differences were made between the ethics and morality, the legal system and theology of the Old and New Testaments. The individual exegete felt himself competent to explain and apply the message of the Bible, and he used his own rules to interpret its words literally. Whatever he considered usable he incorporated into the life and organization of the people. Any belief or practice which was thought to be at variance with the Scriptures was rejected. Hence patristic or papal notions and judgements held little weight with Celtic theologians. No appeal was made to the Apocrypha. The sole use to which it was put was to supply phrases and imagery for expressing any thoughts the Celtic writers desired. Various interpretations and differing points of view among the Celtic theologians themselves finally led to the weakening of their position and eased the conformity of Celtic with Catholic usages, and contributed to the ultimate disappearance of Celtic Christianity as such.

The rules of the Old Testament which shaped the theocracy of Israel were followed by the Celts as a natural consequence of their view of biblical authority. The role of the *Liber ex Lege Moisi* was paramount. The laws defining clean and unclean animals which might or might not be used as food, the methods of slaughtering animals, the advice on hygiene applying to both men and women, the Levirate marriage, the precepts modifying usury and slavery, the treatment of widows and orphans, as well as the payment of tithes and the offering of first-fruits, all were thought necessary. Some Celtic teachers, including Columba himself, went as far as to practise vegetarianism and teetotalism on purely health grounds, regarding their bodies as temples of the Holy Spirit. While fasting was extensively practised, it, too, was carried out much more in the manner of the Old Testament than in accordance with patristic traditions. Any time and any manner was acceptable, provided the fasting was done with a sincere desire to please God.

This emphasis on obedience grew, not only from the Celtic attitude which held the Scriptures in the greatest veneration, but also from the concept that sin was disobedience, and that man's free will was actually capable of rendering obedience to the laws which had been broken. This theory might have developed in consequence of the teaching of Pelagius the Celt. The philosophy which later came to be known as Pelagianism from its most famous advocate, might have been the articulate exposition of this Celtic point of view. While grace was held to be vital to salvation, man also had his part to play in obeying God's commandments, so that the atonement procured by Christ might become effective in the Christian's personal experience.

The observance of the Sabbath of the Old Testament was a natural outgrowth of this tenet. The seventh day was kept from sunset on Friday until sunset on Saturday, and even until dawn on Sunday in some places. No work was done on it, as the laws in the *Liber ex lege Moisi* stipulate. While Sunday was also held to possess minor sanctity, and religious services were carried out on it, the daily chores, the gathering of food, the washing of hair and taking of baths, the going on journeys and carrying out regular business transactions were all permitted upon the first day. There was no Sabbatizing of Sunday during the Celtic period. This eventually came about with the Romanizing of these Christians of the far west. There are records that during the transitional period in places, at least the period of devotion commenced at sunset on Friday and continued until dawn on Monday.

Besides the weekly observance of the Sabbath, with minor religious celebrations on Sundays and other days of minor devotions, the Celts also observed the annual Easter. The divergence of the date they set from the seventh-century Catholic timing of this festival and the grave troubles which this difference caused are well known. The Celts cited apostolic authority for their practice and felt that the invitation to change was tantamount to a request to surrender their independence. The issue was one of authority as well as of principle. They believed they were right. When they eventually stepped into line with Western usages, they accepted the sovereignty of Rome in all things. The same was true of their attitude towards the tonsure. The Celtic cleric evidently wore the hair style of a pre-

Christian teacher in his country, and regarded the giving up of this as a surrender of a symbol of very great value.

The services conducted by the Celtic ministry were for worship, but more especially for the instruction of each member. To this end the preaching was probably conducted in the vernacular. It was simple and practical. The Lord's Supper was performed with the use of both bread and wine, partaken of by all, as emblems of the body and blood of Christ. There is nothing in the sources to suggest that anything of a mystical nature was attached to them. Baptism of instructed and believing candidates was carried out by triple immersion. This was followed by a service of feet-washing and then of Communion, suggesting, from the only records extant, that adult baptism was the practice which was recognized. Pre-Communion feet-washing is also an interesting Celtic usage.

The penitential discipline of the Celts sprang from their veneration of the Scriptures. Sin was disobedience to law, and therefore further rules were devised to aid and define obedience, and hence to assist in virtuous living. Penalties, modelled on those of the Old Testament, exacted what was regarded as justly due, and ranged all the way from "cutting off from the people", banishment or separation from fellowship for life, to going without supper for failure to respect a superior. By taking the substitutionary exactions of the Old Testament to a logical conclusion, all kinds of penalties were concocted by which something might be done or given to compensate for the injury or delinquency or crime. This practice eventually degenerated into great abuses. Confession might be public or private, as might also be the service or act of reconciliation.

The ministry of the early Celtic Christians grew out of New Testament teachings. A bishop-presbyter ministered to each congregation, and hence bishops are found in great numbers scattered over Celtic lands. When a cleric ceased to minister to a congregation, he was still known as a bishop, and hence bishops turn up in the story of the Celtic Church in strange places doing things which would be an outrage to a regularly enthroned metropolitan of later centuries. The clergy were permitted to marry—in fact, during the early Celtic period, marriage prior to ordination was mandatory as it was in New Testament days, but unmarried members of the ministry were tolerated. There is some evidence that women exercised the highest ecclesiastical functions and might even be consecrated as bishops.

The monasticism of the Celts can also be better understood from the standpoint of Old Testament usages. Modelled on the cities of refuge, the monastery consisted of a walled village in which the mixed society of a Christian community lived lives of virtue and devotion separated from the evils of their heathen neighbours. The sacred place was marked by a pillar, and later by a cross, upon which might be depicted scenes from the Bible. These would be used as illustrations for teaching Scripture stories as required by the Mosaic regulations. Within the walls asylum was granted to those in need and hospitality was dispensed. Men, women, and children, single and in families, lived under the guidance of a leader who might be a clergyman or a layman, and was called an abbot. As was the case among the Hebrews, these "cities" were part of the inheritance of the different tribes, and remained as a tribal possession handed down by hereditary laws. Occasionally, as with Hulda the prophetess in Old Testament times, women might preside over such communities. Bishop-presbyters, functioning in religious and cere-monial affairs, would occupy positions inferior to that of the abbot-chieftain. Marriage was permitted to all classes, although celibacy later came to be regarded as the mark of deeper devotion. Poverty was not insisted upon. Individuals and families might grow wealthy. The community consisted, on occasion, of many persons who pooled their abilities and resources for the common good.

Theologically Celtic Christians held ideas which were a natural outgrowth of their view of the Scriptures. Theirs might be called a biblical theology. It was essentially practical and is characterized by a complete absence of discussion and definition and speculation. The supreme authority was the Bible as the revealed word of God. This revelation must be accepted and obeyed in all its parts. God was held to be the supreme Creator and Sustainer of the universe. The Godhead was made up of Three Personages, the Father, his Son, and the Holy Spirit who was sent forth by Christ. Man was created by God and placed on probation on this earth to live in obedience to the divine will. Endowed with freedom of choice man was to exercise his will constantly on the side of right. The fallen angel, Satan, had warred against God in heaven, and continued his warfare against Christ through man whom he seduced to his side. As an

H

antidote God granted fallen man grace through Jesus Christ and the ministry of the Third Person of the Trinity, to help him to obey. The emphasis on the sovereignty of the human will, and the pragmatic individuality to which it gave rise in Celtic circles is a fact which must never be allowed to become obscured. While man is left to choose what he should do in all circumstances, he must remember that, should he prove obdurate in sin, he will be punished in the lake of fire. The righteous, on the other hand, witnessed by their life of obedience, will be resurrected to dwell with Christ for ever. There is no mention in Celtic sources of purgatory or any place of intermediate reformation.

The position of Christ as the substitutionary sacrifice for sin was stressed. He took man's place and died in his stead, meeting the demands of justice, and granting to the penitent hope of eternal life. Adam's sin and fall apparently did not infect mankind with original sin. Each individual himself sinned through the example of Adam by the exercise of his own choice, and was not condemned because of inherent guilt which he had inherited from his parents. As he could accept Christ's gracious life as an example, so he might choose to follow Adam's rebellion in his own personal sinning day by day. Having once made the right choice on behalf of Christ's programme of righteous living, the Christian was freely justified by Christ's righteousness imputed and sanctified by our Lord's righteousness imparted. Both these transactions became operative through faith and obedience on the part of the man, and mercy and grace on the part of God.

Man had been created capable of death. Unending life was conditional on his obedience. When man sinned he became subject to death. This was a natural consequence of the fall, and had nothing penal about it. But when the sinner was finally judged to be guilty, he would be resurrected to receive his sentence and punishment by the infliction of penal death, which would seem, from the sources, to be annihilation. It was in the realm of his body that man was to maintain virtue, for it was the temple of the indwelling Christ. Hence he must guard it against sins and weaknesses of all kinds by carefully disciplining everything he did or thought. As sin resulted in death, so by the final restoration through Christ, those who accepted him would be privileged to live a life that had no end.

To help man Christ provided the ministry not only of the Holy Spirit but also of holy angels. These had themselves resisted the seduction of Satan, and so could succour the needy. There is no mention in the sources of help in any form gained through the mediation of men who had become saints.

Celtic eschatological views were simple and concrete. The Christian was commissioned by his Saviour to preach the gospel to those who were ignorant of it. Then, all men having decided for or against Christ, the Lord will descend to this earth in the last days to judge all mankind. This second advent would be very unlike the first, and might be paralleled with the spectacular descent by God on Sinai to proclaim his law. Final sentence would be given to both the righteous and sinners. The former would be heirs of bliss with Christ, while the latter would be destroyed with the devil and his evil angels. These final events were believed to be near at hand.

There appears to have been no attempt to formulate any sort of doctrine of the Church. There was a concept of Christianity forming God's tribes on earth in contradistinction to the secular septs of the pagans. God's clans were regulated according to Old Testament theocratic ordinances adapted to the tribal organization of the Celtic peoples generally. Each group seems to have been dependent upon the founder and his tribe, but independent of all others. The records note that representatives of various sections met, under the aegis of some venerable saint, to discuss points of controversy, particularly relationships with the Western Church. But in all these discussions democratic freedom seems to have prevailed. No church leader among the Celts was held to be the spokesman of all. Even Adamnan could not persuade those who were directly under his jurisdiction to do what they considered was not according to the Scripture. There was little unity of purpose. Had they presented a united front, the Celtic Church might have lasted for centuries, but they were absorbed into Catholic Christianity piece by piece, and the remnants which withstood, weakened and alone, finally disappeared.

And so passed the Celtic Christians in Britain. Here and there marks of the old saints of these islands remain. Mouldering and roofless shells, with ancient burying grounds hard by, tell of a people who have gone. In some places there may be seen an old stone cross, majestic in its indomitable thrust heavenward even today. Books and artifacts which were beloved by Celtic Christians, and on which they lavished all the skill of their ardent souls are still cherished in museums. Each priceless volume whispers of a culture sometime respected and of a faith once victorious. Celtic bells no longer call the pious to pray, their croziers have no flocks to guide into the the way of life. Some Celtic saints are even now well known; most are records in the annals of their people. Here and there a fountain or a village recalls by its name, twisted by alien tongues, the Celtic ecclesiastic whose memory it commemorates. But save to the historian or antiquary, the Celtic Church has moved into the shadowy legends of the ancient chroniclers. It awaits the loving researches of investigators who will bring back to life the Christian peoples and their ways and culture out of the welter of tradition with which their story has become encrusted.

 appendix

Only four manuscripts of the text of the *Liber ex Lege Moisi* are still extant, all of Irish provenance.

1. Ms. 3182 in the Bibliothèque nationale, of the tenth or eleventh century, was found at the abbey of the Trinity at Fécamp, established during the twelfth century.

2. Ms. Otho E XIII, of the Cotton Collection in the British Museum, is dated from the tenth or eleventh century, and was discovered at the monastery of St Augustine at Canterbury.

3. Ms. 221, in the City Library of Orléans, from the ninth or tenth century, turned up at the abbey of Fleury-sur-Loire.

4. Ms. Corpus Christi College, Cambridge, 279, transferred from the cathedral library at Worcester, dates from the ninth or tenth century.

As has been mentioned, this little work fits in remarkably well with the "books of the Law" which Patrick distributed to his churches, and which had such a pervasive and far-reaching effect upon the beliefs and practices of his followers. This little work has not been published, because it consists solely of biblical texts, but has been described rather inaccurately by Fournier. Like biblical texts of Celtic origin, the *Liber* is replete with readings from the Old Latin, and also contains phrases which cannot be traced to any source, but are part of the "Irish" versions of the Scriptures. The *Liber* contains thirty-five selections from the books of Exodus, Leviticus, Numbers, and Deuteronomy:

1. EXODUS 20.2–17, 22a, 23–6

It is most significant that the *Liber* should commence with the Decalogue, which certainly points to the interest of the Celtic Christian in keeping the Ten Commandments. This passage also includes prohibitions against the forming of idols of silver or gold, and directions for making an altar of earth without steps, under-lining the early stress in the Celtic church of "altars of stone".

2. EXODUS 21.1–36

Hebrew slave laws are here recorded, describing the relationship of the master to his servants. The responsibilities of the husband towards a rejected wife are noted, with the directive that she should be sent back to her own country. Unintentional homicides were allowed to find refuge within the city of refuge, but the murderer must be put to death. Patricide and matricide were capital offences, as was dealing in slaves, the cursing of parents. Bodily injuries must be compensated for. The killing of slaves was forbidden. Injury to pregnant women must be paid for according to the decision of the judges, "an eye for an eye, &c." Should a master knock out his slave's eye or his tooth, he must free his slave. If an ox gored a man to death the ox must be slaughtered. If this tendency were known the owner was to be executed also. Fines were to be paid when the ox merely injured any person. The owner of an open pit must compensate any who might fall into it. If an ox injured another animal, the living ox must be sold and its value divided with the owner of the animal lost, but if the tendency of the ox were known, his whole price must be paid to the injured man.

3. EXODUS 22.1–31

Theft must be compensated for fivefold. Burglars must restore what they have stolen, or be sold to pay for it. Owners must compensate for what their cattle had destroyed. He who lit a fire must pay for any damage it caused. He who loses goods entrusted to him shall recompense their owners. Animals which strayed or were stolen, any torn by other animals while he was responsible for them, must be paid for. What was borrowed must be returned or its value given. The seduced girl must be lawfully married by her seducer. Should her father refuse to allow this, the dowry must be paid as compensation to the girl. No witches were permitted. Beastiality was punishable by death, as was the worship of idols. Strangers were not to be harried, nor widows or orphans. No usury was to be charged on loans; pledges of garments were to be returned on the same day. Rulers were not to be reviled. First-fruits and first-born sons were to be given to God, so, too, the first-born from flocks and herds and domestic birds. No flesh torn by animals was to be eaten; it must be cast to the dogs.

4. EXODUS 23.1–19

No false report is to be spread. It is never right to follow the majority in sinning. The poor must not be defrauded. Straying cattle, even belonging to one's enemies, must be returned. No bribes are to be received. Strangers must not be oppressed. Land can be taken as compensation for debts only for six years, in the seventh year it is to be returned free. The Sabbath is to be kept, as are the three annual feasts. No blood or fat is to be eaten or offered with leavened bread. First-fruits are to be paid. The young of animals are not to be cooked in their mother's milk.

5. EXODUS 31.14

The Sabbath is a sign of God's true people, and must be kept on pain of death.

6. LEVITICUS 5.1

He who learns of a wrong must not hide his knowledge.

7. LEVITICUS 6.1–6a

Fornication, dishonesty, lying regarding stolen property, is prohibited. The culprit must restore, adding one fifth of the value of the article he purloined. He must also present an offering to the Lord.

8. LEVITICUS 7.19, 20

Flesh which has touched anything unclean shall not be eaten, but must be burned; refusal to carry this out is a capital crime. Fat of dead beasts, or those torn by animals, must on no account be eaten, but it might be utilized in other ways. The eating of blood is punishable by death.

9. LEVITICUS 11.33 (fragments), 35, 36

Earthen vessels defiled shall be destroyed. Whatever touches the carcase of unclean animals, birds, fish, or reptiles, becomes unclean. A fountain or well is uncontaminated provided it contains a large quantity of water, but whoever touches the carcase of unclean creatures is rendered unclean thereby.

10. LEVITICUS 12.1–5, 6b

After giving birth to a boy the mother is to be considered unclean for seven days plus thirty-three days; after the birth of a girl, for fourteen days and then sixty-six more. She must bring an offering to the sanctuary after the period of uncleanness is over.

11. LEVITICUS 17.10–11a, 13c, 14b, 15 (fragments)

No blood must ever be eaten, for the life is in the blood. Birds or animals which have been taken by hunting must be slaughtered by blood-letting, or they must not be eaten. Nothing which dies of itself or is slain by animals is to be used as food.

12. LEVITICUS 18.2b, 5–13, 15–21, 22b–24, 29

God's commandments must be observed. Incest is forbidden; the following near of kin are mentioned: parents, mother-in-law, sister, half-sister, daughter-in-law, aunt, mother and daughter, niece, sister-in-law, and women during their periods. Fornication is never allowed, nor is it permissible for children to be passed through the fire to the idols. Sodomy and bestiality were to be punished by death.

13. LEVITICUS 19.11–19b, 20, 21a, 26–28, 31–36b

Stealing, lying, swearing falsely, blasphemy, defrauding wages, cursing or teasing of the deaf or blind, respecting persons in judgement, tale-bearing, false-witnessing, hatred against neighbours, vengeance, are all crimes against God whose statutes must be kept. Fornication should be punished by both partners bringing an offering to the Lord. No blood is to be eaten. No enchantments are to be made. The corners of the beard or hair are not to be cut, nor is any cutting of flesh in mourning to be made. No wizards are to be tolerated. Old age must be respected, and strangers received hospitably. No unrighteous judgements are to be made, nor are false balances to be used.

14. LEVITICUS 20.6, 7, 9–12, 14–19, 21, 23, 27

Wizards are not permitted; cursing of parents, adultery—for which both parties must be put to death—are all crimes against God. Incest is punishable by death, as is lust with a wife and her mother, with a beast, sister, during the woman's period, aunt, sister-in-law. The people of God are not to live as do the heathen nations. All wizards and those with familiar spirits must be cast out of the land.

15. LEVITICUS 22.8a, 14, 21, 22

What dies of itself or is torn by beasts is forbidden as food. If a man eats holy things unwittingly, he must add one fifth of their value as an offering. Only perfect offerings are permissible.

16. LEVITICUS 24.15a, 16ab, 18–22a

Cursing God, blasphemy against his name, are both punishable by death. He who kills a beast must compensate its owner. He who wounds a person shall be wounded in the same way, "an eye for an eye and a tooth for a tooth". There is only one law for the people of God and for the strangers who live among them.

17. LEVITICUS 25.37

No usury is to be taken on money lent.

18. LEVITICUS 27.1–20, 25, 30–4

Vows must be kept, when persons pledge their services to God; on failing to carry out what has been vowed, compensation must be paid in silver. If beasts have been pledged, they must not be substituted; if they are, then a fifth part of their value must certainly be presented. Houses and lands pledged may be redeemed on payment of a set fee. The Jubilee is the deciding factor on the value of property. The standard for all substitutional redemption prices is the shekel of the sanctuary. All the tithe of the land, crops and animals, the fruit of orchard and vineyard, all belong to God. Should they be withheld a fifth part of their value must be added. These are all the commandments of God himself and must be obeyed.

19. NUMBERS 27.7b–11a

Daughters are to receive inheritance with sons. If a father has neither sons nor daughters, he shall give his inheritance to his brothers. If he has no brothers, his nearest kin inherits.

20. NUMBERS 35.30b, 31

One witness is not enough to condemn a person to death. The criminal who flees to a city of refuge must stay within the asylum provided. He cannot come back home nor pay a redemption to do so, if he is a murderer.

21. DEUTERONOMY 1.16b, 17abc

Judgement must be righteous between parties without fear or favour.

22. DEUTERONOMY 6.4–9, 13b, 16

God is One, love him with heart, soul, and might. Obey God and teach his will to the children at all times, and write them on the posts of the home. No idols are allowed. Do not tempt God.

23. DEUTERONOMY 13.1–4a

True prophets will be endorsed by signs and their messages will come to pass; but if the prophet turns from the true God his signs will fail to materialize.

24. DEUTERONOMY 14.21–2

Do not eat what dies a natural death, give it to a stranger. Do not cook a kid in his mother's milk. Tithe all produce and present the various offerings to God.

25. DEUTERONOMY 16.19b

Do not take gifts to prejudice judgement.

26. DEUTERONOMY 17.1, 6

Do not give offerings of blemished animals. Two witnesses are necessary for capital offences.

27. DEUTERONOMY 18.10–12a

God condemns the sending of children through fire; witches and necromancers are put to death, for this is heathenism.

28. DEUTERONOMY 19.4, 5, 11–13a

Cities of refuge must be provided for innocent homicides. For example, if the head of an axe flew off and killed a person, the homicide might find sanctuary in such a city. The murderer must be executed even if he sought asylum.

29. DEUTERONOMY 19.15–19

One witness is not enough to condemn in judgement. False witnesses should be sentenced as they advocated against the accused.

30. DEUTERONOMY 22.5–8, 28, 29

Women are not to wear men's clothes. The mother and its young are not to be snared and slain at the same time, one is to be released. The rapist must pay the girl fifty shekels of silver and marry her.

31. DEUTERONOMY 23.19, 20ac, 21–3

No usury must be taken from a brother, but it is right to impose this on a stranger. Vows must be paid, but if there is no vow made, it is proper to keep one's spoken word.

32. DEUTERONOMY 24.16, 17

Fathers shall not be put to death for the crimes of their children, nor are children to suffer for the crimes of their parents; each is to be punished for his own sin. Strangers, orphans, and widows must be treated justly.

33. DEUTERONOMY 25.13–16a

Diverse unjust weights must not be used. God condemns such action.

34. DEUTERONOMY 27.15–27
Curses against crimes of all kinds condemned in God's law.

35. DEUTERONOMY 28.1–11, 12b–25, 26c–33a, 34–45
Blessings on the obedient and cursing on the disobedient, until they
learn to keep all God's commandments.

To summarize: The *Liber ex Lege Moisi*, starting with its emphasis
on the role of the Decalogue as the foundation of conduct, notes
the following main items, some of which are covered by several
passages and strongly underlined:

1. The seventh day Sabbath.
2. Slavery and the relationship of master to servants.
3. Various capital offences.
4. Compensation in money and "kind" for different crimes.
5. Animals' offences against person and property.
6. Animals used as food, clean and unclean, and slaughtering.
7. Sex and marriage.
8. Feminine hygiene.
9. Tithes, first-fruits, vows, and offerings of all kinds.
10. Justice, bribery, witnesses, traduction, and usury.
11. Cities of refuge, asylum, and hospitality.
12. Wizards and necromancy and human sacrifices.
13. Inheritance, and the Sabbatical and Jubilees years, debts.
14. Signs of a true prophet.
15. Cursing and blessing.

These regulations were modified and adopted by Celtic Christians.

notes

PREFACE

[1] Theodoric, *Historia de Antiqui-tate Regum Norwagiensium*, III; G. Storm, ed., *Monumenta Historica Norvegiae* 8–9.

INTRODUCTION

[1] J. M. C. Toynbee, "Christianity in Roman Britain", *Journal of the British Archaeological Association*, 3rd S., XVI (1953), 2. This contains virtually all the evidence discovered up to 1953.

[2] F. Haverfield, "Early British Christianity", *English Historical Review* XI. 43 (1896), 424.

[3] Toynbee, loc. cit., 9.

[4] Ibid., 15–16.

[5] W. F. Grimes, "Excavations in the City of London", in R. J. S. Bruce-Mitford ed., *Recent Archaeological Excavations in Britain*, 116. This extends the evidence collected by Toynbee.

[6] G. W. Meates, "The Lullingstone Roman Villa", in Bruce-Mitford, op. cit., 103–4.

[7] E. Male, *La fin du paganisme en Guale*, 63ff.

[8] J. Stuart, *The Sculptured Stones of Scotland* II. 35–6.

[9] V. G. Childe and D. Simpson, *Ancient Monuments of Scotland*, 119.

[10] A. O. Curle, *The Treasure of Traprain, passim*.

[11] HS *Councils* I, 3–6.

[12] For a discussion of the suspicious readings see W. Bright, *Chapters in Early English Church History*, 9–11; F. E. Warren, "Conversion of the Kelts", in CMH II, 498.

[13] For arguments on this point see W. L. Alexander, *The Ancient British Church*, 129.

[14] HS *Councils* I, 7.

[15] Gildas, *De Excidio*, XII.

[16] F. L. Cross, ed., *Oxford Diction-ary of the Christian Church*, 552.

[17] M. Deanesly, *The Pre-Conquest Church in England*, 24; Kenney, *Sources*, 500.

[18] Gildas, *De Excidio*, paras. 15–19, 24.

[19] M. Deanesly, *Sidelights on the Anglo-Saxon Church*, 33–6; for a discussion see H. Williams, *Christian-ity in Early Britain*, 306–31.

[20] Bede, HE III, 4.

[21] A. B. Scott, *St Ninian*, 63–9.

22 *Letter*, para. 19.

23 H. E. Maxwell, *The Early Chronicles Relating to Scotland*, 56–7.

24 Ibid., 46–7.

25 TLP I, 95; cf. II, 313; *Book of Armagh*, fol. 11b, 1.

26 TLP II, 337, *Book of Armagh*, fol. 17a, 1; TLP II, 325; *Book of Armagh*, fol. 14a. 1; TLP II, 295; *Book of Armagh*, fol. 8a, 1.

27 *Confession*, para. 51.

28 "Hiberia" should probably be amended to read "Hibernia".

29 KM, *Learning in Ireland in the Fifth Century* 6.

30 J. B. Bury, *Life of St Patrick*, 350–1.

31 Bede, HE III, 27.

32 What is today the territory of Leinster.

33 TLP I, 31.

34 HS, *Councils*, I, 18; II, 2, 290.

35 E. Hogan, ed., *The Irish Nennius*, 15, noted that "Palladius was banished from Ireland".

36 Bede, HE III, 25.

37 Bede, HE II, 19.

38 Bede, HE IV, 15.

39 Published by J. Ussher, *Works* IV, 436.

40 L. Gougaud, *Christianity in Celtic Lands*.

41 Bede, HE II, 2.

42 Ibid.

43 Gildas, *De Excidio*, para. 67.

44 ASC, year 891/2.

45 *Confession*, para. 13.

46 *Confession*, para. 30.

47 *Confession*, para. 61.

48 W. M. Hennessey, tr., "The Old Irish Life of Columba", in W. F. Skene, *Celtic Scotland: A History of Ancient Alban* II, 470.

49 Kenney, *Sources*, 225.

50 Dates range 562–65.

51 Cf. Nennius, *Historia Brittonum*, para. 63. With the Irish 12 suggested perfection or plentitude as did 7 to the Hebrews, *Irish Nenius*, 109, 112.

52 Bede, HE III, 4.

53 J. Stuart, ed., *The Book of Deer*, 91, 92.

54 C. Chisholm, "The Monks of Iona", *Transactions of the Gaelic Society of Inverness*, VIII (1870), 56–63.

55 For a discussion of this phase of church history see J. P. Whitney, "Conversion of the Teutons: The English", in CMH II, 526ff.

56 Bede, HE III, 1.

57 Bede, HE III, 2, 3.

58 Bede, HE III, 5.

59 Plummer, BOH II, 136.

60 Whitney, loc. cit., 524.

61 Bede, *Life of Cuthbert* IX, 185–7.

62 J. B. Lightfoot, *Leaders of the Northern Church*, 81.

63 Ibid., 16.

64 For a discussion of this whole phase of history, see J. A. Duke, *The Columban Church*, 81–92.

65 A. Gwynn, "The date of St Columbanus' birth", *Studies* VII (1918), 474–84; but see H. Concannon, "The date of St Columban's birth, *Studies* VIII (1919), 59–66.

66 Jonas, *Columban* IX.

67 Ibid., IX; cf. Reeves, *Antiquities*, 93, 199.

68 Jonas, *Columban* IX.

69 Ibid., XII.

70 Walker, *Columban*, 147ff.

71 H. Concannon, *The Life of St Columban*, 98–105, and also Appendix D. 295–9; Jonas XVII.

72 Jonas, *Columban* LX.

73 ATig at 671; cf. AFM at 671.

74 AU at 672; AI3F at 672.

75 ATig at 722.

76 W. Reeves, "St Maelrubha: his history and churches", PSAS III (1862), 258–96.

77 *Historia Norwegiae*: Storm's *Monumenta Historica Norvegiae*, 89, tr., Anderson, *Sources* I, 331.

78 Dicuil, *De Mensura*, 41–4, tr. Anderson, *Sources*, I, 341.

79 Anderson, *Sources* I, 340–1.

80 Ibid., I. 341.

81 Ibid., I. 341.

82 Ibid., I. 339.

83 T. C. Lethbridge, *Herdsmen and Hermits*, 84–5.

84 *MHBP*, 108.
85 KM, *SAIP*, 100.
86 *VSH* II. 260, xxiv.
87 KM, *The Old Highlands*, 17; cf. *Eriu* II (1905), 551.
88 KM, "Comad Manchin Leith", *Eriu* I (1904), 40; cf. *SAIP*, 44.
89 Bede, *HE* I, 27.
90 Bede, *HE* I, 29.
91 Bede, *HE* I, 27.
92 Bede, *HE* II, 2.
93 Bede, *HE* V, 15.
94 Bede, *HE* V, 19.
95 Bede, *HE* II, 2.
96 Bede, *HE* II, 2.
97 Bede, *HE* II, 4 (italics supplied).
98 Bede, *HE* II, 4.
99 Bede, *HE* II, 4.
100 C. Baronius, *Annales Ecclesiastici*, Tone VIII, col. 239.
101 Bede, *HE* II, 20.
102 Bede, *HE* III, 29.
103 *MHBP*, 188, 206.
104 Bede's word *argueret* indicates upbraided or censured.
105 Bede, *HE* IV, 2.
106 Bede, *HE* III, 28.
107 Eddius, *Life of Wilfrid* XV.
108 *MHBP*, 207, cr. 88.
109 *MHBP*, 188.
110 Bede, *HE* III, 25.
111 Bede, *HE* III, 25.
112 Eddius, *Life of Wilfrid* V.
113 Bede, *Life of Cuthbert*, VIII.
114 Bede, *HE* III, 25.
115 Bede, *HE* III, 25.
116 B. MacCarthy, *AU* IV, 157.
117 Bede, *HE* III, 26.
118 Bede, *HE* V, 19.
119 Bede, *HE* III, 28.
120 As with Bishop Dagan (see p. 19 above) this attitude stemmed from a literal interpretation of Lev. 6.28, 15.12; Gal. 1.8, 9; 3 John 10, 11; Rom. 16.17. The Romans preached "another gospel".
121 HS *Councils*, III, 271.
122 W. Bright, *Early English Church History*, 467.
123 J. Ussher, *Works* IV, 353.
124 Baronius, op cit. VII, col. 649.
125 Ibid., col. 649.
126 Ibid., VIII, col. 238.
127 Published by Ussher, *Works* IV, 442.
128 Ussher, *Works* IV, 442.
129 Ibid., 439.
130 *VSH* II, 236.
131 *VSH* II, 237.
132 G. T. Stokes, *Ireland and the Celtic Church*, 157.
133 Bede, *HE* III, 3.
134 Ussher, *Works* IV, 438–9.
135 Bede, *HE* II, 19.
136 Bede, *HE* II, 19.
137 Bede, *HE* II, 19.
138 Bede, *HE* V, 15. These "observances" will be considered later.
139 Bede, *HE* V, 15.
140 W. Reeves, *Adamnan's Life of St Columba*, xlix.
141 Bede, *HE* V, 15.
142 J. O'Donovan, *The Annals of Ireland, Three Fragments*, Fragment II, year 704.
143 H. J. Lawlor, *St Bernard's Life of St Malachy*, 17–18.
144 Ibid., 18; cf. 39.
145 Bede, *HE* III, 27.
146 Bede, *HE* V, 9.
147 Bede, *HE* V, 22.
148 *AT*, at 717.
149 Bede, *HE* V, 22; cf. Penitential of Theodore II, ix, 2. "Churches that have been considered by these bishops are to be sprinkled with holy water and confirmed by some collect" (*MHBP*, 206–7).
150 Turgot, *Life of Queen Margaret* VIII.
151 Ninian Hill, *The Story of the Scottish Church*, 32.
152 HS *Councils* II, 159, 167, 191.
153 A. J. Toynbee, *A Study of History* II, 333, holds that the Celtic Church took a very independent attitude toward the Roman Church. For the Roman view see J. C. McNaught, *The Celtic Church and the See of Peter*. But, as K. S. Latourette points out, "the debate is complicated by the ecclesiastical views of the writers, modern Roman Catholics tending to emphasize the

Roman connection and Anglicans to belittle it" (*A History of the Expansion of Christianity* II, 36, n. 87).

CHAPTER 1

[1] N. J. White, "Libri Sancti Patricii, The Latin Writings of St Patrick", *PRIA* XXV, C. 7 (1905), 300–16, 323–5.
[2] *TLP*, II, 567.
[3] *Letter*, para. 20.
[4] L. Bieler, *The Works of St Patrick*, 64–5.
[5] For a discussion of the use of Scripture by Gildas see H. Williams, *Gildas: The Ruin of Britain*, 130–2, where the topic is considered in some detail.
[6] Bede, *HE* III, 4.
[7] Bede, *HE* III, 5.
[8] *Life of Samson*, XIV.
[9] Intro. to Ps. 8, *TP* I, 46. For a discussion of the meaning of the word canon see T. Olden, *The Church of Ireland*, Appendix C, 421–4, (1) the Bible, (2) either testament, (3) any book, (4) any text.
[10] N. J. White, *St Patrick, His Writings and Life*, 3.
[11] HS *Councils* I, 170–98.
[12] *Confession*, para. 40; *Letter*, para. 11.
[13] N. J. White, *Libri Sancti Patricii*, 230–3.
[14] N. J. White, *St Patrick, His Writings and Life*, 4; cf. F. R. M. Hitchcock, *Irenaeus of Lugdunum*, 348 ff.
[15] Kenney, *Sources*, 625.
[16] Gildas, *De Excidio*, para. 103.
[17] A. Souter and C. S. C. Williams, *The Text and Canon of the New Testament*, 200–1.
[18] *MO*, 10 September.
[19] *AFM*, year 1009.
[20] O'Curry, *Lectures*, 78.
[21] C. Patrick McGurk, *Early Gospel Books*, passim.
[22] A. W. Haddon, "Latin Versions of the Holy Scriptures in use in the Scoto-Britannic Churches", in HS *Councils* I, 170, n.a.

[23] Ps. 15.1, *TP* I, 86, 256, Intro. to Ps. 56.
[24] Ps. 12.7, *TP* I, 71.
[25] Ps. 95.8, *TP* I, 389.
[26] MHBP, 109.
[27] O'Curry, *Lectures*, 376–7, from the *Lebar Brecc*.
[28] Cassian, *Institutiones* V, 34.
[29] Cassian, *Collationes* XIV, 10.
[30] J. Ussher, *Works* VII, 30.
[31] Bede, *HE* III, 7.
[32] Bede, *HE* III, 27.
[33] Bede, *HE* III, 27.
[34] M. L. W. Laistner, *Thought and Letters in Western Europe*, 146.
[35] T. P. O'Nowlan, "A Prayer to the Archangel", *Eriu* II, 1 (1905), 92–4.
[36] R. H. Charles, ed., *Apocrypha and Pseudepigrapha of the Old Testament* II, 432–42, 448.
[37] R. E. McNally, *The Bible in the Early Middle Ages*, 26.
[38] Cf. R. E. McNally, op. cit., 42 ff; T. Olden, *The Holy Scriptures in Ireland One Thousand Years Ago*, 117–31.
[39] *TP* II, 314.
[40] *TP* I, 54.
[41] *TP* I, 681.
[42] *TP* II, 95, 150.
[43] *TP* I, 570, 647.
[44] *TP* I, 503.
[45] *TP* I, 515.
[46] *TP* I, 256, 548.
[47] *TP* I, 534.
[48] *TP* I, 501, &c.
[49] *TP* I, 585, &c.
[50] *TP* II, 78, &c.
[51] *TP* I, 397.
[52] *TP* I, XVI, n.
[53] *TP* I, 137, &c.
[54] *TP* I, 233, &c.
[55] Kenney, *Sources*, 635–6.
[56] Walker, *Columban*, 25.
[57] Boniface, *Epistola* xlvii, *PL*, LXXXIX, col. 753.
[58] Alcuin, *Epistola ad Colcu*, 790; J. Ussher, *Works* IV, 466–7.
[59] Cassian, *Collationes* VIII, 3.
[60] Ps. 9.3, *TP* I, 51.
[61] Ps. 14.1, *TP* I, 77.

[62] 2 Thess. 2.3, TP I, 665.

[63] 2 Cor. 12.7, TP I, 616. Did Pelagius suffer from headaches?

[64] 1 Cor. 14.8, TP I, 577.

[65] 1 Cor. 5.7, TP I, 552.

[66] Ps. 8, TP I, 48.

[67] Ps. 21, TP I, 125.

[68] KM, *Hibernica Minora*, 31.

[69] R. L. Ramsay, "Theodore of Mopsuestia in England and Ireland", ZCP VIII (1912), 470.

[70] WS suggests that the Irish word means "allegory".

[71] WS, ACC, 257.

[72] Ramsay, loc. cit., 474–6, versified by Eleanor Hull.

[73] Ps. 130.4, TP I, 463.

[74] Ps. 83.5, TP I, 352.

[75] KM, op. cit., 35–7.

[76] Ibid., 35.

[77] TP I, 656, 667.

[78] TP I, 588.

[79] Ps. 11.2, TP I, 64.

[80] TP I, 153. To "cover up" sin is the technical meaning of the Hebrew verb *kāphār*, to forgive, and had reference to the idea of cleansing by means of the blood of the sacrificial victim.

[81] Ps. 72.6, TP I, 301.

[82] TP I, 52.

[83] A. W. Haddan, *Remains*, 293.

[84] 1 Cor. 12.10, TP I, 572.

[85] Matt. 28.19, 20.

[86] TLP I, 65–7.

[87] J. Strachan, "An Old-Irish Homily", *Eriu* III, 1 (1907), 1–10.

[88] 1 Pet. 2.18–21.

[89] 1 Pet. 5.8.

[90] R. E. McNally, *The Bible in the Early Middle Ages*, 38–9, a translation of Ms. 908, "The Ioca monachorum".

[91] R. E. McNally, op. cit., 39.

[92] C. W. Dugmore, *The Influence of the Synagogue upon the Divine Office*, 104, 105.

[93] C. L. Kraemer, "Pliny and the Early Church Service", *Journal of Classical Philology* XXIX (1934), 294–6.

[94] Dugmore, op. cit., 105.

[95] 1 Tim. 1.7, TP I, 679.

[96] AFM year 438; cf. ALI III, 27–31.

[97] ALI I, 17; cf. Rom. 2.14–15.

[98] ALI I. 23.

[99] Paul Fournier, "Le Liber ex Lege Moysi et les tendances bibliques du droit canonique irlandais", RC, XXX (1909), 221–34.

[100] ALI I, 17; III 29, cf. Rom. 2.14–15.

[101] Gal. 3.22; Rom. 3.19.

[102] ALI I, 43.

[103] TLP II, 300.

[104] Kenney, *Sources*, 250.

[105] MHBP, 130.

[106] LSBL, 1. 1412.

[107] WS, ACC, 169.

[108] MO, 30 July, p. 165; cf. for others who kept the commandments, LCBS, 299.

CHAPTER 2

[1] *Confession*, para. 14, emphasis added.

[2] ISBL, 1. 3390.

[3] Kenney, *Sources*, 635.

[4] 1 Cor. 13.9, TP I, 575.

[5] *Confession*, para. 4, 35.

[6] *Confession*, para. 19.

[7] *Hymn of Secundus*, xxii.

[8] *Confession*, para. 4.

[9] *Confession*, para. 4; on Patrick's expression "We adore . . ." P. Freeman, *Principles of Divine Service* II, 340, pointed out that the singular, "I adore . . ." is peculiar to the third century. This underlines the early date of Patrick's view.

[10] Gildas, *De Excidio* XII.

[11] F. C. Conybeare, "The Character of the Heresy of the Early British Church", THSCymm. (1897–8), 84–177.

[12] 2 Thess. 2.15, TP I, 666.

[13] WS, *Goidelica*, 102–3.

[14] TP I, 490; cf. 1 Cor. 6.11, TP I, 554; *Letter*, para. 21.

[15] Ps. 130.5, TP I, 464.

[16] *Confession*, para. 4.

[17] Cf. Col. 1.17, TP I, 669.

[18] Heb. 1.5, TP I, 705.

[19] Ps. 109.1 TP I, 435.

[20] Phil. 2.6, TP I, 647.

[21] Col. 4.3, TP I, 673.

[22] Ps. 2.1; 7.14, TP I, 16, 19.
[23] Intro. to Ps. 2, TP I, 21.
[24] 1 Cor. 15.27, TP I, 585.
[25] Rom. 1.20, TP I, 500.
[26] Ps. 2.1, TP I, 19.
[27] Col. 1.15, TP I, 669.
[28] Heb. 3.1, TP I, 705.
[29] Intro. to Ps. 8, TP I, 45.
[30] Ps. 109.1, TP I, 435.
[31] Titus 3.4, TP I, 701.
[32] Rom. 15.12, TP I, 539.
[33] *Lorica*, stanza 2.
[34] *Salthir na Rann* 11. 7529–30.
[35] *LSBL*, cv.
[36] *LSBL*, 11. 4600–1.
[37] *LSBL*, 1. 4602.
[38] Rom. 14.15, TP I, 537.
[39] Rom. 8.32, TP I, 519.
[40] Eph. 1.7, TP I, 631.
[41] Rom. 3.25, TP I, 505.
[42] Rom. 8.29, TP I, 518.
[43] Rom. 6.10, TP I, 510.
[44] 1 Cor. 15.17, TP I, 584.
[45] 1 Cor. 15.32, TP I, 586.
[46] Assumption rather than ascension, cf. *Confession*, para. 4.
[47] Eph. 1.21, TP I, 632.
[48] 1 Tim. 2.5, TP I, 681.
[49] Rom. 5.11, TP I, 509.
[50] Rom. 3.25, TP I, 505.
[51] Col. 1.14, TP I, 669.
[52] Rom. 8.34, TP I, 519.
[53] Rom. 8.34, TP I, 519, ALI IV, 419, "frisindlim", TP II, 351.
[54] E. Hull, *The Poem Book of the Gael*, 119–20.
[55] Eph. 1.9 TP I, 631.
[56] Col. 4.3, TP I, 676.
[57] 1 Cor. 1.17, TP I, 545.
[58] Col. 4.3, TP I, 676.
[59] Phil. 4.7, TP I, 651.
[60] *Confession*, para. 4; TP I, 571.
[61] TLP II, 316.
[62] *Confession*, para. 4.
[63] Eph. 2.16, TP I, 634.
[64] 1 Cor. 12.9, TP I, 571.
[65] Following the period of the Danish invasions the *Lives* were filled with all kinds of miraculous occurrences which were said to have been wrought by the Spirit, such as resuscitating cows! *LSBL* 1, 100.

[66] Col. 4.3, TP I, 676.
[67] Heb. 1.7, TP I, 705.
[68] *Confession*, para. 4.
[69] Eph. 1.13, TP I, 632.
[70] 2 Cor. 3.3, TP I, 598.
[71] 1 Cor. 12.13, TP I, 572.
[72] Eph. 4.30, TP I, 638.
[73] *Confession*, para. 33.
[74] Rom. 8.11, TP I, 516.
[75] Rom. 8.9, TP I, 516.
[76] 2 Cor. 4.6, TP I, 601.
[77] *LSBL*, 1. 163.
[78] Rom. 8.26, TP I, 518.
[79] Rom. 8.26, TP I, 518.
[80] Rom. 8.27, TP I, 518.
[81] TP, II, 359.
[82] Ps. 33.9, TP I, 163.
[83] Ps. 2.1, TP I, 19.
[84] Ps. 19.1, TP I, 115.
[85] Ps. 19.3, TP I, 115.
[86] Ps. 19.2–3, TP I, 116.
[87] Cf. G. Murphy, "The Origin of Irish Nature Poetry", *Studies* XX (1931), 87–102.
[88] WS, *Anecdota Oxoniensia* (Medieval and Modern Series), I, iii; cf. E. Hull, *Poem Book of the Gael*, 3–50.
[89] WS, "The Evernew Tongue", *Eriu* II. 2 (1905), 96–162.
[90] *Confession*, para. 4.
[91] *Altus Prosator*, stanza 5.
[92] 1 Thess. 5.23, TP I, 662.
[93] Heb. 4.13, TP I, 710.
[94] Rom. 8.26, TP I, 518.
[95] Rom. 7.22, TP I, 515.
[96] *Altus Prosator*, stanza 7.
[97] Rom. 7.13, TP I, 514; cf. Eph. 2.3, TP I, 633.
[98] 1 Cor. 15.32, TP I, 586.
[99] 2 Cor. 5.2, TP I, 602.
[100] Rom. 8.13, TP I, 517.
[101] *Letter*, para. 6.
[102] Rom. 9.11, TP I, 521.
[103] 1 Tim. 2.5, TP I, 681.
[104] Eph. 1.5, TP I, 631.
[105] 1 Tim. 2.4, TP I, 681.
[106] Rom. 11.32, TP I, 530.
[107] Ps. 4.1, TP I, 27.
[108] Ps. 10.1, TP I, 57.
[109] *Hymn of Secundus*, stanza x.
[110] *Confession*, para. 44.

111 *Confession*, para. 59.
112 2 Tim. 2.18, *TP* I, 693.
113 Rom. 8.28, *TP* I, 518.
114 Gal. 6.9, *TP* I, 629.
115 *Confession*, para. 60, 49; cf. *Letter*, 18; *Hymn of Secundus*, stanza v.
116 *Letter*, para. 4.
117 *ALI* I, 281–3, 261.
118 Rom. 8.2 *TP* I, 515.
119 Rom. 5.15, *TP* I, 509; Gal. 3.22, *TP* I, 624.
120 Rom. 7.6, *TP* I, 513.
121 Ps. 25.12, *TP* I, 139.
122 Rom. 7.22, *TP* I, 515.
123 Rom. 2.13, *TP* I, 502.
124 Rom. 4.15, *TP* I, 507.
125 Rom. 7.10, *TP* I, 513.
126 Ps. 94.12, *TP* I, 387.
127 Ps. 73.9, *TP* I, 307.
128 Rom. 8.3, *TP* I, 515.
129 Rom. 5.20,*TP* I, 510.
130 Gal. 1.7, *TP* I, 619.
131 Rom. 7.13, *TP* I, 514.
132 Rom. 7.7, *TP* I, 513.
133 Rom. 5.6, *TP* I, 509.
134 Rom. 10.19, *TP* I, 525.
135 *Confession*, para. 2.
136 *Confession*, para. 4.
137 Rom. 6.18, *TP* I, 511
138 TLP II, 283.
139 Rom. 11.31, *TP* I, 529.
140 Rom. 10.10, *TP* I, 524.
141 Rom. 7.6, *TP* I, 513.
142 Gal. 2.20, *TP* I, 622.
143 Rom. 3.24, *TP* I, 505.
144 Rom. 8.2, *TP* I, 515.
145 Rom. 4.3, *TP* I, 506.
146 Rom. 4.4, *TP* I, 507.
147 *Letter*, para. 1.
148 *Confession*, para. 57.
149 Eph. 4.22, *TP* I, 638.
150 Rom. 7.14, *TP* I, 514.
151 Rom. 5.14, *TP* I, 509.
152 Rom. 5.15, *TP* I, 509.
153 Rom. 5.16, *TP* I, 509.
154 Eph. 2.3, *TP* I, 633.
155 1 Cor. 15.26, *TP* I, 585.
156 Ps. 34.21, *TP* I, 171.
157 *TP* I, 517, 585, 706.
158 Mark 14.64, *TP* I, 490–1.
159 *Confession*, para. 16.
160 Ps. 5.2, *TP* I, 32.
161 Ps. 54.6, *TP* I, 248.
162 Ps. 72.6, *TP* I, 295.
163 Ps. 51.7, *TP* I, 243.
164 Warren, *Liturgy*, 96.
165 MO, 271.
166 MO, 279, 282, 283.
167 2 Cor. 12.8, *TP* I, 616.
168 *Life of Samson* I, xiv.
169 Col. 4.2, *TP* I, 676.
170 Rom. 15.30, *TP* I, 540.
171 1 Thess. 5.17, *TP* I, 662
172 *Adomnan*, 121–2.
173 *Life of Malachy*, xviii, xxxix.
174 MO, 17, 35, 80.
175 TLP I, clxv–clxviii.
176 MO, 163, 274.
177 M. E. Byrne, "Féilire Adam-náin", *Eriu* I, 2 (1904), 255–8.
178 MHBP, 82.
179 MHBP, 166.
180 *Letter*, paras. 8, 20; *Confession*, para. 61; *Lorica*, stanzas 3, 5.
181 Ps. 90. 1ff, *TP* I, 380.
182 LSBL, II, 4520–1.
183 LSBL, I, 238.
184 LSBL, I, 4514.
185 1 Cor. 6.3, *TP* I, 553.
186 *Altus Prosator*, 3, 4.
187 Gal. 1.8, *TP* I, 619.
188 ISBL, II. 124–5.
189 LSBL, I, 1885.
190 LSBL, I, 4127.
191 LSBL, I, 4166.
192 LSBL, I, 550; cf. TLP I, 227.
193 LSBL, II, 3545–6.
194 LSBL, II, 2582–3.
195 LSBL, II, 3388–92.
196 LSBL, II, 2493–6.
197 TLP I, 169.
198 TLP II, 396.
199 TLP II, 487.
200 TLP II, 415.
201 *Confession*, para. 20.
202 Eph. 2.2, *TP* I, 633.
203 2 Cor. 2.11, *TP* I, 597.
204 MO, 75.
205 Eph. 4.27, *TP* I, 638.
206 LSBL, xix.
207 LSBL, II, 1408–10.
208 LSBL, I, 3626.
209 LSBL, II, 3712–16.

[210] *Confession*, para. 4; cf. *Letter*, paras. 5, 11.
[211] *Lorica*, stanza 2.
[212] *Altus Prosator*, stanza 20.
[213] 2 Thess. 1.8, TP I, 664.
[214] 1 Thess. 4.16, TP I, 660.
[215] 1 Cor. 1.7, TP I, 548.
[216] 1 Cor. 15.32, TP I, 588.
[217] 2 Thess. 1.8, TP I, 664.
[218] 1 Cor. 4.5. TP I, 549.
[219] *Confession*, para. 8.
[220] Rom. 2.15, TP I, 502.
[221] Ps. 1.5, TP I, 16.
[222] Rom. 14.11, TP I, 536.
[223] 2. Thess. 2.10, TP I, 666.
[224] 1 Cor. 7.29, TP I, 559.
[225] *Confession*, para. 34.
[226] *Confession*, para. 4.
[227] Walker, *Columban*, 41.

CHAPTER 3
[1] Luke 4.16–18.
[2] S. V. McCasland, "The Origin of the Lord's Day", *Journal of Biblical Literature* XLIX (1930), 65–82.
[3] A. Neander, *General History of the Christian Religion and Church* II, 194.
[4] G. L. Laing, *Survivals of Roman Religion*, 148.
[5] Codex Justinianus, Lib. III, tit. 12, 3, translated by Philip Schaff, *History of the Christian Church* III, 380, n.1.
[6] For a discussion of this complex topic see R. Cox, *Literature of the Sabbath Question*, 2 vols.; J. N. Andrews and L. R. Conradi, *A History of the Sabbath*.
[7] *Sabbatum*.
[8] Canon 29, C. J. Hefele, *A History of the Christian Councils*, tr. and ed. H. N. Oxenham, II, 316.
[9] Socrates, *HE* V, 22; cf. *NPNF*, 2nd Series, II, 132.
[10] Augustine, *Letter* 54, "Ad Januarium", cap. 2, PL XXXIII, 200–1.
[11] Jerome, *Letter* 108, "Ad Eustochium Virginem", PL XXII, c. 896.
[12] LHP, VII, 58.
[13] LHP, XXXII, 113.
[14] κριακή κάιυ σάββατον

[15] LHP XXV, 121.
[16] κυριακή καὶ σάββατον
[17] LHP XIV, 68.
[18] LHP XIV, 68.
[19] σάββατον
[20] LHP XLVIII, 155.
[21] LHP XVIII, 81, 82.
[22] LHP LIX, 165.
[23] σάββατον
[24] LHP XVI, 72.
[25] Irrefutable because uncontrived.
[26] E. C. Butler, *Lausiac History of Palladius* II, 198.
[27] This section is an attempt to clarify the points raised by D. McLean, *The Law of the Lord's Day in the Celtic Church*.
[28] N. J. White, *St Patrick, His Writings and Life*, 109.
[29] Ibid., 104.
[30] In Ms. C. of the *Confession*, the form "Victricius" is found. Cf. White, op. cit., 115.
[31] *Confession*, para. 23.
[32] A. Anscombe, "St Victricius of Rouen and St Patrick", *Eriu* VII, (1913), 13–7.
[33] N. J. White, *St Patrick, His Writings and Life*, 109.
[34] Ibid., 98–9.
[35] TLP I, 147, 175, 183.
[36] TLP I, 193; cf. 223, 225.
[37] TLP I, 125.
[38] Adomnan, 27.
[39] ALI III, 41.
[40] ALI III, 43.
[41] Skene, *Scotland* II, 71.
[42] TLP I, 117.
[43] LSBL, 1, 430.
[44] Cf. "eve of Sunday", or "vespers on Sunday".
[45] MHBP, 173.
[46] LCBS, 582.
[47] LCBS, 416.
[48] LCBS, 444–5.
[49] LCBS, 335.
[50] LCBS, 335–6.
[51] E. J. Gwynn and W. J. Purton, "The Monastery of Tallaght", *PRIA* XXIX, Section C, 5 (1912), 115–17, para. 69.
[52] Adomnan, 120; cf. L. Gougaud,

53 *MHBP*, 194: "Those who labour on the Lord's day . . . shall do penance . . ."

54 Walker, *Columban*, lxi.

55 Ibid., 203.

56 Ibid., 201.

57 *Adomnan*, 521.

58 The phrase "I keep sabbath" is translated from the verb *sabbatizo*, from *sabbatizare*, to observe the Sabbath.

59 *Adomnan*, 523: other saints also apparently wished for their deaths to fall on the Sabbath; cf. *LSBL*, 11. 4375, 4452.

60 Adamnan mentions Lord's day six times, Sabbath five, and uses *sabbatizo* once.

61 *Adomnan*, 29, (c. 690–700).

62 *MHBP*, 96.

63 *Historia Norwegiae*, ed. G. Storm, *Monumenta Historica Norvegiae*, 89, tr. O. A. Anderson, *Sources* I, 331.

64 Gregory I, *Selected Epistles*, Book 13, Epistle 1, translated in NPNF, 2nd Series, XIII, 92, 93.

65 *MHBP*, 186, 194, 206.

66 *MHBP*, 194.

67 *MHBP*, 159.

68 R. Atkinson, *The Passions and the Homilies from the Leabhar Breac*, 274 (*na dena obair domnaig*); 490 ("do no work on Sunday").

69 Walker, *Columban*, 155, 181.

70 *Adomnan*, 293.

71 *Adomnan*, 293.

72 *Adomnan*, 535.

73 *VSH* II, 25.

74 Kenney, *Sources*, 476.

75 J. G. O'Keefe, "The Law of Sunday—The Epistle of Jesus", *Eriu* II, 2 (1907), 201, hereinafter designated O'Keefe.

76 *AU*, at 886.

77 O'Keefe, 193.

78 Ibid., 195.

79 Ibid., 197.

80 Ibid., 203–5.

81 Ibid., 203.

82 Ibid., 209–11.

83 Ibid., 211.

84 D. MacLean, *The Law of the Lord's Day in the Celtic Church*, 13–15.

85 *VSH* I, 43.

86 *VSH*, I, 263.

87 S. H. O'Grady, *Silva Gadelica* I, 55.

88 O'Curry, *Lectures*, 293. This is one of the threats recorded in the "Epistle of Christ"; see O'Keefe, 195, para. 9: "Whatsoever horse is ridden on Sunday, it is a horse of fire in the fork of its rider in hell."

89 Julius Pokorny, *Old Irish Grammar*, 15.

90 L. Gougaud, *Christianity in Celtic Lands*, 323.

91 *Life of St Margaret*, xix.

92 Ibid., xix.

93 *Njal's Saga*, 226.

94 Lev. 23.32.

95 McLean, op. cit. 3.

96 *Adomnan*, 259–61.

97 *TP* I, 385.

98 Bede, *HE* III, 5.

99 Ibid.

100 *MHBP*, 105.

101 *MHBP*, 193.

102 *MHBP*, 193, 195–6.

103 *MHBP*, 270 (Ps. Cum).

104 WS, ACC, 179; cf. R. Tall., ref. to Thursday, 31, 23, 49, 51; cf. Rule of the Culdee, in the same work, 67, 69.

105 *TLP* I, 117.

106 Neh. 2.1; Esther 3.7; Exodus 13.4; Josephus, *Antiquities* III, X. 5; H. Danby, *The Mishnah*, "Menahoth", x, iii, 505–6,

107 1 Cor. 5.7; cf. John 1.29.

108 1 Cor. 15.23.

109 Socrates, *HE* V, 22; translated in NPNF, 2nd Series, II, 130–1.

110 *Liber Pontificalis* XI, 14, 15.

111 There is no mention of "the Lord's day" in the extant book of

Hermas, called the *Pastor* or *Shepherd*.

[112] Eusebius, *HE* V, 24.

[113] Epiphanius, *Haereses*, PG XLII, 355, tr. by Lewis Hensley, in *Dictionary of Christian Antiquities* I, 589, in which will be found a good summary of the entire topic.

[114] B. MacCarthy, *Annals of Ulster*, IV. 144 ff.

[115] MacCarthy, AU, IV, lxxix, recorded an entry in the Chronicle of Marius, bishop of Avenchis (560) which suggested that the eighty-four-year cycle was also surviving in Gaul. Cf. Bede, *HE* III, 17.

[116] Bury, *Patrick*, 372.

[117] Bede, *HE* II, 2; III, 28; but cf. III, 3, 25, V, 21.

[118] Bede, *HE* III, 25.

[119] Bede, *HE* III, 25.

[120] Bede, *HE* II, 2.

[121] Bede, *HE* III, 4, 17, 25.

[122] *Life of Wilfrid*, 10, 12, 14, 15.

[123] *Life of Wilfrid*, 10; Bede, *HE* III, 25.

[124] AI3F, Fragment II at 704.

[125] Skene, *Scotland*, 12, 13.

[126] MHBP, 188, No. 3.

[127] MHBP, 189, No. 13.

[128] Walker, *Columban*, 7.

[129] *Life of Samson*, V. 65–6; cf. XI, 74.

[130] MO, 35.

[131] MO, 58.

[132] MG, 63.

[133] R. Tall., 63.

[134] TLP I, 41–3.

[135] *Antiphonary of Bangor* II, xi.

[136] MO, 165.

[137] MHBP, 96.

[138] Ryan, *Monasticism*, 392.

[139] Bede, *HE* III, 27.

[140] Ryan, op. cit., 392.

[141] *Life of St Margaret*, VI.

[142] Bede, *HE* III, 23.

[143] MHBP, 160.

[144] Epiphany.

[145] O'Keefe, 2309.

[146] TLP II, 433; LSBL, II. 151–2.

[147] ALI II, 215; cf. Lev. 25.

[148] ALI III, 31.

[149] MHBP, 86.

[150] ALI V, 315–17.

CHAPTER 4

[1] John 3.3,5.

[2] Acts 8.15–17.

[3] Rom. 6.4, TP I, 510.

[4] Eph. 4.5, TP I, 636.

[5] Col. 2.12, TP I, 672; cf. Mark 13.21, TP I, 495.

[6] 1 Cor. 14.6, TP I, 577.

[7] Mark 13.10, TP I, 487.

[8] Unbaptized.

[9] MHBP, 79–80.

[10] 1 Cor. 14.6, TP I, 577.

[11] LSBL, II. 156.

[12] LSBL, II. 497–8.

[13] LSBL, II. 280–1.

[14] LSBL, II. 2840.

[15] TP II, 240; cf. *Adomnan*, 201.

[16] TP I, 487.

[17] Mark 1.1–6, TP I, 487.

[18] Mark 1.1–6, TP I, 487.

[19] Rom. 8.10, TP I, 516.

[20] TP I, 488.

[21] *Letter*, para. 3.

[22] Ps. 45.16, TP I, 223.

[23] 1 Cor. 12.13, TP I, 572.

[24] Gal. 3.26, TP I, 624.

[25] TP I, 487.

[26] 2 Cor. 1.15, TP I, 593.

[27] Rom. 6.3, TP I, 510.

[28] MHBP, 86.

[29] F. C. Conybeare, "The Character of the Heresy of the Early British Church", THSCymm. (1899) 84–117.

[30] S. Gregorii Papae II, *Epistola* xiv, PL, LXXXIX, col. 543, tr. Conybeare, loc. cit., 96.

[31] HS, *Councils* I, 153.

[32] Warren, *Liturgy*, 217.

[33] LSBL, 184.

[34] LSBL, 184.

[35] LSBL, 232.

[36] LSBL, 265.

[37] LSBL, 249.

[38] LSBL, 278.

[39] MHBP, 97.

[40] TLP I, 185: LSBL, II.396–8.

[41] LSBL, II.2521–4; TLP I, 135.

[42] LSBL, II. 1807–11.

[43] Cf. Adomnan, 275.

[44] MHBP, 114; Adomnan, 347.

[45] MHBP, 114.

[46] TLP I, 161, 169, 225, &c.

[47] Adomnan, 397; cf. 493.

[48] MHBP, 97.

[49] TLP I, 103; II, 316.

[50] TLP I, 175.

[51] TP II, 238, 330.

[52] Letter, para. 3.

[53] Mark 1.1–6, TP I, 487.

[54] Warren, Liturgy, 207–20.

[55] TLP I, 9.

[56] TLP I, 77.

[57] T. Thompson, The Offices of Baptism and Confirmation, 253.

[58] Rom. 8.10, TP I, 516.

[59] J. G. O'Keefe, "The Rule of Patrick", Eriu I. 2 (1904), 221.

[60] Bede's Life of Cuthbert, xxix.

[61] TLP, I, clxxxiv.

[62] MHBP, 202.

[63] MHBP, 202.

[64] For the best account of the history of pedilavium see ERE v, 814–23, by G. A. Frank Knight.

[65] Augustine, Epistola 54, "Ad Januarum", PL, XXXIII, col. 220.

[66] E. C. Hoskyns, The Fourth Gospel, 444.

[67] A. A. King, Liturgies of the Past, 116.

[68] W. B. Marriott, "Baptism", DCA I, 158.

[69] King, op. cit., 116.

[70] E. A. Love, ed., The Bobbio Missal, A Gallican Mass-Book (HBS LVIII), 75, nos. 251, 252.

[71] ERE v, 817.

[72] Warren, Liturgy 217–18, n.4.

[72a] Bede's Life of Cuthbert, xviii.

[73] LSBL, 186; for a discussion see E. Hull, Early Christian Ireland, 141–5.

[74] Adomnan, 221.

[75] LSBL, 325.

[76] LSBL, 326.

[77] LSBL, 277.

[78] Anonymous Life of Cuthbert, ii.

[79] Adomnan, 349–51.

[80] TLP I, 145.

[81] LSBL, 196.

[82] Skene. Scotland II, 504, "The Old-Irish Life of Columba".

[83] Wm. Hone, Every-day Book I, 402; cf. BNE II, para. 38, pp. 56, 329, 331, n. 65, for a discussion of ancient Maundy Thursday ceremonies." 'Here ye are to keep this Saturday and vigil, and on yonder island that ye now see in the offing shall ye celebrate the Easter Masses.' And having said thus he began to render the service [of the day, i.e. foot-washing] to Brendan and the brethren" (BNE II, 56).

[84] F. E. Warren, Missale vetus Hibernicum, 119–20, where footwashing and Communion follow each other; cf. R. Tall, 17, for a description of foot-washing at Tallaght.

[85] LSBL, 190–1.

[86] 1 Tim. 5.10.

[87] Cf. John 13.1 ff.

[88] Bede's Life of Cuthbert, xviii, "coena Domini".

[89] BNE II, 59.

[90] R. C. Maclagan, Scottish Myths, 139, where evidence of Kentigern's vegetarianism and teetotalism is adduced.

[91] Bede's Life of Cuthbert. xxix.

[92] MHBP, 260.

[93] Adomnan, 459.

[94] L. Gougaud, Christianity in Celtic Lands, 324.

[95] W. Reeves, ed. and tr., "Prose Rules of the Celi De", TRIA XXIV (1873), 206; cf. R.Tall., 68–9.

[96] MHBP, 206.

[97] Gildas, Epistola II; HS, Councils I, 112.

[98] HS, Councils III, 367.

[99] Bede, HE II, 2.

[100] Life of St Margaret, VIII.

[101] A. A. King, Liturgies of the Past, "The Celtic Rite, 186–275".

[102] H. Leclercq, "La Messe dans les liturgies Celtique", DACL XI, sec. xxxiv.

[103] L. Gougaud, "Celtique Liturgies", DACL II, sec. ii.

[104] Warren, Liturgy, 96.

[105] Warren, Liturgy, 127–8.

[106] Adomnan, 305.

107 *Adomnan*, 293.
108 Walker, *Columban*, Sermon 13, p. 119.
109 Walker, *Columban*, 143.
110 *Liber Hymnorum*, 19; TLP II, 388.
111 *TLP* I, 103.
112 *Antiphonary of Bangor* II, 10, Hymn No. 8.
113 *VSH* II, 196.
114 Eph. 1.7, TP I, 631.
115 *Adomnan*, 197, 325–7.
116 *TLP* II, 327.
117 *TLP* I, clxxxvi.
118 *TLP* I, clxxxvi.
119 *TLP* I, 171.
120 L. Todd, *St Patrick*, 460; cf. VSH II.
121 Bede's *Life of Cuthbert*, xv.
122 Ibid., xxxix.
123 *AFM*, 801–1022; see 981, year 1105 and 995 year 1113.
124 James 5.14–16.
125 *Life of Samson* I, liv.
126 Warren, *Liturgy*, 220–3.
127 Kenney, *Sources*, 712.
128 Ibid., 711–12.

CHAPTER 5

1 Matt. 28.16–20.
2 Acts 2.41–7; 3.1; 4.32–7; 5.25; 41.
3 Acts 6.1–8.
4 Skene, *Scotland* II, 12.
5 Cf. H. Williams, *Christianity in Early Britain*, 456.
6 1 Tim. 3.4, TP I, 682.
7 1 Tim. 3.7, TP I, 682.
8 1 Tim. 3.3, TP I, 682.
9 Titus 1.7, TP I, 698.
10 1 Tim. 3.2, TP I, 682.
11 1 Tim. 3.2, TP I, 682.
12 1 Tim. 3.3, TP I, 682.
13 1 Tim. 3.1, TP I, 682.
14 1 Tim. 3.2, TP I, 682.
15 1 Tim. 5.21, TP I, 687.
16 1 Tim. 5.22, TP I, 687.
17 1 Tim. 3.4 TP I, 682.
18 Titus 1.9, TP I, 698.
19 1 Tim. 3.2, TP I, 682.
20 Titus 1.9, TP I, 699.
21 *TLP* II, 241; cf. 403.

22 Titus 1.6, TP I, 698.
23 1 Tim. 3.2, TP I, 682.
24 *ALI* V, 235, 237.
25 *TLP* I, 69.
26 *TLP* I, xlviii.
27 *TLP* II, 441–3.
28 *TLP* I, 89–91.
29 MHBP, 77, and Gildas, *De Excidio*, 66, 108, 118, noted with approval a bishop who was married to one wife only.
30 Bede, HE I, 27.
31 MHBP, 92, 27.
32 MHBP, 97.
33 MHBP, 159–60.
34 MHBP, 275, 302.
35 MO, 205.
36 MHBP, 239, "The Dialogue of Egbert"; 275, "Burgundian Penitential"; 302, so-called "Roman Penitential".
37 Gildas, *De Excidio*, cix.
38 For a discussion of this point see J. Ussher, *Works* IV, 295.
39 MD, 249; cf. ALI V, 129, where a married clergy is recognized.
40 *AI3F*, Frag. III, 241.
41 *AFM* I, 564, n. 6.
42 *Life of St Malachy* IV, 45, see also pp. 48, 148, 165, and for further consideration of this subject G. Stokes, *Ireland and the Celtic Church*, 339 ff, on the continuing anomalies at Armagh.
43 1 Cor. 11.5, TP I, 563.
44 1 Cor. 7.19, TP I, 558.
45 Mark 1.6, TP I, 489.
46 TP I, 490.
47 Gildas, *De Excidio*, cvi–cvii, 1 Pet. 1.3, 13, 14, 22; 2.1, 9; Acts 1.15–26; "Secunda lectio", 1 Tim. 3.1; Matt. 16.13–19; 1 Pet. 1.13–32.
48 Warren, *Liturgy*, 72.
49 Ibid., 68–9.
50 Ibid., 73–4.
51 Bede, HE III, 5.
52 For a discussion of this point see H. Heron, *The Celtic Church in Ireland*, 184–8.
53 Acts 13.2, 3, where ordination was by the whole congregation.
54 Reeves, *Antiquities*, 161.
55 Ibid., 162.

56 Gildas, *De Excidio*, lxxvi.
57 Ibid., xxxii, cix.
58 *Adomnan*, 305.
59 1 Tim. 3.12, TP I, 683.
60 1 Tim. 3.13, TP I, 683.
61 1 Tim. 3.10, TP I, 683.
62 1 Tim. 3.9, TP I, 683.
63 1 Tim. 3.8, TP I, 683.
64 1 Tim. 3.3, TP I, 683.
65 1 Tim. 3.13, TP I, 683.

CHAPTER 6

1 *Didache* IV, 14.
2 *Didache* XIV, 1.
3 James 5.16.
4 E. Amann, "Penitence-sacrament", DTC XII, 783, 837.
5 Ambrose, "De penitentia", II, i, 5, PL XVI, col. 497.
6 Ibid., col. 518.
7 Socrates, HE V, 19.
8 O. D. Watkins, *History of Penance* I, 491 ff.
9 M. J. O'Donnell, *Penance in the Early Church*, 119.
10 Watkins, op. cit. I, 439.
11 Ambrose, "De penitentia" II, 10, PL XVI, col. 520.
12 Eva M. Sanford, ed., *On the Government of God: A Treatise by Salvian* VI, 1.
13 Ibid., VII, 5.
14 Watkins, op. cit. I, 465.
15 MHBP, 101–11; cf. Cummean's discussion of methodology.
16 For a discussion of this point see MHBP, 25.
17 Eph. 4.11, TP I, 637.
18 1 Cor. 9.1, TP I, 562.
19 Caesar, *De bello Gallico* VI, 12.
20 G. Keating, *History of Ireland* II, 273, 405.
21 E. Hull, *Folklore in the British Isles*, 290.
22 But see Skene, *Scotland* II, 88, n.11, who sought to debunk the idea.
23 Hull, op. cit., 300.
24 F. Seebohm, *Tribal System of Wales*, 58; cf. his *Anglo-Saxon Law*, 42.

25 A. Owen, *Ancient Laws and Institutes of Wales* II, 478.
26 Caesar, *De bello Gallico* III, 9, 17; IV, 20.
27 2 Thess. 2.9; TP I, 666; T. Olden rendered the Irish word which WS translated "wizard" as "druid".
28 LSBL, 215.
29 VSH I, 103.
30 TLP II, 564.
31 WS, ACC, 285.
32 Reeves, *Columba*, 43, 150.
33 A. Owen, *Ancient Laws and Institutes of Wales*, I, 28.
34 Reeves, *Columba*, 305.
35 MO, 65, 191–2.
36 VSH I, 136; cf. MHBP, 28.
37 MO, 65.
38 Walker, *Columban*, 145, 179; cf. Jonas, *Columban*, viii.
39 MHBP, 87.
40 MHBP, 88.
41 MHBP, 78.
42 MHBP, 78.
43 Bede's *Life of Cuthbert*, ix.
44 MHBP, 163.
45 MHBP, 123, no. 4.
46 MHBP, 123, no. 3.
47 *Life of Samson*, xxix.
48 MHBP, 28.
49 MHBP, 163.
50 MHBP, 397–8 discusses Alcuin's letter to the Irish on this point.
51 1 Cor. 11.28, TP I, 570.
52 1 Tim. 2.21, TP I, 694; Irish *treathirgi*, not penance.
53 Ps. 24.2, TP I, 137.
54 TP I, 73.
55 Ps. 32.5, 6, TP I, 158.
56 Ps. 32.1, TP I, 153.
57 J. T. McNeill, "The Celtic Penitentials", RC XL (1923), 79.
58 MHBP, 78.
59 MHBP, 89.
60 Cf. MHBP, 44.
61 MHBP, 92–3.
62 MHBP, 265.
63 MHBP, 108, 161, no. 5.
64 MHBP, 88, nos. 6, 7.
65 MHBP, 137, no. 45.
66 ALI I, 15.
67 ALI I, 69.

[68] MHBP, 124.
[69] MHBP, 91.
[70] MHBP, 253, 254; cf. David's penitential ruling, 173.
[71] See T. P. Oakley, "Commutations and Redemptions of Penance", *Catholic Historical Review* XVIII (1933), 341–51.
[72] KM, "An Old Irish Treatise De Arries", *RC* XV (1894), 484–98.
[73] MHBP, 141.
[74] MHBP, 122.
[75] MHBP, 123.
[76] MHBP, 124.
[77] MHBP, 81.
[78] MHBP, 160.
[79] MHBP, 155.
[80] MHBP, 111.
[81] MHBP, 110.
[82] MHBP, 173, no. 9.
[83] MHBP, 173, no. 8.
[84] MHBP, 111, no. 26.
[85] MHBP, 122.
[86] McNeill, loc. cit., 340.
[87] MHBP, 104.
[88] MHBP, 145.
[89] MHBP, 145.
[90] MO, 247.
[91] MHBP, 144.
[92] R.Tall., 61.
[93] MO, 246; LSBL, 235.
[94] MO, 43.
[95] MO, 280.
[96] MHBP, 115.
[97] MHBP, 142.
[98] MHBP, 163.
[99] MHBP, 231.
[100] MHBP, 104, 141.
[101] MHBP, 91.
[102] MHBP, 252.
[103] MHBP, 170.
[104] MHBP, 170, 102.
[105] LSBL, 11. 700–7.
[106] MHBP, 110.
[107] MHBP, 110.
[108] MHBP, 83.
[109] MHBP, 174–5.
[110] MHBP, 88.
[111] MHBP, 110.
[112] MHBP, 115.
[113] MHBP, 120.
[114] MHBP, 174.

[115] McNeill, loc. cit., 330–4.
[116] MHBP, 424.
[117] MHBP, 124.
[118] MHBP, 136.
[119] MHBP, 34.
[120] MHBP, 122; TLP II, 484.
[121] MHBP, 36.
[122] T. P. Oakley, *English Penitential Discipline*, 193–6.
[123] MHBP, 25–6.
[124] MGH, *Concilia*, II, i, 278 ff.
[125] MGH, *Concilia*, II, ii, 633.
[126] H. S. Lea, *History of Auricular Confession*, II, 106–7.
[127] Cf. J. T. McNeill, "Folk-paganism in the Penitentials", *Journal of Religion* XIII (1933), 450–66.
[128] MHBP, 77.
[129] MHBP, 78.
[130] MHBP, 166.
[131] MHBP, 121.
[132] MHBP, 90
[133] MHBP, 120, 103.
[134] MHBP, 198.
[135] BOH I, 157–8; but see MHBP, 397.
[136] MHBP, 142 ff; 268 ff; 319ff; 48.
[137] MHBP, 394, 405.

CHAPTER 7

[1] E. C. Butler, *Lausiac History of Palladius* II, 211.
[2] LHP VII, 5.
[3] Sozomen, HE I, 2.
[4] For a discussion of the origins of monasticism see U. Berlière, *L'ordre monastique.*
[5] LHP, XVIII, 29.
[6] LHP XVIII, 2.
[7] LHP II, 1.
[8] LHP II, 1.
[9] LHP XXXVII, 1.
[10] LHP II, 3; XVIII, 3.
[11] LHP XVIII, 4.
[12] LHP XVIII, 4.
[13] LHP, XXIV, 5.
[14] Sulpicius Severus, *Dialogue* I, 8. PL XX, 186.
[15] J. B. Bury, *Life of St Patrick*, 39.
[16] E. C. Butler, *Lausiac History of Palladius* II, 254.

17 Athanasius, "Epistola and Dracon", PG xxv, col. 534.
18 Augustine, *de Haeresibus*, xl., PL xl, col. 32.
19 *Confession*, para. 41; cf. 49 and *Letter*, para. 12.
20 Brigit's founding of Kildare in 480 cannot yet be established.
21 HS, *Councils* II, 2, 295 for all the evidence.
22 ALI v, 25.
23 *Tuath* or tribe.
24 Ps. 75.1, TP I, 318.
25 Cf. the careful way in which the cities of the clerics of Israel had been chosen (Josh. chs. 20 and 21.)
26 VSH II, 27.
27 L. de Paor, "A Survey of Sceil Mhichil", JRSAI lxxxv (1955), 174 ff.
28 M. Stokes, *Early Christian Architecture in Ireland*, 32.
29 Lord Dunraven, *Notes on Irish Architecture* I, 28.
30 Cf. Murphy, loc. cit.; K. Jackson, *Early Celtic Nature Poetry*, 82.
31 Cf. *Life of Samson* I, xl–xli.
32 KM, SAIP, 30-1.
33 Num. 35.1–8.
34 TLP I, 67.
35 TLP I, 229.
36 Bede, HE III, 4.
37 Bede, HE III, 3.
38 TLP I, 191–3.
39 ALI v, 269.
40 TLP II, 473.
41 ALI v, 429.
42 ALI v, 431.
43 Lev. 27.30–4.
44 Giraldus Cambrensis, *Description of Wales*, xviii.
45 LCBS, 381.
46 Bede, HE IV, 29.
47 Mal. 3.10–12.
48 ALI III, 13–15.
49 ALI I, 53.
50 MHBP, 129.
51 MHBP, 128; cf. ALI III, 39.
52 ALI III, 41.
53 ALI III, 41.
54 MHBP, 128.
55 MHBP, 128.
56 ALI III, 23.

57 J. G. O'Keefe, "The Rule of Patrick", Eriu I (1904), 222, Rule 8.
58 Ibid., 223, Rule 11.
59 I.e. the *manach* tenant.
60 Ibid., 223, Rule 14.
61 Kenney, *Sources*, 237.
62 AFM, 435, 437, 453.
63 AU, at 733, 742, 752, 771; cf. AFM, 417, 441.
64 AFM, 437, 451, 543, 577.
65 BNE II, 216; VSH I, xciii, cx.
66 O'Keefe, loc. cit., 216.
67 MHBP, 78.
68 MHBP, 78.
69 MHBP, 81.
70 1 Thess. 4.11, TP I, 660.
71 1 Thess. 4.10, TP I, 660.
72 2 Thess. 3.7, TP I, 667–8.
73 Titus 1.2, TP I, 698.
74 MHBP, 97.
75 Barry Island and Flat Holmes in the Bristol Channel.
76 LCBS, 336.
77 LSBL, 1. 4113.
78 For his discussion of this topic see LSBL, cxix.
79 MD, 331.
80 LSBL, 1. 2361.
81 LSBL, 11. 4425–7.
82 LSBL, xliii.
83 J. O'Neill, "The Rule of Ailbe of Emly", Eriu III (1906) 107.
84 LSBL, 11. 2090–2.
85 LSBL, 1. 4460.
86 LSBL, 11. 4379, 4399.
87 LSBL, 11. 2552, 2583–4.
88 Adomnan, 455.
89 Bede, HE III, 25.
90 LSBL, 11. 3789–91.
91 LSBL, 11. 1570–8.
92 LCBS, 338.
93 MHBP, 164.
94 MHBP, 109.
95 KM, SAIP, "The gloom of a prayer house", 90.
96 MHBP, 147.
97 MD, 83.
98 MHBP, 116.
99 R.Tall., 53.
100 W. Stokes, "Right-hand and Left-hand", Eriu III. 1 (1907), 11, 12.
101 LSBL, 11. 2237–9.

[102] Bede, *HE* III, 23.
[103] *MHBP*, 79.
[104] L. Haly, *The Ancient Irish Church*, 47.
[105] *ALI* V, 228–9; cf. Josh. 3.4.
[106] *TLP* I, 71.
[107] *TLP* I, 236.
[108] *Adomnan*, 495.
[109] H. C. Lawlor, *Chapters on the Book of Mulling*, 181.
[110] *Bede's Life of Cuthbert*, xvii.
[111] *LSBL*, xxviii.
[112] Reeves, *Antiquities*, 182.
[113] *LCBS*, xxviii, 11. 1–3.
[114] *ALI* IV, 227–37.
[115] *ALI* V, 221.
[116] For a discussion of this point see Lawlor, op. cit., 173–85.
[117] R. A. S. Macalister, *Guide to Monasterboice*, 18.
[118] Cf. the pillar which Jacob set up as a dividing limit between him and the hostile Laban (Gen. 31.44–9; cf. also Gen. 28.18).

CHAPTER 8

[1] *ALI* IV, 235.
[2] Adomnan, 383.
[3] *AFM* I, year 555.
[4] *LSBL*, xxvii.
[5] 1 Sam. 1.1, 2; cf. H. Williams, *Christianity in Early Britain*, 322.
[6] *MHBP*, 158.
[7] *MHBP*, 113.
[8] *BNE* I, 125, 128.
[9] 1 Thess. 2.7, *TP* I, 656.
[10] *LSBL*, 1. 4126.
[11] *VSB et G*, 57 (14).
[12] Joyce, *Social History* I, 437.
[13] *LSBL*, 173.
[14] *ALI* II, 147.
[15] *ALI* III, 71–3.
[16] *R.Tall.*, 83.
[17] 1 Tim. 5.18, *TP* I, 686.
[18] Bede, *HE* III, 27.
[19] *ALI* III, 409–11.
[20] *MHBP*, 336.
[21] *LSBL*, 191–2; cf. L. Gwynn, "The life of Lasair", *Eriu* V. 1 (1911), 73–103.
[22] KM, *SAIP*, 100.
[23] O'Curry, *Lectures*, 616.

[24] *ALI* IV, 375.
[25] *ALI* II, 279–81.
[26] *Life of Samson*, xvi.
[27] *ALI* IV, 383.
[28] Giraldus Cambrensis, Gemma Ecclesiastica, Disert. II, 22; cf. H. C. Lea, *History of Sacerdotal Celibacy* I, 347, 360–4.
[29] *ALI* III, 73.
[30] *LSBL*, 11. 815–18.
[31] *ALI* III, 73–9.
[32] *ALI* III, 73.
[33] *ALI* II, 345.
[34] *ALI* III, 75.
[35] *AFM*, 437, 441.
[36] *TLP* I, 69.
[37] For a discussion of this topic see W. H. Todd, *St Patrick*, 171–2, and W. Reeves, *Ecclesiastical Antiquities*, 136.
[38] *Life of Malachy*, 45.
[39] Skene, *Scotland* II, 12, 13.
[40] T. Olden, "On the consortia of the first order of Irish saints", *PRIA*, 3rd Series, II, no. 3 (1894), 415–20.
[41] A. H. Sayce, "The Indebtedness of Celtic Christianity to Egypt", *Scottish Ecclesiological Society Transactions* III (1912), 257; cf. H. C. Lea, *History of Sacerdotal Celibacy* I, 96; II, 316.
[42] *ALI* IV, 363–5.
[43] *ALI* IV, 369.
[44] *ALI* IV, 367.
[45] *LCBS*, 343.
[46] *LCBS*, 348.
[47] *LCBS*, 356.
[48] *ALI* III, 63.
[49] E. Hull, *Poem Book of the Gael*, 148.
[50] Moling had eight carpenters and their wives in his "family" (O'Curry, *Manners* III, 34).
[51] *AFM*, I, 135–41, year 448.
[52] *MO*, 93.
[53] *BNE*, 287–8.
[54] *MO*, 95.
[55] *LSBL*, 226.
[56] J. Ryan, *Irish Monasticism*, 193 ff.
[57] Dubliter sought to persuade Mael Ruain to drink (*R.Tall.*, 25).

[58] M. Bateson, "Origins and early history of double Monasteries", TRHS, New Series, XII (1899), 141; several of the facts presented here emanate from this article.

[59] MHBP, 204.

[60] J. Coglan, Trias Thaumaturga, 523.

[61] Ibid., 521.

[62] C. de Smedt and J. de Backer, Acta SS Hiberniae, col. 36.

[63] Bede's Life of Cuthbert x.

[64] Ibid., XXXV.

[65] Ibid., XXXIV.

[66] O. J. Bergin, "A Fragment of Old Irish", Eriu II (1906), 223–5.

[67] MO, xxxvii.

[68] MO, 41.

[69] LSBL, 269–70.

[70] TLP I, 233.

[71] TLP I, 233.

[72] TLP I, 267.

[73] WS, ACC, 177.

[74] MO, 43.

[75] MO, 147.

[76] MO, 147.

[77] TLP I, 235.

[78] A name for Ireland.

[79] KM, SAIP, 37–8.

[80] MHBP, 77.

[81] MHBP, 205.

[82] MO, 67; Lib. Hymn II, 41, 192, 193.

[83] MD, 331.

[84] S. Roberts, Boswell's Life of Johnson II, 82.

[85] W. Turner, "Irish Teachers in the Carolingian Revival of Learning", Catholic University Bulletin XIII (1907), 579–80.

[86] LSBL, 282; for a discussion of education in Welsh monastic schools see H. Williams, Christianity in Early Britain, 330–1.

[87] L. Gougaud, "The Remains of Irish Monastic Libraries", in J. Ryan, ed., Féil-sqribhinn Eoin Mich Neill, 319–34.

[88] M. Esposito, "The knowledge of Greek in Ireland during the Middle Ages", Studies I (1912), 665–83.

[89] Jonas, Columban VII.

[90] Ibid., IX.

[91] LSBL, 304.

[92] Adomnan, 525–7.

[93] T. Olden, "On the Geography of Ros Ailthir", PRIA, II (1883), 219–52; cf. Dicuil, Sedulius, and John Scotus Erigena, A.D. 800–75.

[94] O'Curry, Manners, III, 31–8.

[95] Bede, HE III, 27.

[96] VSH I, 115.

[96a] TP I. 516.

[97] Book of Leinster, 135, 32n.

[98] TLP I, 111, 113, 138; I, 320, 322.

[99] LSBL, 172.

[100] Adomnan, 203; Kenney, Sources, 254.

[101] Eoin Mac Neill, "The Vita Tripartita of St Patrick", Eriu XI (1932), 1–31.

[102] VSH I, 11.

[103] K. Hughes, "The Distribution of Irish Scriptoria and Centres of Learning from 730–1111", in Nora K. Chadwick, ed., Studies in the Early British Church, 243–72.

[104] G. Coffey, Guide to Celtic Antiquities of the Christian Period, 82–4.

[105] Joyce, Social History I, 482–4.

[106] LSBL, 11 4049–52.

[107] Cf. ALI III, 89.

[108] Joyce, op. cit. I, 480.

[109] VSH I, 59.

[110] KM, SAIP, 87.

[111] F. Keller, "Illustrations and Fac-Similes from Irish Manuscripts in the Libraries of Switzerland", The Ulster Journal of Archaeology VIII (1860), 222.

[112] AU, 697, 730, 796, 830, and many others in AFM.

[113] E. Hull, Early Christian Ireland, 224–5.

[114] Ibid., 225.

[115] O. J. Bergin, "A Fragment in Old Irish", Eriu II. 2 (1905), 225.

[116] Kenney, Sources, 648.

[117] R. Flower, Poems and Translations, 116.

[118] E. Hull, Early Christian Ireland, 270.

[119] Muratori, *Antiquates Italicae* I, Dissertatio xliii, 493–505.

[120] Bede, *HE* V, 21.

[121] J. Dowden, "An Examination of Original Documents on the Question of the Form of the Celtic Tonsure", *PSAS* VI, 3rd Ser. (1895), 325–7.

[122] O'Curry, *Lectures*, 271–2.

[123] *TLP* II, 561.

[124] *TLP* II, 509–10.

[125] *TLP* II, 317, line 11.

[126] Walker, *Columban*, 155.

[127] de Paor, op. cit., 103.

[128] Salvian, op. cit. VIII, 22.

[129] *Annals of Inifallen*, year 889.

[130] *MHBP*, 382.

[131] *Life of Samson* I, 15.

[132] Ibid., I, 16.

[133] WS, ACC, 263.

[134] Ibid., 263–5.

[135] Ibid., 403.

[136] Skene, *Scotland* II, 505.

[137] 1 Cor. 6.13, TP I, 555.

[138] Rom. 14.17, TP I, 537.

[139] Lev. 11.7.

[140] *MHBP*, 132.

[141] Exod. 21.29, 36.

[142] *MHBP*, 132.

[143] *MHBP*, 134.

[144] *MHBP*, 174.

[145] *MHBP*, 174.

[146] *MHBP*, 105.

[147] Exod. 15.19–17; Lev. 18.19.

[148] *MHBP*, 105.

[149] Lev. 12.2–4, 5–6.

[150] Gen. 19–22; for a discussion of this point see N. Power, "Classes of Women Described in the Senchas Mar", in R. Thurneysen, ed., *Studies in Early Irish Law*, 81–108.

[151] Giraldus Cambrensis, *The Topography of Ireland* XIX, 135.

[152] *Life of Margaret* VIII.

[153] See Deut. 25.5; Mark 12.19; Luke 20.28.

BIBLIOGRAPHY

More than twenty-five thousand works on Celtic studies exist, but only those have been included in this Bibliography which have direct bearing on the topic of this thesis. They are divided into two sections;

SOURCES

Adamnan, Cain Adamnain, or The Law of Adamnan (c. 697)

    Meyer, Kuno, *Cain Adamnain, An Old Irish Treatise on the Law of Adamnan.* Oxford 1905.

Adamnan, Vita Sancti Columbae (c. 700)

    Anderson, A. O. and M. O., *Adomnan's Life of St Columba.* London 1961.

    Fowler, J. T., *Adamnani Vita S. Columbae.* Oxford 1920.

Altus Prosator (Hymn attributed to Columba ?)

    Bernard, J. H., and Atkinson, R., *The Irish Liber Hymnorum.* 2 vols. Dublin 1898. (See vol. I, 62–83)

Alcuin's Letters (+ 804)

    Duemmler, E. L., *Monumenta Alcuiniana. Bibliotheca Rerum Germanicarum* VI. Berlin 1873.

Ambrose, *De Penitentia* (+ 397)

    Migne, J. P., PL. XVI. Paris 1864.

Amhra Choluimb Chille, or The Praise of Columba (*c.* sixth century?)
 Stokes, W., "The Bodleian Amra Choluimb Chille". RC XX (1899) and XXI (1900), being the text of Rawlinson B 502.
 Crowe, J. O'Beirne, *Amra Choluim Chilli*. Dublin 1871.

Ancient Laws of England (seventh and subsequent centuries)
 Attenborough, F. L., ed., *Laws of the Earliest English Kings*. Cambridge 1922.
 Thorpe, B., ed., *Ancient Laws and Institutes of England*. London 1840.

Ancient Laws of Ireland (? *c.* 440 to 795)
 Hancock, W. N., and others, *The Ancient Laws of Ireland*. 6 vols. Dublin 1865–1901.

Ancient Laws of Wales (seventh and subsequent centuries)
 Watson, W. K., *Ancient Laws and Institutions of Wales*. 2 vols. London 1841.

Annales Ecclesiastici (1588 to 1607)
 Baronius, C., *Annales Ecclesiastici*. 12 vols. Rome 1739.

Annals of the Four Masters (to 1171)
 O'Donovan, J., ed., *Annals of the Kingdom of Ireland by the Four Masters*. 4 vols. Dublin 1856.

Annals of Innisfallen (to 1319)
 Best, R. I., and MacNeill, E., ed., *Annals of Innisfallen*. Dublin 1933.
 MacAirt, Sean, ed., *Annals of Innisfallen*. Dublin 1951.

Annals of Ireland, Three Fragments (573–753; 662–704; 651–913)
 O'Donovan, J., ed., *Annals of Ireland, Three Fragments*, copied from ancient sources by Dubhaltach Mac Firbisigh. Dublin 1860.

Annals of Tigernach (+ 1088)
 Stokes, W., ed. and trs., "The Annals of Tigernach", RC. XVI–XVIII 1895–97)
 MacNeill, Eoin, "The Authorship and Structure of the Annals of Trigernach", *Eriu* VII (1913), 30–113.

Annals of Ulster or Annals of Senat (to 1540)
 Hennessy, W. M., and MacCarthy, B., ed., *Annals of Ulster*. 4 vols. Dublin 1887–1901.

Anonymous Life of Saint Cuthbert, see Colgrave, B. (under Bede)

Antiphonary of Bangor (*c.* 680–91)
Warren, F. E., ed., *The Antiphonary of Bangor.* 2 vols. London
1893, 1895.

Apocrypha and Pseudepigrapha, see Charles, R. H.

Athanasius, Bishop of Alexandria (+ 373)—Letters
Athanasius, *Epistola ad Dracontium,* PG, xxv, col. 534.

Augustine of Hippo (+ 430)—Letters and Sermons
Augustine, *De Haeresibus,* PL XLIII, cols. 21 to 50.
            Epistola ad Januarium, PL XXXIII, col. 200.
            De Genesi ad Literam, PL XXXIV.

Baronius, Caesare, *Annales Ecclesiastici,* see *Annales Ecclesiastici.*

Bede, *Historica Ecclesiastica Gentis Anglorum* (731)
Plummer, C., *Baedae Opera Historica.* 2 vols. Oxford 1896.
Sherley-Price, Leo, *Bede: A History of the English Church and
People.* London 1960.

Bede, *Life of Saint Cuthbert* (first quarter of eighth century)
Colgrave, B., *Two Lives of St Cuthbert.* Cambridge 1940.

Bernard of Clairvaux, *Vita Sancti Malachiae* (1152)
Lawlor, H. J., *St Bernard of Clairvaux's Life of St Malachy of
Armagh.* London 1920.

Bobbio Missal (seventh or eighth centuries)
Lowe, E., and Wilson, H., *The Bobbio Missal.* HBS LXI. London
1924.
Neale, J. M., and Forbes, G. H., *The Ancient Liturgies of the Gallican Church.* Burntisland 1853.

Boniface, Letters (+ 754)
Giles, J. A., *S. Bonifacii opera.* 2 vols. London 1844.
Kylie, E., *The English Correspondence of St Boniface.* New York
1940.

Book of Armagh (807)
Gwynn, J., *Liber Ardmachamus: The Book of Armagh.* Dublin
1913.
Gwynn, E., *Book of Armagh: The Patrician Documents.* Dublin
1937.

Book of Deer (*c.* 1150)
Stuart, J., ed. and trs., *The Book of Deer.* The Spalding Club,
No. 36. Edinburgh 1896.

Book of Kells (? eighth century)
Sullivan, E., *The Book of Kells, Described and Illustrated*. London 1914.

Book of Lismore (fifteenth century ?)
Stokes, W., *Lives of Irish Saints from the Book of Lismore*. Anecdota Oxoniensia. Oxford 1890.

Book of Llandav (*c.* 1132)
Rees, W. J., *Liber Landavensis*. Llandovery 1840.
Evans, J. G., and Rhys, J., *The Book of Llandaff*. Series of old Welsh Texts, No. 4. Oxford 1894.

Book of Popes, see *Liber Pontificalis*.

Caesar, Julius, *Commentarii de bello Gallico* (*c.* 58–50 B.C.).

Cain Domnaig, or the Law of Sunday (late sixth or seventh century)
MacLean, D., ed. and trs., *The Law of the Lord's Day in the Celtic Church*. Edinburgh 1926.
O'Keefee, J. G., "Cain Domnaig—Letter of Jesus", *Eriu*, II (1905), 189–211.

Cassian, J., *Collationes et Instituta* (+ 435)
Cassian, J., *Collationes et Instituta*, PL XLIX, XL.
Gibson, E., *Cassian: De Institutis Coenobium. Collationes. Nicene and Post-Nicene Christian Fathers*, Series 2, XI, 161–641.
Chadwick, O., *John Cassian: A Study in Primitive Monasticism*. Cambridge 1950.

Catalogue of the Saints of Ireland (first half of eighth century)
Ussher, J., *Works* IV, *Sylloge*, no. xi, 441ff. Dublin 1847–64.
Bury, J. B., *The Life of St Patrick*, 285–7. London 1905.

Columbanus, Epistolar, *Regulae et Instructiones* (+ 615)
Walker, G. S. W., ed., *S. Columbani Opera*. Dublin 1957.

Consilia
Monumenta Germaniae Historica: Scriptores Rerum Merovingicarum. Hanover 1885–1909.

Cummian, Letter to Segene, abbot of Iona (*c.* 632–3)
Ussher, J., *Works* IV, *Sylloge*, no. xi, 441ff. Dublin 1847–64.

Didache
Lightfoot, J. B., and Harmer, J. R., in *Anti-Nicene Christian Library*. London 1891.

Gildas, *De Excidio et Conquestu Brittaniae* (*c.* 500–70)
Giles, J. A., ed. and trs., *Six Old English Chronicles*. London 1848.
Giles, J. A., *The Works of Gildas, Surnamed the Wise.* London 1841.

Giraldi Cambrensis Opera (+ 1223)
Wright, T., ed. and trs., *The Historical Works of Giraldus Cambrensis*. London 1892.
O'Meara, J. J., *Topographia Hibernica: Topography of Ireland by Giraldus Cambrensis*. Dundalk 1951.

Gregory the Great, Letters (+ 604)
Gregory the Great, *Works*, PL LXXV–LXXVIII.

Historia Ecclesiastica
Bede—see Bede.
Eusebius, *Ecclesiastical History*, ed. and trs., McGiffert, A. C., London 1890.
Socrates, *Ecclesiastical History*, ed. and trs., Zenos, A., *Nicene and Post-Nicene Christian Fathers*, Series 2, II. London 1890.
Sozomen, *Ecclesiastical History*, PG LXVII, cols. 843–1630.

Josephus, Antiquities and Wars (first century)
Josephus, *Works*, ed. and trs., Shilleto, A. R., and Wilson, C. W., Bohn's edn. 5 vols. London 1889–90.

Historia Norvegiae (? end of twelfth century)
Storm, G., ed., *Monumenta Historica Norvegiae*. Kristiania 1880.

Jonas, *Vita S. Columbani* (*c.* 639)
Munro, D. C., *Life of St Columbanus by the Monk Jonas*. Philadelphia 1902.

Lausiac History of Palladius
Butler, E. C., *The Lausiac History of Palladius*. 2 vols. Texts and Studies VI. Cambridge 1904.
Clarke, W. H. L., trs., *The Lausiac History of Palladius*. London 1918.

Law of Sunday, see *Cain Domnaig*.

Liber ex Lege Moisi (? eighth to ninth centuries)
Corpus Christi College, Cambridge, Ms. 279.
Fournier, Paul, "Le Liber ex Lege Moysi et les tendances bibliques du droit canonique irlandais", RC XXX (1909), 221–34.

Lebar Brecc, or The Speckled Book (fourteenth century)
Stokes, W., ed. and trs., *Three Middle-Irish Homilies on the Lives of Saints Patrick, Bridget and Columba*. Calcutta 1877.

Atkinson, R., *The Passions and Homilies from the Leabhar Brecc.* RIA Todd Lectures, Series 2. Dublin 1887.

Liber Hymnorum
Bernard, J. H., and Atkinson, R., ed. and trs., *The Irish Liber Hymnorum.* 2 vols. London 1898.
Stokes, W., *Goidelica.* London 1872.

Liturgy, see Warren, F. E.

Lives of the various Saints (from the seventh century)
Anonymous Life of Cuthbert, see Colgrave, R., *Two Lives of St Cuthbert.* Cambridge 1940.
Colgan, J., *Acta Sanctorum Veteris Scottiae seu Hiberniae.* 2 vols. Louvain 1645–47.
Doble, H. G., *Cornish Saints Series.* London 1923–43.
—— *Welsh Saints Series.* Guildford and Esher 1942–3.
—— *St Illtyd.* Cardiff 1944.
Forbes, A. P., *Lives of St Ninian and St Kentigern.* HS v. Edinburgh 1874.
Forbes-Leith, W., *Turgot's Life of St Margaret.* Edinburgh 1896.
—— *The Life of St Cuthbert.* Edinburgh 1888.
Hennessy, W. M., "The Old Irish Life of St Columba", in Skene, W., *Celtic Scotland* II, 467–507. Edinburgh 1877.
Gwynn, L., "The Life of Lassair", *Eriu* V (1911), 73–109.
Joynt, M., trs., *The Life of St Gall.* London 1927.
Metcalfe, W. K., *Ancient Lives of Scottish Saints.* 2 vols. Paisley 1899.
Pinkerton, J., *Vitae Antiquae Sanctorum,* revised and enlarged by Metcalfe, W. M. Paisley 1889.
Plummer, C., *Bethada Naem nErenn or The Lives of Irish Saints.* Oxford 1922.
—— *Vitae Sanctorum Hiberniciae.* 2 vols. Oxford 1910.
Rees, W. J., *Lives of Cambro-British Saints.* Llandovery 1853.
Stokes, W., *Lives of Saints from the Book of Lismore.* Oxford 1890.
—— *The Tripartite Life of St Patrick, with other documents relating to that Saint.* 2 vols. London 1887.
Wade-Evans, A. W., *The Life of St David.* Cardiff 1923.
—— *Vitae Sanctorum Britanniae et Genelogiae.* Cardiff 1944.

Martyrologies (from the ninth century)
Adamnan—Byrne, M. E., "Feilire Adamnain", *Eriu* I, 225–8.
Donegal—O'Donovan, J., *The Martyrology of Donegal,* ed. Todd, J. H., and Reeves, W. Dublin 1864.

Gorman—Stokes, W., *Felire Hui Gormain, The Martyrology of Gorman.* HBS IX. London 1895.

Oengus—Stokes, W., *Felire Oengusso Celi De, The Martyrology of Oengus the Culdee.* HBS XXIX. London 1905.

Tallaght—Kelley, M., *Calendar of Irish Saints, the Martyrology of Tallagh; with notices of the patron saints of Ireland and select poems and hymns.* Dublin 1857.

MGH, *Monumenta Germaniae Historica*

Auctores Antiquissimi. Berlin 1877–1905.

Gesta Pontificum Romanorum. Berlin 1898.

Scriptores. Hanover 1826–1905.

Scriptores Rerum Merovingicarum. Hanover 1885–1909.

Migne, J. P., *Patrologiae Cursus Completus, Series Latina.* Paris 1844–64.

Migne, J. P., *Patrologiae Cursus Completus. Series Graeca.* Paris 1857–66; 1912.

Muirchu Maccu-mactheni, Life of Patrick, see Patrick.

Mishnah (*c.* 133 to 220)
Darnby, H., ed. and trs., *The Mishnah.* Oxford 1933.

Missals
Bobbio—Lowe, E. A., *The Bobbio Missal.* 3 vols. HBS LIII, LVIII, LXI. London 1917, 1920, 1924.

Stowe—Warner, G. F., *The Stowe Missal.* 2 vols. HBS XXXI, XXXII. London 1906, 1915.

Njal's Saga (*c.* 1280)
Magnusson, M., and Palsson, H., ed. and trs., *Njal's Saga.* London 1960.

Patrick, *Confession, Letter,* and *Lorica* (fifth century)
Bieler, L., *The Works of St Patrick.* London 1953.

Penitentials
McNeill, J. T., and Gamer, H. M., *Medieval Handbooks of Penance.* Records of Civilization XXIX. New York 1965.

Wasserschleben, F. W., *Die irische Kanonensammlung.* Leipzig 1885.

Rules
Ailbe—O'Neill, J., ed. and trs., "The Rule of St Ailbe of Emly", *Eriu* III (1907), 92–115.

Celi De—Reeves, W., "The Prose Rule of the Celi De", *TRIA* XXIV. 3 (1873), 202–15.

Patrick—O'Keefee, J. G., ed. and trs., "The Rule of St Patrick", *Eriu* I. 1 (1904), 216–24.

Tallaght—Gwynn, ed., "The Rule of Tallaght", *Hermathena* XLIV (2nd supplemental volume 1927), 1–109.
Gwynn, E. J., and Purton, W. J., "The Monastery of Tallaght", *PRIA* XXIX. C. 5 (1912), 115–79.

Salvian, De Gubernatione Dei (+ 480)

Sanford, E. M., ed. and trs., *De Gubernatione Dei, On God's Providence.* Records of Civilization. New York 1930.

Stephanus, Eddius, Vita S. Wilfridi (c. 730)

Colgrave, B., *The Life of Bishop Wilfrid by Eddius Stephanus.* Cambridge 1927.

Sulpicius Severus (c. 363–c. 420/5), Dialogues
Sulpicius Severus, *Works, PL* XX, 95–248.

Turgot's Life of Queen Margaret (c. 1100)

Forbes-Leith, W., *Turgot's Life of Queen Margaret.* **Edinburgh** 1896.

Various:

Bergin, O. J., "A Fragment of Old-Irish", *Eriu* II. 2 (1906), 221–6.
—— "The Harrowing of Hell", *Eriu* IV. 1 (1908), 112–19.

Best, R. I., ed., "The Lebar Brecc Tractate on the Canonical Hours", text, trans. and notes in *Miscellany Presented to Kuno Meyer*, ed., 142–66. Halle 1912.

Best, R. I., and Lawlor, H. J., ed., *The Martyrology of Tallaght from the Book of Leinster.* HBS LXVIII. London 1931.

Carmichael, A., *Carmina Gadelica, Hymns and Incantations.* 2 vols. Edinburgh 1928.

Colgan, *Trias Thaumaturga.* Louvain 1647.

de Smedt, C., and de Backer, J., *Acta Sanctorum Hiberniae.* Edinburgh and London 1888.

Flower, R. E. W., *Poems and Translations.* London 1931.

Hefele, C. J., *History of the Christian Councils*, trs., Oxenham, H. N. Edinburgh 1896.

Hull, E., *The Poem Book of the Gael.* London 1912.
—— *Folklore of the British Isles.* London 1928.

Jackson, K., *A Celtic Miscellany: Transcriptions from the Celtic Literature.* Cambridge 1951.
—— *Studies in Early Celtic Nature Poetry.* Cambridge 1935.

Lawlor, H. J., *Chapters on the Book of Mulling.* Edinburgh 1897.

Meyer, K., trs. and ed., "An Old-Irish Treatise De Arries", *RC* xv (1894), 485–98.

—— *Hibernica Minora: being a fragment of an Old Irish treatise on the Psalter.* Oxford 1894.

—— *Selections from Ancient Irish Poetry.* London 1928.

—— *The Triads of Ireland*, Todd Lectures Series xiii, Dublin 1906.

Murphy, G., *Early Irish Lyrics.* Oxford 1956.

O'Curry, E., *Lectures on the Manuscript Materials of Ancient Irish History*, ed. O'Brien, S. Dublin 1944.

—— *On the Manners and Customs of the Ancient Irish.* 3 vols. London 1873.

O'Grady, S. H., *Silva Gadelica: A Collection of Tales in Irish.* 2 vols. London 1892.

O'Nowland, T. P., ed. and trs., "A Prayer to the Archangels", *Eriu* ii. 2 (1905), 92–4.

Reeves, W., *Ecclesiastical Antiquities of Down, Connor and Dromore.* Dublin 1847.

Sabatier, P., ed., *Bibliorum Sacrum Latinae Versiones Antiquae.* Paris 1751.

Stokes, W., and Strachan, J., *Thesaurus Palaeohibernicus: A Collection of Old-Irish Glosses, Scholia, Prose and Verse.* 2 vols. Cambridge 1901–03. *Supplement*, Halle 1910.

Strachan, J., ed. and trs., "An Old Irish Homily", *Eriu* iii (1907), 1–10.

Warren, F. E., *The Liturgy and Ritual of the Celtic Church.* Oxford 1881.

White, N. J. D., "Libri Sancti Patricii: The Latin Writings of Saint Patrick", *PRIA* xxv. C. 7 (1905), 201–326.

—— *Libri Sancti Patricii.* London 1918.

—— *St Patrick, His Writings and Life.* Dublin 1920.

SECONDARY SOURCES: BOOKS AND ARTICLES

Allen, J. R., *The Early Christian Monuments of Scotland.* Rhind Lectures. Edinburgh 1903.

—— *A Monumental History of the Early British Church.* London. 1889.

Aman, E., "Penitence-Sacrament", *DTC* xii.

Anderson, A. O., *Early Sources of Scottish History*, A.D. 500–1286. 2 vols. London 1922.

—— "Ninian and the southern Picts", *SHR* xxvii (1948), 25–27.

—— *Scottish Annals from English Chroniclers.* London 1908.

Anderson, J., *Scotland in Early Christian Times.* Edinburgh 1881.

Anderson, J. N., and Conradie, L. R., *A History of the Sabbath.* Washington 1913.

Anonymous, "The Liturgy and Ritual of the Celtic Church", CQR x (1880), 50–84.

—— "Liturgy and Ritual of the Anglo-Saxon Church", CQR XIV (1882), 276–94.

Anscombe, A., *The Date of the Obit of St Columba: A vindication and refutation of those writers who would apply a cycle of 84 years to the computation of the British and Irish Easter.* Tottenham 1893.

—— "St Victricius of Rouen and St Patrick", *Eriu* VII (1913), 13–17.

Bateson, Mary, "Origin and Early History of Double Monasteries", TRHS XIII (1899), 137–98.

Beck, H. G. J., *The Pastoral Care of Souls in South-East France during the Sixth Century.* Anelecta Gregoriana LI. Rome 1950.

Bellesheim, A., *History of the Catholic Church of Scotland,* tr. Blair, D. O. H., 4 vols. Edinburgh 1887–90.

Berlière, U., *L'Ordre Monastique.* Paris 1921.

Bernard, J. H., "On the Stowe St John", TRIA XXX (1893), 313–21.

Best, R. I., and O'Brien, M. A., ed., *The Book of Leinster formerly Lebar in Nuachongabala.* 2 vols. DIAS. Dublin 1956–57.

Bieler, L., *The Life and Legend of St Patrick.* Dublin 1949.

—— "The Island of Scholars", IHS VIII (1952), 213–34.

—— "The Mission of Palladius", *Traditio* VI (1948), 1–33.

—— "Recent Research on Irish Hagiography", *Studies* XXXV (1946), 230–9, 536–44.

—— "Sidelights on the Chronology of St Patrick" IHS VI (1949), 247–60.

—— "Was Palladius surnamed Patricus?" *Studies* XXXII (1943), 323–6.

Binchy, D. A., "The Fair of Taltui and the Feast of Tara", *Eriu* XVII (1944), 113–38.

—— *The Linguistic and Historical Value of the Irish Law Tracts.* London 1944.

——Studies in Early Irish Law. Dublin 1936.

Bingham, J., The Antiquities of the Christian Church. London 1845.

Birkett, F. C., "The Bible of Gildas", RB XLVII (1934).

Bischoff, B., "Wendepunkte in der Geschichte der lateinischen Exegese im Frühmittelalter", Sacris Erudiri VI (1954), 189–281.

Bishop, E., Liturgica Historica: Papers on the Liturgy and Religious Life of the Western Church. Oxford 1918.

Bishop, W. C., "A Service Book of the Seventh Century (Antiphonary of Bangor)", CQR XXXVII (1893–4) 337–63.

—— "The Stowe Missal", CQR (1918) 302–14.

Bolton, C. A., "St Patrick and the Easter Fire", IER, 5th Series, LXX (1948), 680–6.

—— "St Patrick's Breastplate: a new interpretation", IER, 5th Series, LXXV (1951), 226–31.

Bonser, W., An Anglo-Saxon and Celtic Bibliography, 450–1087. 2 vols. Oxford 1957.

Bowen, E. G., The Celtic Church in Wales. Cardiff 1954.

—— The Settlements of Celtic Saints in South Wales. Cardiff 1954.

—— "The Travels of the Celtic Saints", Antiquity XVIII (1944), 16–28.

Bradshaw, H., The Early Collection of Canons known as the Hibernensis, Two Unfinished Papers. Cambridge 1893.

Brewer, J. S. and Dimmock, J. F., Giraldus Cambrensis Opera. 8 vols. London 1861–91.

Bright, W., Chapters of Early English Church History. Oxford 1897.

—— The Roman See in the Early Church. London 1896.

Browne, G. F., The Christian Church in these Islands before the Coming of Augustine. London 1899.

Brynmor-Jones, D., "The Brehon Laws and their relation to the Ancient Welsh Institutes", THSCymm, (1904–5), 7–36.

Bulloch, James, The Life of the Celtic Church, Edinburgh 1963.

Bund, J. W., The Celtic Church in Wales. London 1897.

Butler, E. C., "Monasticism", CMH I, 521–42. Cambridge 1911.

Cabrol, F., ed. DACL. Paris 1903 ff.

Carney, J., The Problem of St Patrick. DIAS. Dublin 1961.

—— *Studies in Irish Literature and History.* Dublin 1955.

Cathcart, W., *The Ancient British and Irish Churches, including the Life and Labours of St Patrick.* London 1894.

Chadwick, H. M., *Early Scotland: the Picts, the Scots and the Welsh of Southern Scotland,* ed. N. K. Chadwick. Cambridge 1949.

Chadwick, N. K., and others, *Studies in the Early British Church.* Cambridge 1958.

Charles, R. H., *The Apocrypha and Pseudepigrapha of the Old Testament.* Oxford 1913.

Clark, J. M., *The Abbey of St Gall as a centre of Literature and Art.* Cambridge 1926.

Concannon, H., *The Life of St Columban: A study of ancient Irish Monastic Life.* Dublin 1915.

—— *St Patrick: His life and Mission.* London 1913.

Conybeare, F. C., "The Character of the Heresy of the Early British Church", THSCymm (1897–8), 84–177.

Cox, R., *The Literature of the Sabbath Question.* 2 vols. Edinburgh 1865.

Cross, F. L., *Oxford Dictionary of the Christian Church.* Oxford 1957.

Deanesly, M., *The Pre-Conquest Church in England.* London 1961.

—— *Sidelights on the Anglo-Saxon Church.* London 1962.

De Paor, see Paor, de.

Dowden, J., "An Examination of Original Documents on the Question of the Form of the Celtic Tonsure", PSAS xxx, 3rd series, 6 (1896), 325–7.

—— *The Celtic Church in Scotland.* London 1894.

Duckett, Eleanor, *The Wandering Saints.* London 1959.

Duchesne, L., *Christian Worship: Its Origin and Evolution.* 2nd English edn. London 1904.

Dugmore, C. W., *The Influence of the Synagogue upon the Divine Office.* Oxford 1944.

Duke, J. A., *The Columban Church.* Edinburgh and London 1957.

Dunraven, E. R. W. Wyndham-Quin, the Earl of, *Notes on Irish Architecture,* ed. M. Stokes. 2 vols. London 1875–77.

Emerton, Ephraim, tr., *The Letters of St Boniface.* New York 1940.

Esposito, M., "The knowledge of Greek in Ireland during the Middle Ages", *Studies* I (1912), 665–83.

Esposito, M., "A Seventh-Century Commentary on the Catholic Commentary Epistles", *JTS* XXI (1920), 316–18.

—— "Notes on Latin Learning and Literature in Medieval Ireland", *Hermathena* XIV (1907) to XLVII (1932); XLIX (1933); L (1937).

—— "The Patrician Problem and a Possible Solution", *IHS* X (1956), 131–55.

Evans, A. W., see Wade-Evans.

Eyre, C., *The History of St Cuthbert*. London 1887.

Feasy, H. J., *Ancient English Holy Week Ceremonial*. London 1897.

Flick, A. C., *The Rise of the Medieval Church*. New York 1901.

Flower, R. E. W., "Irish High Crosses", *Journal of the Warburg and Courtauld Institutes* XVII (1954), 87 ff.

—— *The Irish Tradition*. Oxford 1947.

—— "The Two Eyes of Ireland", in *The Church of Ireland*, 432 ff, ed. Bell, W., and Emerson, N. O., Dublin 1932.

—— "Religion and Literature in Ireland in the Eighth and Ninth Centuries", *Ibid*.

Freeman, P., *The Principles of Divine Service*. 2 vols. Oxford 1880.

Gougaud, L., "Celtiques (Liturgies)" *DACL* II, cols 2969–3032.

—— *Christianity in Celtic Lands*, tr. Joynt, M. London, 1932.

—— *Devotional and Ascetic Practices in the Middle Ages*. London 1927.

—— *Gaelic Pioneers of Christianity: The Work of Irish Monks and Saints in Continental Europe*, VI–XII *Centuries*, tr. Collins, V., Dublin 1923.

—— *Modern Research with special reference to Early Irish Ecclesiastical History*. Dublin 1929.

—— "The Remains of Irish Monastic Libraries", in *Feilsg. Mic Neill*, 319–34. See Ryan, J.

—— "Mulierum Consortia: étude sur le syneisaktisme chez les ascètes celtiques", *Eriu* IX (1921), 147–56.

Graham, H., *The Early Irish Monastic Schools: A Study of Ireland's contribution to early medieval culture.* Dublin 1923.

Grosjean, P., "Recent Research on the Life of St Patrick", *Thought* V (1930), 22ff.

—— "Le martyrologue de Tallaght", AB LI (1933), 117–30.

—— "Hagiographica Celtica", *AB* LV (1937), 96–108, 284–99.

—— "Notes sur les documents anciens concernant S. Patrice", AB LXII (1944), 42–73.

Gross, C., *The Sources and Literature of English Church History, from the Earliest Times to about 1485.* London 1915.

Gwynn, A., "St Malachy of Armagh", IER LXX (1948), 961–78.

—— "St Patrick and Rome", IER, LXXXII (1961), 217–22.

Gwynn, E. J., "An Irish Penitential", *Eriu* VII (1914), 121–95.

—— "De Arreis", *Eriu* V (1911), 45–8.

Haddan, A. W., *Remains,* ed. Forbes, A. P., Oxford 1876.

Haddan, A. W., and Stubbs, W., *Councils and Ecclesiastical Documents Relating to Great Britain and Ireland.* 3 vols. in 4. Oxford 1869–78.

Hancock, P. D., *A Bibliography of Works Relating to Scotland.* Edinburgh 1960.

Hanson, R. P. C., *Saint Patrick, his Origins and Career.* Oxford 1968.

Hanson, W. G., *The Early Monastic Schools of Ireland: Their Missionaries, Saints and Scholars.* Cambridge 1927.

Hastings, J. ed., *Encyclopedia of Religion and Ethics,* 12 vols. New York 1922.

Healy, J., *The Ancient Irish Church.* London 1892.

—— *Insula Sanctorum et Doctorum, or Ireland's Ancient Schools and Scholars.* Dublin 1902.

Henning, J., "Studies in the Liturgy of the Early Irish Church", IER, 5th series, LXXV (1951), 318–33.

Hill, R. M. T., "The Northumbrian Church", CQR CLXIV (1963), 160–72.

Hitchcock, F. R. M., "The Irish Mission to England", *Churchman,* New Series 3 (1963), 189–200.

—— *Irenaeus of Lugdunum*. Cambridge 1914.

—— "The Creeds of SS. Irenaeus and Patrick", *Hermathena* XIV (1907).

Hogan, J. F., "The Monastery and Library of St Gall", *IER* XV (1894).

Hole, Ch., *Early Missions to and within the British Islands*. London 1895.

Hone, Wm. *Every-Day Book*. London 1840.

Hoskyns, E. C., *The Fourth Gospel*. London 1947.

Hughes, K., "On an Irish Litany of Pilgrim Saints compiled *c.* 800", AB, LXXVII (1959), 305–31.

—— "The Changing Theory and Practice of Irish Pilgrimage", *JEH* XI (1960), 143–51.

—— "The Church and the World in Early Christian Ireland", *IHS* XIII (1962), 99–116.

—— "Irish Monks and Learning", *Los Monjes y los Estudios* IV *Semana de Estudios Monasticos Poblet* 1961. Poblet 1963.

—— "The Celtic Church and the Papacy", in *The English Church and the Papacy in the Middle Ages*, ed. C. H. Laurence. London 1965.

—— "The Distribution of Irish Scriptoria and Centres of Learning from 730–1111", see Chadwick, N. K., *Studies in the Early British Church*, 243–72.

Hull, E., *Early Christian Ireland*. London 1905.

—— ed., *Lives of the Celtic Saints*. London 1926.

Hyde, D., *A Literary History of Ireland from the Earliest Times to the Present Day*. London 1899.

Jamieson, J., *An Historical Account of the Ancient Culdees of Iona, and of their Settlements in Scotland, England and Ireland*. Glasgow 1890.

Jenkins, T. R. and Rees, W., *A Bibliography of the History of Wales*. Cardiff 1931.

Jones, G. H., "Celtic Britain and the Pilgrim Movements", *Y Cymmrodor* XXIII (1912), 1–581.

—— "Early Celtic Missionaries", *Y Cymmrodor* XXXIX (1928), 39–67.

Joyce, P. W., *A Social History of Ancient Ireland*. 2 vols. Dublin 1913.

Joynt, M., "Tonsure", *Eriu* X (1928), 130–4.

Keller, F., "Illustrations and Fac-Similes from Irish Manuscripts in the Libraries of Switzerland", *Ulster Journal of Archaeology* VIII (1860), 212–30.

Kellner, K. A. H., *Heortology: A History of the Christian Festivals from their origin to the present day*. London 1908.

Kenney, J. F., "The Earliest Life of St Columcille", *Catholic Historical Review* (January 1926), 636–44.

—— *The Sources for the Early History of Ireland*, I *Ecclesiastical*. New York 1929.

Kerr, W. S., *The Independence of the Celtic Church in Ireland*. London 1931.

Kidd, B. J., *Documents Illustrative of the History of the Church*. 2 vols. London n.d.

Killen, W. D., *The Ecclesiastical History of Ireland*. 2 vols. London 1875.

—— *The Old Catholic Church*. Edinburgh 1871.

King, A. A., *Liturgies of the Past*. London 1959.

Kraemer, C. L., "Pliny and the Early Church Service", *Journal of Classical Philology* XXIX (1934), 293–300.

Laing, G. L., *Survivals of Roman Religion*. London 1931.

Laistner, M. L. W., "A Ninth-Century Commentator on the Gospel according to Matthew", *Harvard Theological Review* XX (1927), 129–49.

—— *Thought and Letters in Western Europe, A.D. 500–900*. London 1957.

La Pina, G., ed., *The Letters of St Boniface*, tr. with an introduction by Emerton, E. Records of Civilization. New York 1940.

Lawlor, H. J., "The Cathact of St Columba", *PRIA* XXXIII C (1916), 241–443.

Lawlor, H. J., and Best, R. I., "Ancient lists of the coarbs of St Patrick", *PRIA* XII (1919), 316–62.

Lea, H. C., A History of Auricular Confession and Indulgences in the Latin Church. 3 vols. London 1896.
—— A History of Sacerdotal Celibacy in the Christian Church. 2 vols. London 1907.
Leask, H. C., Irish Churches and Monastic Buildings. Dundalk 1955.
—— Glendalough, Co. Wicklow. Official Guide. Dublin 1951.
Leclercq, H., "La messe celtique dans les liturgies", DACL XI.
Levison, W., England and the Continent in the Eighth Century. Oxford 1946.
Lightfoot, J. B., Leaders in the Northern Church. London 1891.
Lingard, J., The History and Antiquities of the Anglo-Saxon Church. 2 vols. London 1858.
Loomis, L. R., ed. and tr., The Book of the Popes (Liber Pontificalis). Records of Civilization. New York 1920.
Luddy, A. J., Life of St Malachy. Dublin 1930.

Macalister, R. A. S., Ancient Ireland: A Study in the Lessons of Archaeology and History. London 1935.
McAlpine, R. G., Celtic Christianity. London 1967.
——Monasterboice. Dundalk 1946.
McGurk, Pat., Early Gospel Books. Paris, &c. 1961.
MacKinlay, K. M., "In oceano desertum — Celtic anchorites and their island retreats", PSAS XXXIII (1899), 129–33.
M'Lauchlan, Th., Celtic Gleanings: or Notices of the History and Literature of the Scottish Gael. Edinburgh 1857.
—— The Early Scottish Church. Edinburgh 1865.
MacNaught, J. C., The Celtic Church and the See of Peter. Oxford 1927.
McNally, R. E., The Bible in the Early Middle Ages. Westminster, Md 1959.
—— "The 'Tres linguae sacrae' in Early Irish Bible Exegesis", Theological Studies XIX (1958), 395–403.
MacNeill, Eoin, Early Irish Laws and Institutions. Dublin 1935.
——St Patrick: Apostle of Ireland. Dublin 1934.
—— Phases of Irish History. Dublin 1937.
—— "The Vita Tripartita of St Patrick", Eriu XI (1932), 1–41.

McNeill, J. T., "The Celtic Penitentials", RC XXXIX (1922), 257–300; XL (1923), 51–103, 320–41.

—— "Folk-paganism in the Penitentials", *Journal of Religion* XIII (1933), 450–66.

—— "Medicine for sin as prescribed in the Penitentials", *Church History* I (1932), 14–26.

Macpherson, J. R., ed. and tr., *De Locis Sanctis*. Pilgrim Trust Society Publication X. London 1889.

Mâle, E., *La fin du paganisme en Gaule*. Paris 1950.

Maxwell, H. E., *The Early Chronicles Relating to Scotland*. Rhind Lectures. Glasgow 1912.

Megaw, J. V. S., "Iona and Celtic Britain", *Journal of Religious History* 3 (June 1965), 212–37.

Meissner, J. L. G., "Essays on the History of the Early Church in Ireland", see Phillips, W. A., *History of the Church of Ireland*.

—— *The Celtic Church in England after the Synod of Whitby*. London 1929.

Meyer, Kuno, *Learning in Ireland in the Fifth Century and the Transmission of Letters*. Dublin 1913.

Mitchell, G., "Commutations of Penances in the Celtic Penitentials", IER, 5th series, XL (1932), 225–39.

Montalembert, Count de, *Monks of the West*, English tr. by Gasquet, F. A. London 1896.

Morris, J., "Dates of the Celtic Saints", JTS, new series 17 (October 1966), 342–91.

Morris, R., "Theology of the Early British Church", Y *Cymmrodor* XXIII (1914–15).

Mortimer, R. C., *Origin of Private Penance in the Western Church*. Oxford 1939.

Mullinger, J. B., *The Schools of Charles the Great and the Restoration of Education in the Ninth Century*. London 1877.

Murphy, G., "The Origin of Irish Nature Poetry", *Studies* XX (1931), 87–102.

—— "The Two Patricks", *Studies* XXXII (1934), 297–307.

Newell, E. J., *A Popular History of the Ancient British Church, with special reference to the Church in Wales*. London 1887.

—— A History of the Welsh Church to the Dissolution of the Monasteries. London 1895.

Neander, A., General History of the Christian Religion and Church, tr. Torrey, J. 9 vols. London 1847–55.

Oakley, T. P., "Celtic Penance: Its sources, affiliations, and influences" IER, 5th series, LII (1938), 147–64, 581–601.

—— "Commutations and Redemption of Penance in the Penitentials", Catholic Historical Review XVII (1933), 341–51.

—— "The co-operation of medieval penance and secular law", Speculum VII (1932), 515–24.

—— English Penitential Discipline and Anglo-Saxon Law in their Joint Influence. New York 1923.

—— "The Origins of Irish Penitential Discipline", Catholic Historical Review XIX (1933), 320–32.

—— "The Penitentials as Sources for Medieval History", Speculum XV (1940), 210–23.

O'Connell, D. J. K., "Eastern cycles in the early Irish Church", JRSAI LXVI, 7th series, 6 (1936) 67–106.

O'Keefe, J. G., "A Poem on the Day of Judgment", Eriu III (1907), 29–33.

Olden, T., The Church of Ireland. London 1895.

—— tr., "Early Irish Service of the Consecration of a Church", Transactions of St Paul's Ecclesiological Society IV (1897), 98–104, 177–80.

—— The Epistles and Hymns of St Patrick. London 1889.

—— "On the 'Consortia' of the first order of Irish Saints", PRIA, 3rd series, III (1894) 415–20.

——Holy Scriptures in Ireland one Thousand Years Ago. Dublin 1888.

O'Lochlain, C., "Roadways in Ancient Ireland", in Essays Presented to Eoin Mac Neill, ed. Ryan, J., 465–73.

O'Rahilly, C., Ireland and Wales: Their Historical and Literary Associations. London 1924.

O'Rahilly, T. F., The Two Patricks. Dublin 1924.

O'Riordain, Sean, P., Antiquities of the Irish Countryside. London 1953.

Oulton, J. E. L., *The Credal Statements of St Patrick as contained in the fourth chapter of his Confession.* Dublin 1940.

Owen, A., *Ancient Laws and Institutes of Wales.* 2 vols. London 1841.

Paor de, L., "A Survery of Cheilg Mhichil", *JRSAI* LXXXV (1955), 177ff.

Paor de, M. and L., *Early Christian Ireland.* London 1958.

Parthey, G., *Dicuili liber de mensura orbis terrae.* Berlin 1870.

Petrie, G., *The Ecclesiastical Architecture of Ireland Anterior to the Norman Invasion.* Dublin 1845.

—— *Christian Inscriptions in the Irish Language,* ed. Stokes, M. 2 vols. Dublin 1872, 1878.

Phillimore, E., "Annales Cambriae", *Y Cymmrodor* IX (1888), 141–83.

Plummer, A., *The Churches in Britain before 1000 A.D.* 2 vols. London 1911, 1912.

Pokorny, Julius, *Concise Old-Irish Grammar and Reader.* Halle and Dublin 1914.

Poole, R. L., *Illustrations of the History of Medieval Thought and Learning.* London 1920.

Power, P., tr., *Lives of Declan and Mochuda.* Irish Text Society. London 1914.

—— "The Mass in the Early Irish Church", *IER,* 5th series, LX (1942), 197–206.

—— *Early Christian Ireland: A Manual of Irish Christian Archaeology.* Dublin 1925.

Pryce, J., *The Ancient British Church.* London 1878.

Quasten, J., and Plumpe, J. C., *Ancient Christian Writers.* London 1953.

Ramsay, R. L., "Theodore of Mopsuestia in England and Ireland", *ZCP* VIII (1912), 452–97.

—— "Theodore of Mopsuestia and St Columban on the Psalms", *ZCP* VIII (1912), 421–51.

Rees, W., *An Historical Atlas of Wales.* Cardiff 1951.

Reeves, W., *The Culdees of the British Islands, as they appear in History*. Dublin 1864.

—— "On Augustine, Irish Writer of the seventh century", *PRIA* VII (1881), 514–22.

—— "On the Celi-De, commonly called Culdees", *TRIA* XXIV. 3 (1873), 119–264.

—— *The Life of St Columba, founder of Hy, written by Adamnan, ninth abbot of that monastery*. Edinburgh, the Bannatine Club, 1857.

—— *St Maelrubha: His History and Churches*. Edinburgh 1861.

Robertson, J. A., *The Laws of the Kings of England from Edmund to Henry I*. Cambridge, Mass. 1925.

Robinson, G. W., *The Life of St Boniface by Willibaldus*. Cambridge Mass. 1916.

Rock, D., *The Church of Our Fathers*, ed. Hart, G. W., and Frere, W. H., 4 vols. London 1905.

Roberts, S., ed., *Boswell's Life of Johnson*. 2 vols. London 1960.

Ryan, J., *Irish Monasticism: Origins and Early Development*. Dublin 1931.

—— ed., *Essays and Studies Presented to Professor Eoin MacNeill*. Dublin 1946.

Salagnac, G., and Cerbeland, B., *Ireland, Isle of Saints*, Dublin 1966.

Sayce, H. A., "The Indebtedness of Keltic Christianity to Egypt", *Transactions of the Scottish Ecclesiological Society* III. 3 (1911–12), 250–60.

Scott, W. H., "Celtic Culture and the Conversion of Ireland", *International Review of Missions* 56 (April 1967), 193–204.

Seebohm, F., *Tribal Custom in Anglo-Saxon Law*. London 1911.

—— *The Tribal System in Wales*. London 1904.

Simpson, W. D., *The Celtic Church in Scotland*. Aberdeen 1935.

—— *The Historical St Columba*. Aberdeen 1927.

——*St Ninian and the Origin of the Christian Church in Scotland*. Edinburgh 1940.

Skene, W. F., *Celtic Scotland: A History of Ancient Alban*. 3 vols. Edinburgh 1886–90.

Smalley, B., *The Study of the Bible in the Middle Ages*. Oxford 1952.

Smith, W., and Cheetham, S., *A Dictionary of Christian Antiquities*. 2 vols. London 1875–80.

Smith, W., and Wace, H., *Dictionary of Christian Biography, Literature, Sects and Doctrines*. 4 vols. London 1877–87.

Souter, A., *Pelagius' Expositions of 13 Epistles of St Paul*. 2 vols. Cambridge 1926.

—— "The Commentary of Pelagius on the Epistles of Paul". *Proceedings of the British Academy* (1905–6), 409–39.

—— Pelagius' Doctrine in relation to his Early Life", *Expositor*, 8th series, IX (1915), 180–2.

Souter, A., and Williams, C. S. C., *The Text and Canon of the New Testament*. London 1954.

Spence-Jones, H. D. M., "The Celtic Church—A Tragedy in History", *THSCymm* (1913–14), 1–82.

Stenton, E., *Anglo-Saxon England*. Oxford 1957.

Stephen, L., and Lee, S., ed., *Dictionary of National Biography*. 66 vols. London 1885–1901–1913.

Stokes, G. T., "Ancient Celtic Expositors: St Columbanus and his Teaching", *The Expositor*, 3rd Series, X (1889), 136–50.

Stokes, G. T., and Lawlor, H. J., *Ireland and the Celtic Church*. Dublin and London 1928.

Stokes, M., *Early Christian Architecture in Ireland*. London 1878.

Stokes, W., "Cross Vigils", *Academy* XLV (1894), 125–6.

—— "St Patrick's Doctrines", *Academy* XXXIV (1888), 26, 54–5, 104.

—— "On Two Irish expressions for 'Right Hand' and 'Left Hand'", *Eriu* III. 1 (1907), 11–12.

—— *Saltair na Rann*. Anecdota Oxoniensis, Medieval and Modern Series, I. 3. Oxford 1883.

—— "The Ever New Tongue", *Eriu* II (1905), 96–162; III (1907), 34–5.

—— Strachan, J., ed. and trs., "Cormac's Rule", *Eriu* II (1905), 62–68.

—— "Two Monastic Rules", *Eriu* II (1905), 227–9.

Taylor, H. O., *The Medieval Mind: A History of the Development of Thought and Emotion in the Middle Ages*. 2 vols. London 1921.

—— ed. and trs., *The Life of St Samson of Dol*. London 1925.

Todd, J. H., *St Patrick, Apostle of Ireland*. Dublin 1864.

Todd, J. H., and Reeves, W., ed., *The Martyrology of Donegal*, tr. Donovan, J. Dublin 1864.

Todd, J. H., and Herbert, A., *Leabhar Breathnach annso sis: The Irish Version of the Historia Brittonum of Nennius*. Dublin 1848.

Todd, J. H., *Leabhar Imuinn, The Book of Hymns of the Ancient Church of Ireland*. Dublin 1898.

Tyrer, J. W., *Historical Survey of Holy Week: Its Services and Ceremonial*. London 1932.

Ussher, J., *British Ecclesiastical Antiquities*. Dublin 1639.

Waddell, H. J., *Beasts and Saints*. London 1934.

—— *The Desert Fathers*. London 1946.

—— *The Wandering Scholars*. London 1954.

Wade-Evans, A. W., *The Emergence of England and Wales*. Oxford 1956.

—— *Welsh Christian Origins*. Oxford 1934.

—— *Welsh Medieval Laws*. Oxford 1909.

Watkins, O. D., *History of Penance, being a study of authorities*. 2 vols. London 1920.

Williams, H., *Christianity in Early Britain*. Oxford 1912.

—— *Gildas: The Ruin of Britain*. Cym. Record Series No. 3. Hon. Soc. of Cymmrodorion. London 1899.

—— "A Review of Dr Heinrich Zimmer's 'Pelagius in Ireland' and 'The Celtic Church in Britain and Ireland' ", ZCP IV. 3 (1903).

—— "Some Aspects of the Christian Church in Wales During the Fifth and Sixth Centuries", THSCym (1893–4).

Willis-Bund, J. W., *The Celtic Church of Wales*. London 1897.

Young, J. P. W., "Greek Influence in the Early British Church", *Tran. of the Scottish Ecclesiological Society* VIII (1926), 110–20.

Zimmer, H., *The Celtic Church in Britain and Ireland*, tr. Meyer, Antoine. London 1902.

—— *Pelagius in Ireland*. Berlin 1901.

—— *The Irish Element in Medieval Culture*, tr. Edmonds, J. L. New York 1891.

index

PROPER NAMES

Adamnan of Iona 5, 25–7, 35, 68, 84, 86, 90, 95, 116, 132, 134, 139, 143, 164, 174, 192, 197–8, 207
Aldhelm, abbot of Malmesbury 22
Aidan 10, 41, 90, 132, 139, 161
Ailred 3
Alcuin 37
Alfred, King 8, 25, 50
Ambrose, St 112, 136
Anthony 153
Armagh 27, 156
Athanasius 155
Augustine 2–8, 17–18, 37, 76, 91, 94, 111, 128, 155–6

Bangor 10, 156
Baronius, Cardinal Caesare 19, 23–4
Bede 7, 18, 21–2, 25, 30, 95, 115, 117, 168, 191, 194–5
Bernard of Clairvaux 27
Bobbio 11
Boniface, 37, 106
Brigit of Kildare 113–15, 139, 157, 169, 174, 176, 184, 190
Brendan 24, 156
Bruide, King 9

Canones Hibernenses 50
Cassian, John 33, 37, 154

Catholic Rite 22
Chad, Bishop 20
Clonmacnoise 156–7
Colman 21–2
Columba 3, 9, 11, 21, 27, 30, 39, 41, 50, 54, 71,
    82, 84–6, 91, 108, 113–20, 133, 138–9, 156–8, 160,
    169, 174, 183, 187–8, 191–3, 197, 202 *passim*
Columbanus 10–11, 19, 41, 68, 72, 83, 85, 96,
    116, 119, 139, 143–6, 158, 161, 183, 191, 195
    passim
Columbkille 26, 95
Comgell 10, 156
Constantine 1–2, 76, 93
Cormac, son of Culennan 14
Councils of Agade 184; Arles 2, 93; Clovesho 117;
    Laodicea 76; Nicaea 5, 93–5, 189; Rimini 2;
    Toledo 112; Whitby 21; Windsor 28
Cummian 5, 23–5
Cuthbert 10, 21, 113

Dagan, Bishop 19
David, King of Wales 81–2, 147, 158
Devon 22

Eata 21
Eddius 20, 95
Egbert 27–8, 98
Elbodus, bishop of Bangor 22

Faroes 12
Finan 20
Finnian 34, 105, 156; penitential of 108

Gildas the Briton 30–1, 35
Gregory, Pope 17–18, 54, 85, 96, 128
Gregory II, Pope 106

Honorius, Pope 4, 25

Ia 26, 95
Iceland 11–12
Inishbofin 22
Iona 5, 9–10, 24, 26–8, 160
Ireland 3–4, 8, 23–4, 26, 48, 113
Irish Christians 108

Jerome 31, 76
Jocelyn 3
John, Pope 25
Justinian 184

Kentingern 3
Kieran of Clonmacnoise 24
Kirkmandarine gravestones 2

Lanfrance 28

Lavrentius 18–19, 24
Lindisfarne 10, 20, 113
Lullingstone 1

Macarius 154
MacCoelmaine, Conall 87
Malachy O' Morgair, bishop of Rome 27
Margaret, bride of Malcolm 28
Meyer, Kuno 4
Middle Angles, Kingdom of 10

Nectan, King 12, 28
Ninian 3
Novationists 147

Old Irish Life of Columba 9
Oswald, King 9–10
Oswy, King 21–2

Pachomius 153
Palladius 4, 77, 153–4, 184
Parpar, Celtic missionaries 12
Patrick 3–9, 26, 29, 31, 35, 41, 48–72, 78–81, 85,
    91, 94–110, 114, 119–20, 124–7, 131, 137, 139–40,
    142, 156, 160–4, 169–70, 179, 187, 189; parents
    of 48; Rule of 111
Paulinus 9
Pelagius 61–7, 70, 72, 203
Picts 2–3, 21, 108

Severus, Sulpicius 2, 94, 154
Simplicius, Pope 136
Skellig, Michael 158
Synod of Campus Lene 23–4; Chalons-sur-Saône
    149; Elvira 112; Nicaea 111; Paris 149; Patrick,
    First 150; Rathbreasil 133; Tars 26; Whitby 22

Theodore of Mopsuestia 39
Theodore of Tarsus 19–20, 85

Ussher 23

Vandals 4
Victor, bishop of Rome 92–3
Victricius, bishop of Roven 79

Wilfred 21
Wini, Bishop 20

York, Archbishop of 28

GENERAL

Abbot 131, 141, 182
Adoption of children 61
Allegorizing Scriptures 37–8
Alms 164–5
Angels 68–72, 207
Annihilation of sinners 56, 60, 206
Antinomianism 48, 64
Anti-Semitism 48, 76, 92
Arianism 2, 54–5
Artifacts, Christian 2
Asylum, of monastery 173

Baptism: by fees 107; immersion 20, 59, 88, 101–113, 116, 128, 204; infant 108, 111, 119, 139; prerequisites 103; rituals 109; trine 102
Baptistery 110
Bible: analogical meaning of 37; literal meaning of 38; moral or tropological meaning of 38; mystical meaning of 38
Bishops: monarchial 124; ordination 20, 132–4; overseer 124; simply priests 124–34, 143, 149
Book of Armagh 3
Brahminism 154
Brehon Laws 49

Cain Domnaig 86, 88
Canon of Scriptures 31
Celibacy 125–30, 154–5, 180, 186, 189, 205
Celtic Christians, original 18–28
Cenobitism 154
Chi-rho monogram 1
Christ: Christmas 89; mediator 68; nativity 99; nature 55; resurrection 56; second advent 71; virgin birth 56;
Christology 58
Church, construction of 167–9
"Cities": asylum 173; monastic 160, 166, 183; precincts 170, 173
Coarbs 177–9
Communion 20, 77, 88, 101, 105, 110–20, 133, 136, 204
Confession 140–2, 204
"Confirmation" 111
Cosmology 59
Councils 37
Creationism 60
Crucifixion as penance 145, 148
Cryptogram, Christian 1

Deacon 124–8, 131–4
Deaconess 124

Death: man's condition in 56, 60; natural, a sleep 66; penal, annihilation 66
Decalogue, must be obeyed 48–50, 63–4, 72
Devil, doctrine of 70–2
Discipline 135
Docetism 75
Doctrines of Celts 18, 53–4
Double monasteries 184–5
Druid 138–9, 195

Easter controversy 5, 18, 20–1, 25–6, 84–100, 111, 115, 163
Ecclesiastical loan words 4
Education 175, 191–2
Election, views of 61
End of the world 72
"Epistle of Christ" 86–9, 99
Eternal life, views of 56
Etymology in homiletics 40
Eucharist 105, 118–19
Evangelism 8
Exegesis 37, 72
Existence of man, views of 57

Fall of man 60–3, 65
"Family", monastic 181
Fasting 90–1, 146–7, 154, 168, 202
Feminine hygiene from O.T. 198
Fiat creation 59
Food, "clean and unclean" 196–7
Fostering, *see* Adoption 174–5
Freedom of will 62

Glorification of man 62
Gnosticism 75, 153
God, nature of Trinity 43–4, 53, 58–9, 101, 106, 109, 206
Godhead 205

Hades 46
Hagiographers 3, 113
Hagiography 29
Heaven, doctrine of 46–7
Hebrew year 91
Hell, doctrine of 46–7, 63
Holy Spirit 58–9
Homily 47
Hospitality 166–7

Imagery, biblical in homiletics 29
Incarnation 58
Invocation of saints 68, 97
Iona accepts Romanism 27
Ireland accepts Romanism 26–7

Jewish Sabbath, *see* Sabbath
Jubilee: Great 100; Little 99–100
Judaism, Judaizing 11, 84–5, 92
Judgement 71

Kentish Christianity 10

Law, v grace 65
Lent 98
Leviticus, laws from 50
Liber ex Lege Moisi 50, 100, 161–95, 197–8, 202–3
Liquor, prohibited 197
Liturgical objects 3
Lord's day: prayer 118; supper, *see* Communion; *and see* Sunday

Man, doctrine of 60–3
Married clergy 106
Mediation of Christ 68
Ministry 123
Missionary zeal 11
Mithraism 75–6
Monachism 153–4, 185
Monastery, Celtic 11, 173
Monastic communities of families 181–2, 187–99; rules 183; schools 174
Monasticism, 77, 124, 130, 153–99
Mosaic legislation 49–50
Muratorian fragment 31

Nicene Creed, the 58
Northern heathen tribes 9

Offerings 80, 163–4, 202
Old Latin Bible 31, 47
Ordination, *see* Bishops
Original sin 66
Overseer, *see* Bishops

Pasch, order of 24
Passover 25, 92–4
Pelagianism 2
Penitentials 148–51, 162–5, 169, 174, 191, 204
Pentecost 98–9, 163
Pilgrimages: general 8, 14; to Rome 14
Practices of Celts 50
Prayer 67–8
Preacher, Irish 45
Preaching 41–2; analysis 47
Predestination 61
Presbyter 124, 126, 128–9, 131, 137, 139–40, 149
Presbyter-bishops 130–1, 204–5

"Quartodecimans" 20, 95–6

Resurrection of man 63, 71
Ritual 18, 109
Romanizing of Celtic Christianity 9, 15, 23
Romans leave Britain 2

Sabbath (Saturday) 12, 75–90, 100, 121, 203;
   changed to Sunday 75–6; eve of 81; Friday
   sundown commencement of 81; *see Senchus
   Mor*
Salt 109
Salvation, doctrine of 65–6, 72
"Schismatici Britanniae" 20
Schools, development of 33; Irish education 4;
   monastic 174; students 175
Schism 23
Scribes 193
Scriptorium 193–4
Scriptures in Celtic lands 29; commentaries 34;
   interpretation 35; veneration for 33
Second advent, *see* Christ
Sees, fourfold 24
Semi-Arianism 59
Senchus Mor 49, 80–1
Sermons 42–3; construction of 42, 45
Sin 66; original 66
"Soul-friend" 9, 137–9, 168
Soul, man's not immortal 60
Spirit, Holy, 59; deity of 58
Students, *see* Schools
Sunday 75–100, 121, 164; observed with Sabbath
   77–8
Sundown Friday, *see* Sabbath
Swine's flesh prohibited 197
Symbols, Christian 1

Teachers, *see* Schools
Theologians, Celtic 48
Theology 51
Tithes 80, 161–3, 202
Tonsure 18, 95 195–6, 203
Tribal organization 157
Trinity, *see* God

Vegetarianism 197, 202
Vellum 193
Virgin birth, *see* Christ
Vulgate 32, 47

Western Christian thought 5
World, end of 71–2
Würtzberg glosses 36